PROFIT PLANNING

through

VOLUME-COST ANALYSIS

THE MACMILLAN COMPANY
NEW YORK · CHICAGO
DALLAS · ATLANTA · SAN FRANCISCO
LONDON · MANILA
IN CANADA
BRETT-MACMILLAN LTD.
GALT, ONTARIO

John Y. D. Tse, D.C.S.

PROFESSOR OF
INDUSTRIAL ADMINISTRATION
PURDUE UNIVERSITY

PROFIT PLANNING
through
VOLUME-COST ANALYSIS

NEW YORK

The Macmillan Company

First printing

Library of Congress Catalog Card Number: 60–13230
The Macmillan Company, New York
Brett-Macmillan Ltd., Galt, Ontario
Printed in the United States of America

Dedicated to
the Memory of My Father

K. Y.

PREFACE

Volume-cost analysis is a modern tool of management, a tool which can be used to help management make better planning decisions and do a better job of controlling the operation of the business. When management is confronted with problems such as planning capital expenditures, selecting a product, pricing, deciding whether to make or buy, controlling cost, where cost and profit play an important role in the final decision, volume-cost studies have been found of genuine value in helping management in selecting the proper course of action.

It is believed, however, that in many companies the need for volume-cost analysis and the potential application of volume-cost studies have not been widely recognized. One of the main objectives of this book is to show, through analysis of actual business problems, a variety of important uses of volume-cost studies, uses which help management in making more intelligent business decisions and thus lead toward better profit. Included among the analyses is the application of the author's formula, table and charts for helping management evaluate price reductions, which were developed by him several years ago and which are now made available to the public for the first time.

The introduction of a formal system of volume-cost analysis to a business organization, like that of any other new management tool, may create problems if the company is not fully prepared. The second objective of this book is to show some of the key factors underlying the successful application of this new tool, so that those contemplating the introduction of the new system may avoid the pitfalls which have already been experienced by others.

The size of this study does not permit a full discussion of all the uses and all the issues involved in the application of volume-cost analysis. Nor does this study purport to be a statistical review of practices in volume-cost analysis. Instead, topics have been selected on the basis of their educational value for management.

A unique feature of this book is that it contains a number of actual cases covering a variety of situations. The findings are based primarily upon the experience of more than ten companies in several different industries. Most of these companies have annual sales ranging from $10,000,000 to $60,-000,000. Large companies with annual sales exceeding $100,000,000 and smaller ones with annual sales of less than $1,000,000 have also been included.

Since it is necessary to conceal the identity of these companies, all names, including both corporations and individuals as well as product and brand names, used in this book are fictitious. All figures and statistics contained in this book are likewise fictitious and are for the purpose of illustration only. Hence, any similarity which the reader may find with him or his own company is purely coincidental.

The organization of this book follows closely its main objectives. Part I deals with the uses of volume-cost analysis and should, therefore, be of particular interest to executives who are primarily interested in knowing how volume-cost analysis can help them make better decisions. Part II deals with factors underlying the successful application of formal volume-cost analysis systems and should, therefore, be of interest to those who are responsible for the installation and administration of such systems. In the appendices, three comprehensive cases showing the evolutionary experience at three different companies are presented.

* * *

The successful undertaking of a project like this one would not have been possible without the assistance of many other persons. While the author cannot name here individually the executives who so generously contributed their time and experience to this study without disclosing the identity of their companies, he is indebted to all of them for their courtesy and assistance. In the process of planning and writing this book, many helpful suggestions were received from Professors Clarence B. Nickerson and Charles A. Bliss of Harvard Graduate School of Business Administration, Dr. Herbert F. Klingman, formerly Research Director of Controllership Foundation and now Director, Division of Commerce, University of Wisconsin-Milwaukee, Mr. John W. Gladson, of Esso Standard Oil Company and Columbia Graduate School of Business, Mr. Harry P. Kelley, of American Viscose Corporation, and Mrs. Helen E. Haworth, of Purdue University. To all of them, the author is deeply grateful. Special gratitude is owed to Mr. Robert Shenton of Harvard University who cheerfully read several drafts of this manuscript and whose invaluable help and incessant encouragement will always be remembered. Finally to the author's wife, Emma, profound appreciation is due for her moral support and understanding throughout this project. While the help of all the persons mentioned above is gratefully acknowledged, the responsibility for the study and the views expressed therein rest entirely with the author.

JOHN Y. D. TSE

CONTENTS

LIST OF CASES

PROFIT PLANNING

through

VOLUME-COST ANALYSIS

Part I

THE USES OF
VOLUME-COST
ANALYSIS IN
PROFIT PLANNING

CHAPTER 1

Introduction to
Profit Planning

In a free enterprise system, there is probably no privately operated business that does not hope to make a profit from its operations. Profit is invariably one of the key criteria used by management in evaluating and selecting its operating plans.[1] Whenever any person translates his operating plans into financial terms and uses his estimates of the probable income expense and profit as a guide in planning and conducting the operation of a business, he is in fact profit planning. The practice of profit planning is, therefore, as old as the history of business itself. The underlying concept, if not the term, of profit planning is thus familiar.

Profit planning through volume-cost analysis, however, is a modern concept of management planning, a tool designed primarily for industrial enterprises. It involves a study of what a business' costs and expenses should be and will be at different levels of operation, and it includes a study of the resultant effect upon profit due to this changing relationship between volume and cost.

Prior to the introduction of volume-cost analysis, the type of profit planning generally used, including both formal and informal planning, was what is called today a fixed budget. Essentially, a fixed budget is a projection of a company's revenue, costs, and expenses on the basis of management's expec-

[1] Profit, of course, should not be the sole determinant of a business' operating plans. Other criteria which may be used by management are to maintain steady employment, to provide customers with satisfactory products and services, to fulfill a business' social responsibilities, and so forth. However, except for government operated enterprises, the ability of privately operated businesses to fulfill and maintain these other objectives over any extended period of time will be very much limited if a healthy profit cannot be made at the same time.

3

tation of a certain fixed volume of business for a given period. While the fixed budget is still an indispensable part of profit planning, management of a number of companies found that fixed budgets alone were not adequate.

As an illustration, assume that XYZ Manufacturing Company estimates that its sales this year would be $10,000,000. Its costs would be $9,000,000, and its resulting profit would be $1,000,000. Suppose that this company's sales are now running at the rate of $7,000,000 a year. Could the management of this company assume that a 30 per cent reduction in volume of business should and would be accompanied by a similar percentage reduction in costs and profit? In such case, there would still be a profit of $700,000. Although this $700,000 is less than the original estimate of $1,000,000, it might still be satisfactory to the management. Hence, no modification in operating plans would necessarily be considered. Or, could the management of this company assume that, although its sales were only 70 per cent of its original expectation, its costs would remain at $9,000,000? It would therefore lose $2,000,000 this year.

The answer to both these questions is no. But how much would the cost of this company be when its sales are at the level of $7,000,000? How much profit could it make at this level? The answer will have to depend upon this company's cost structure.

Those who are familiar with the actual conduct of a modern business know that the various costs and expenses of a company do not respond uniformly to changes in volume of operation. Certain costs will fluctuate in direct proportion to changes in volume of business. Others will remain fixed regardless of changes in volume. Still others will respond only in part to these changes. The nonuniform response of different costs and expenses to changes in volume of business has a serious effect upon profits. A seemingly insignificant decline in volume from an expected level can often be accompanied by a serious drop in expected profit. Depending upon the cost structure and existing level of business, such decline in volume can often result in substantial losses.

For many industrial enterprises, it is extremely difficult to predict with certainty the *exact* volume of business in the period ahead, because of the constant presence of such uncertain factors as competition, consumer attitudes, general economic conditions, government regulations, union relations, and many others that may affect sales and production. Most managements find that a reasoned estimate based upon informed and experienced judgment of the most probable range of volume of business is the best they can do.

Owing to the difficulty of predicting the exact volume of business in the period ahead, managements of a number of companies studied by the author found that intelligent evaluation of operating plans could often be sharpened by analyzing the probable costs and profits at several different volumes of business, instead of the cost and profit at only one volume level. By analyzing the changing volume-cost relationship of a business, management not only learns what should be and will be its costs and expenses at different volumes of business, including the one which will actually be realized by the company under different operating plans, but it also acquires additional information, which is often crucial in the final decision of the operating plan under consideration, but which is not provided if no volume-cost analysis has been made. Examples of such information are: (1) the minimum volume of business which a company must achieve in order to keep itself out of loss, (2) the minimum volume of business which the company must attain in order to reach its profit objectives, (3) the probable profit or loss at different volumes of business within the range which management can reasonably expect, and (4) the relevant cost information in decisions of whether a company should keep or drop a line of product or whether it should accept or reject a particular order from a customer at a certain specified price, and so forth. It was found that with information of this type management could make a better evaluation of the profit opportunities or lack thereof of any operating plans under consideration. On the other hand, ignorance of the volume-cost relationship and lack of such information could on many occasions lead management into improper and erroneous decisions on future operating plans. These poor decisions might well have been avoided if the proper knowledge of volume-cost relationships had been available.

For example, the success or failure of many new businesses or products can often be traced to the wisdom displayed by management at the time when the investment decision is being made. Not infrequently, estimates of costs and profit used in investment decisions were based upon a certain assumed "normal," "average," "optimum," or sometimes even "maximum" level of production, with no consideration being given to whether and when the company's sales would be able to reach such a level and what would happen if the company did not reach that level. Then, after the investments had already been made, many of these companies were jolted into realization that it would usually take some time to build up a business and that, when sales volumes were less than what had been assumed, the costs of running a business did not come down proportionately. Depending upon their volume-cost structure and rate of growth, some of these companies would have to face a sustained period of deficit operation. If their financial resources were limited, many of them would be extinguished long before they could reach their normal, average or optimum level of operation, even if such a level might eventually be reached when enough time was allowed.

Mistakes of this nature could often have been prevented and better courses of action could have been selected if the management of these companies had analyzed their volume-cost structure at the time when investment decisions were made. As pointed out earlier, by analyzing the changing volume-cost relationships of a business, management not only learns what should be and will be its costs and expenses at different volumes of business, it also learns the profit or loss that it will make or incur at various levels of operation. In addition, it also learns the minimum sales volumes that are necessary to keep it out of loss and to enable it to reach its profit objectives. By learning the minimum sales volumes necessary to keep a company out of loss and to enable it to reach its profit objectives, management will be forced to study whether or not and when the company will be able to reach such volumes. The knowledge of profit or loss to be expected under different sales volumes can serve as an important aid to management in studying whether or not, and how much, additional funds over and above the initial investment in plant and equipment will be needed to keep the business going before it becomes self-sufficient. This knowledge of profit or loss at different volumes of business can also provide management with a convenient means of studying if and when the original investment can be recovered and how much profit in the aggregate can be expected from the investment during its life span. Although no scientific method can ever completely eliminate management's judgment in the planning and operation of a business, by dealing on an objective basis, volume-cost analysis provides management with a means of making sounder appraisals of the future of a capital investment and forces management's attention on those critical areas where its judgment can most effectively focus for the successful operation of a business.

Besides capital investment, pricing is another area where the wisdom of management decisions plays a very important role in the success or failure of many companies. Experience shows that unsound pricing decisions not only can bring misfortune to individual companies, but can also lead an entire industry into chaotic conditions. While there are many factors which management must take into consideration in any pricing decision, cost is certainly one that can hardly be ignored.

In considering the cost of a product for pricing purposes, management again must analyze the volume-cost relationship of its particular business. Otherwise, it can be easily misled into erroneous decisions. It is a common practice that, since the price of a product has to be expressed in terms of a certain monetary value per unit of product, the cost figure used for pricing purposes also has to be expressed in terms of cost per unit of product. Because of the changing relationship between volume and cost in a manufacturing company, the unit cost of its product will vary with the volume of business selected or assumed by the company in its cost computations. Failure to recognize the changing volume-cost relationships of a business and to question the reasonableness of the volume assumed in cost computation is found to be one of the major causes of many unsound pricing decisions leading toward unprofitable operations. On the other hand, one company, which had been operating at a loss, was able to turn its operation into a profitable one through a change of its pricing policy, following a study of its volume-cost relationship. The experience of some of the companies studied as well as the use of the knowledge of volume-cost relationships in helping management make more intelligent pricing decisions will be discussed in detail in a later chapter.

For companies that do not set the prices of their own products but choose to follow the prices set by others in the same industry for similar products, decisions of adding, pushing, or dropping a product are often based upon the profitability of that product under a certain prevailing or expected price. In determining the profit of any product, cost again is a key factor which management has to take into consideration. Since adding, pushing, or dropping a product invariably involves a change in volume of operation, a proper understanding of the volume-cost relationship of the particular business is needed in determining the profitability of any product under consideration. Without volume-cost analysis, management can easily be misled by conventional cost or accounting reports as to the profitability of a product in deciding whether such a product should be pushed or dropped from operations.

In addition to the selection of intelligent operating plans in advance, the successful reaching of the profit goal of a business depends also upon the ability of management to keep its costs and expenses under proper control. Effective cost control requires an understanding of what and how much should be or should have been spent for different types of costs and expenses. Because of the difficulty in predicting the exact volume of business in the period ahead and of the changing relationship between volume and cost, the value of many of the older devices of cost control, including fixed budget and standard cost, is limited to only those costs or expenses which are either completely fixed or completely variable in relation to changes in volume of operation. But the total cost of a business and many individual expenses in a manufacturing company are neither completely fixed nor completely variable. This is particularly true of overhead expenses, because these are made up of a conglomeration of expenses, each of which behaves differently in response to changes in volume of business. Furthermore, overhead expenses in many industrial companies appear to have grown higher and higher in relation to productive labor. In order to keep these costs under proper control, it is necessary for management to know what should be spent at different levels of operation and what should have been spent at the actual level of operation experienced by the company. This again necessitates studies of the changing relationship between volume and cost of the particular company.

It is believed that the concepts of volume-cost analysis or the practicality

of applying such concepts are still foreign to the mind of many managements. The cases presented in the following chapters will show specific
examples in which the lack of knowledge of volume-cost relationships of a
particular business led to erroneous decisions which could otherwise have
been avoided. They include problems such as those of planning capital
expenditures, make or buy, keeping or dropping an unprofitable product,
price determination, cost control, and so forth. All these cases show that
better decisions can be made with an intelligent study of volume-cost relationships.

CHAPTER 2

Planning Capital Expenditures

One of the most perplexing yet extremely important business problems is the planning of capital expenditures for a "new" product. Frequently involved in one single decision are hundreds of thousands of dollars for smaller firms, millions of dollars for larger companies. The success or failure of a number of businesses can often be traced to the wisdom displayed in their early investment decisions. Management is not infrequently led into unsound investment decisions by deceptive cost and profit analyses. Common to these misleading analyses are assumptions of an unrealistically high volume of operation in the computation of cost and profit and ignorance of the changing volume-cost-profit relationships. The need and value of studying the changing relationships among volume, cost, and profit of a business for helping management make better investment decisions on capital expenditures will thus be brought out by the experience of Hobson Pigment Company.

Hobson Pigment Company

Hobson Pigment Company, a subsidiary of Montana Metals Company, mines and processes octahedrite into titanium pigment for use in the paint and ceramic industries. The titanium pigment manufactured and marketed by Hobson was a new product recently developed by the research laboratory of Montana Metals Company, which has been undertaking an extensive program of diversification and expansion since the end of World War II. According to Montana's laboratory reports, the Hobson pigment is the most

9

versatile pigment on the market. The use of this pigment will not only give finished paints higher brilliancy and greater durability, but will also make possible a reduction in paint manufacturing costs by eliminating a number of other "extenders" currently used in the manufacture of a variety of paints. To bring this new laboratory development into commercial operation, a subsidiary, Hobson Pigment Company, was formed in 1953. Mining rights to more than 5,000,000 tons of proved octahedrite near Hobson, Montana, were acquired. A new plant equipped with the most modern machinery to

TABLE 2–1

Montana Metal Company

Estimates of Income, Expenses, and Profit on Proposed Investment in
Hobson Pigment Company

		Total	Average per Ton
Sales (100,000 tons)		$3,000,000	$30.00
Costs and expenses:			
Mining royalties		$ 200,000	$ 2.00
Operating labor	$425,000		$4.25
Maintenance labor	210,000		2.10
Packing and shipping labor	158,000		1.58
Administrative labor	22,000		0.22
Supervision	35,000		0.35
	$850,000		$8.50
Fringe benefits	170,000		1.70
		1,020,000	10.20
Operating supplies	$200,000		$2.00
Maintenance supplies	250,000		2.50
Light, power, and fuel	300,000		3.00
Packing and shipping supplies	200,000		2.00
General supplies and services	150,000		1.50
Property insurance and taxes	5,000		0.05
		1,105,000	11.05
Depreciation		125,000	1.25
Market development		150,000	1.50
Total cost and expense		$2,600,000	$26.00
Pre-tax profit		$ 400,000	$ 4.00
Income taxes at 50%		200,000	2.00
Net profit after taxes		$ 200,000	$ 2.00

Estimated life of plant: 12 years
Years to pay off $1,500,000 investment in plant and equipment: 4.6 years
Rate of return on investment of
    $1,500,000 (plant and equipment)   13.3%
    $1,600,000 (plant and equipment and land)   12.5%
    $2,000,000 (fixed property and working capital) 10.0%

process 300 tons of finished pigment a day was built at a cost of $1,600,000.

Preliminary estimates indicated that a yearly pre-tax profit of $400,000 and an after-tax profit of $200,000 could be obtained on an annual sales volume of 100,000 tons.[1] The new pigment was expected to be sold at a price of $30 against an average cost of $26 per ton. The entire investment of $1,500,000 in plant and equipment (exclusive of a $100,000 investment in land) was expected to be recovered in less than 5 years. An after-tax rate of return ranging from 10 to 13.3 per cent was expected. Details of these estimates are shown in Table 2–1. Commercial production was started by Hobson early in 1954, management of Montana being confident of the future of this new product.

However, despite Montana's high optimism, the actual operating results of Hobson during its first 3 years of operation were far from satisfactory. Its sales during each of these years were

1954	1,000 tons
1955	2,000 tons
1956	4,000 tons

which represented only a small proportion of the company's productive capacity and estimated volume. During this 3-year period, the total operating loss amounted to $1,144,000, and additional cash had to be supplied by the parent company to keep it going. A statement of income and expenses for the year ended December 31, 1956, is shown in Table 2–2.

One of the major difficulties encountered by Hobson in trying to sell to paint and ceramic manufacturers was the reluctance of prospective customers to change their raw-material formulas or manufacturing processes until the improved performance of a new ingredient could be ascertained. Although some paint manufacturers were willing to experiment with Hobson pigment in their laboratories, complete laboratory evaluation of the qualities of any paint usually involved a long waiting period.[2] Therefore, even to these cooperative customers, few immediate sales could be made.

The operating executive of Hobson Pigment Company felt that, although sales volume had not reached a satisfactory level, its selling efforts had, nevertheless, met with satisfying success. He pointed out the fact that, despite the difficult selling job which Hobson had to face, the company had been able to double its sales each year since it started operation. While its operation had not been profitable, he felt that acceptable operating profit was within sight, justifying continued optimism by Montana's management.

[1] 48 weeks at 7 days = 336 days at 300 tons a day = 100,800 tons. An annual volume of 100,000 tons was used in the estimate.

[2] One of the testing procedures used by many paint manufacturers is to prepare a batch of paint through pilot grinders and mixers. The finished paint will then be subjected to actual atmospheric conditions for durability and brilliancy for a minimum period of 12 months to 5 years.

TABLE 2–2

Hobson Pigment Company

Statement of Income and Expenses
Year Ended December 31, 1956

Net sales	*4,000 tons*		$120,000
Manufacturing cost of goods sold:			
Inventory at beginning	*AVG. PER TON*		...
Manufacturing expenses:			
Mining royalties	*2.00*	$ 8,000	
Operating labor	*10.25*	$ 41,000	
Maintenance labor		18,000	
Packing and shipping labor		14,000	
Administrative labor		22,000	
Supervision		35,000	
		$130,000	
Payroll fringe benefits		26,000	
		$156,000	
Operating supplies		$ 8,000	
Maintenance supplies		10,000	
Light, power, and fuel		12,000	
Packing and shipping supplies		8,000	
General supplies		6,000	
Property insurance and taxes		5,000	
		$ 49,000	
Depreciation		$125,000	
Total manufacturing expenses			338,000
Inventory at end			(...)
Manufacturing cost of goods sold			$338,000
Market development expenses			150,000
Total costs and expenses			$488,000
Operating profit (loss)			($368,000)

(handwritten annotation: "labor varied" with bracket beside Operating labor through Packing and shipping labor)

Operating statistics:

Inventory at beginning	None
Production	4,000 tons
Sales	4,000 tons
Inventory at end	None
Net realized selling price	$30.00 per ton
Average manufacturing cost	$84.50 per ton

Up until 1957, Mr. Frank A. Payne, controller of Montana Metals Company, was responsible to its top management in reporting only past financial histories and on matters related to corporate income taxes. Analysis for capital expenditures was the function of another department. Although his opinion had never been sought prior to Montana's decision to commit

$1,500,000 in the new plant, Mr. Payne had been carefully watching the operation of Hobson since its start.

The continuous cash drain of Hobson on Montana in the past few years had now caused considerable concern among several members of the parent company's executive committee. Although they had been assured from time to time that profitable operation would be in sight soon, they wondered if this would ever happen. After a full discussion among its members, the committee decided that an independent study should be made in this case, and Mr. Payne was asked to do the job.

Mr. Payne, although sharing the optimistic outlook about the expanding sales of Hobson pigment, was, nevertheless, less enthusiastic about the prediction of Hobson's reaching a satisfactory profit level in the early future. From the experience of the past 3 years, a study of Hobson's volume-cost-

TABLE 2–3

Hobson Pigment Company

Summary of Variable and Fixed Expenses—1956

	Variable Cost per Ton of Pigment	Total Variable Cost	Fixed Cost	Total Cost
Mining royalties	$ 2.00	$ 8,000	...	$ 8,000
Operating labor	$ 4.00	$16,000	$ 25,000	$ 41,000
Maintenance labor	2.00	8,000	10,000	18,000
Packing and shipping labor	1.50	6,000	8,000	14,000
Administrative labor	...	...	22,000	22,000
Supervision	...	...	35,000	35,000
	$ 7.50	$30,000	$100,000	$130,000
Payroll fringe benefits	1.50	6,000	20,000	26,000
Total wages and salaries including fringe benefits	$ 9.00	$36,000	$120,000	$156,000
Operating supplies	$ 2.00	$ 8,000	...	$ 8,000
Maintenance supplies	2.50	10,000	...	10,000
Light, power, and fuel	3.00	12,000	...	12,000
Packing and shipping supplies	2.00	8,000	...	8,000
General supplies and services	1.50	6,000	...	6,000
Property insurance and taxes	...	...	$ 5,000	5,000
Total supplies and expenses	$11.00	$44,000	$ 5,000	$ 49,000
Depreciation	...	...	$125,000	$125,000
Market development	...	...	150,000	150,000
Total cost and expenses	$22.00	$88,000	$400,000	$488,000

Total sales and production in 1956: 4,000 tons
Net selling price realized: $30 per ton

profit relationships was made by him. He found that, during 1956 for every ton of pigment produced and sold, Hobson's variable cost of production amounted to $22 against a net realized selling price of $30. Only $8 a ton or $32,000 was left to cover the company's fixed costs and expenses, which amounted to $400,000. Under this cost structure, Hobson would have to sell a minimum of 50,000 tons a year before it could start to earn any profit. If it wanted to earn a pre-tax profit of $400,000, it would have to sell 100,000 tons. Compare these figures with the 4,000 tons which were actually sold in 1956. A summary of Hobson's variable and fixed costs by types of expense is shown in Table 2–3. Its volume-cost-profit relationships in 1956 are shown in Fig. 2–1.

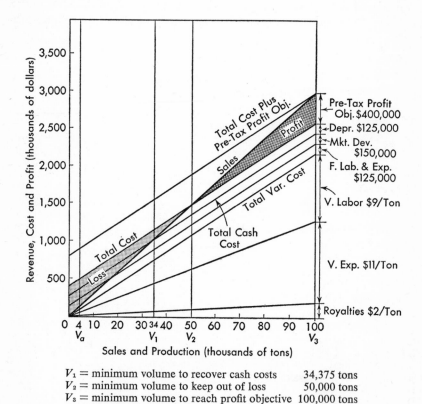

V_1 = minimum volume to recover cash costs   34,375 tons
V_2 = minimum volume to keep out of loss   50,000 tons
V_3 = minimum volume to reach profit objective 100,000 tons
V_a = actual volume in 1956   4,000 tons

Fig. 2–1.   Hobson Pigment Company. Volume-cost-profit relationships for 1956.

In order to give the executive committee some rough idea as to when Hobson would be able to stand "on its own feet," how much additional cash Montana would have to provide to carry Hobson through, and how much profit Hobson would be able to make after it was "broken in," three different sales estimates were made by Mr. Payne. Under the first, or conservative, estimate Hobson's sales would double each year for the first three years of operation, and would then increase at the rate of 2,000 tons a year. Under the second, medium optimistic, estimate Hobson's sales would continue to double until they reached a level of 16,000 tons a year in 1958. Thereafter, its sales would increase at the rate of 8,000 tons a year, reaching a level of 72,000 tons by 1965. Under the third, very optimistic, estimate Hobson's sales would continue to double each year until they reached the maximum productive capacity of 100,000 tons a year in 1961 and would remain at that level until the end of the economic life of the present productive facility.

The economic life of Hobson's productive facilities represents the length of useful service which Montana's management can most reasonably expect from its investment. Twelve years was considered to be the economic life of Hobson's present productive facility.

Based upon the volume-cost relationships shown in Fig. 2–1 and Table 2–3, the expected yearly profit or loss and the cumulative profit or loss during the entire economic life of Hobson's present productive facility under the three different sales estimates were computed. The results of these computations are shown in Tables 2–4, 2–5, and 2–6, and Figs. 2–2, 2–3, and 2–4.

TABLE 2–4

Hobson Pigment Company

Estimates of Sales, Profit, and Cash Deficit—Conservative
1954–1965

	Year	Sales	Net Pre-tax Profit (*Loss*)	Pre-tax Cash Profit (*Loss*)	Cumulative Profit (*Loss*)	Cumulative Cash Profit (*Loss*)
		Tons	(000 omitted)	(000 omitted)	(000 omitted)	(000 omitted)
1	1954	1,000	($392)	($267)	($ 392)	($ 267)
2	1955	2,000	(384)	(259)	(776)	(526)
3	1956	4,000	(368)	(243)	(1,144)	(769)
4	1957	6,000	(352)	(227)*	(1,496)	(996)
5	1958	8,000	(336)	(211)*	(1,832)	(1,207)
6	1959	10,000	(320)	(195)*	(2,152)	(1,402)
7	1960	12,000	(304)	(179)*	(2,456)	(1,581)
8	1961	14,000	(288)	(163)*	(2,744)	(1,744)
9	1962	16,000	(272)	(147)*	(3,016)	(1,891)
10	1963	18,000	(256)	(131)*	(3,272)	(2,022)
11	1964	20,000	(240)	(115)*	(3,512)	(2,187)
12	1965	22,000	(224)	(99)*	(3,736)	(2,236)

* Total cash deficit 1957 to 1965: $1,467,000.

While all three estimates were optimistic about the future outlook for Hobson's expanding volume of business, the profit or loss that might be expected from these sales presents three entirely different pictures. With a rate of expansion such as that indicated by the conservative estimate (Table 2–4 and Fig. 2–2), Hobson would never have any opportunity to show a

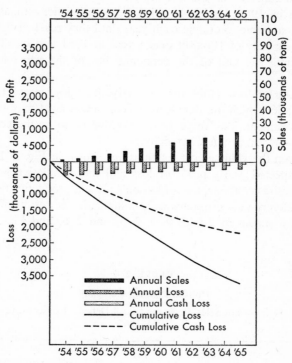

Fig. 2–2. Hobson Pigment Company. Estimates of sales, profit, and cash deficit— conservative—for 1954–1965.

profit within the life span of its present productive facility. This rate of expansion is too slow to provide an adequate sales volume to "break in" the company. To keep itself out of loss, Hobson needs a minimum sales volume of 50,000 tons a year under its present cost structure. But at the rate of increase of 2,000 tons a year, its annual sales would be only 22,000 tons by 1965. Additional cash would, therefore, have to be continuously poured in by Montana to keep Hobson going. The sum of $1,467,000 would be needed over the next 9 years (1957–1965) merely to cover Hobson's cash operating deficit during this period. When Hobson's present productive facility came to the end of its economic life, Montana's investment would be completely dissipated, resulting in a total loss of $3,736,000 over a 12-year period.

A much-improved profit picture could, nevertheless, be obtained if Hob-

TABLE 2–5

Hobson Pigment Company

Estimates of Sales, Profit, and Cash Deficit—Medium Optimistic
1954–1965

	Year	Sales	Net Pre-tax Profit (Loss)	Pre-tax Cash Profit (Loss)	Cumulative Profit (Loss)	Cumulative Cash Profit (Loss)
		Tons	(000 omitted)	(000 omitted)	(000 omitted)	(000 omitted)
1	1954	1,000	($392)	($267)	($ 392)	($ 267)
2	1955	2,000	(384)	(259)	(776)	(526)
3	1956	4,000	(368)	(243)	(1,144)	(769)
4	1957	8,000	(336)	(211)*	(1,480)	(980)
5	1958	16,000	(272)	(147)*	(1,752)	(1,127)
6	1959	24,000	(208)	(83)*	(1,960)	(1,210)
7	1960	32,000	(144)	(19)*	(2,104)	(1,229)
8	1961	40,000	(80)	45	(2,184)	(1,184)
9	1962	48,000	(16)	109	(2,200)	(1,075)
10	1963	56,000	48	173	(2,152)	(902)
11	1964	64,000	112	237	(2,040)	(665)
12	1965	72,000	176	301	(1,864)	(364)

* Total cash deficit 1957 to 1960: $460,000.

son could expand its sales at a faster rate, such as the one shown under the
medium optimistic sales estimate (Table 2–5 and Fig. 2–3). Under this
accelerated rate of expansion, the company would continue to lose money
through 1962. However, after 1962 its sales would reach a level high enough
to yield some profit. Furthermore, not only would Hobson have an opportunity to make some profit, but its reliance upon Montana for continued
financial support to carry it through would also be limited to the next 4
years (1957–1960) only. Total cash required during this period was estimated at $460,000. Hobson's operating profit during the later years would
enable it to recover a large portion, though not all, of its operating losses
incurred during the earlier years. Over the entire life span of its productive
facility, Hobson's net cash operating deficit would be $364,000 in contrast
with $2,236,000 under the conservative sales estimate. While the cash
operating loss would be greatly reduced, the $1,500,000 investment in the
present productive facility would, nevertheless, be dissipated as it would
under the conservative estimate.

A still better profit picture might be obtained if Hobson could continue
to double its sales as shown under the third, very optimistic, estimate (Table
2–6 and Fig. 2–4). Although the company would continue to lose money
through 1959, it would finally reach, by 1961, an annual sales volume of
100,000 tons a year. At this level, the company would be able to earn the
$400,000 pre-tax profit desired by its management. Only $377,000 addi-

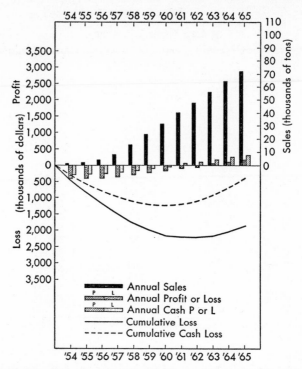

Fig. 2–3. Hobson Pigment Company. Estimates of sales, profit, and cash deficit —medium optimistic—for 1954–1965.

tional cash would be needed from the parent company to cover the cash operating deficit of the subsidiary through the next 3 years (1957–1959). Thereafter, Hobson would be able to "stand on its own feet." When the economic life of its present productive facility came to its end by 1965, the $1,500,000 investment in this facility would be fully recovered. In addition, a small net profit would be made over this period. However, because of the heavy operating losses during the early years, this net pre-tax profit (over the entire life span) would amount to only $216,000.

Mr. Payne's analysis of Hobson's future profitability was presented at the executive meeting of Montana Metals Company. Top management of Montana was greatly impressed with this analysis and regarded it as the first realistic approach to the evaluation of Hobson's future. As pointed out previously, some of the executives had been very distressed by the heavy operating loss of Hobson during the past 3 years and had been extremely concerned as to how long this would continue. Mr. Payne's analysis distinctly showed whether Hobson would ever have a chance of being self-sufficient and clearly indicated the minimum sales volumes Hobson must achieve in order to keep itself out of loss and to reach its profit objective. Another

TABLE 2-6

Hobson Pigment Company

Estimates of Sales, Profit, and Cash Deficit—Very Optimistic
1954–1965

	Year	Sales	Net Pre-tax Profit (Loss)	Pre-tax Cash Profit (Loss)	Cumulative Profit (Loss)	Cumulative Cash Profit (Loss)
		Tons	(000 omitted)	(000 omitted)	(000 omitted)	(000 omitted)
1	1954	1,000	($392)	($267)	($ 392)	($ 267)
2	1955	2,000	(384)	(259)	(776)	(526)
3	1956	4,000	(368)	(243)	(1,144)	(769)
4	1957	8,000	(336)	(211)*	(1,480)	(980)
5	1958	16,000	(272)	(147)*	(1,752)	(1,127)
6	1959	32,000	(144)	(19)*	(1,896)	(1,146)
7	1960	64,000	112	237	(1,784)	(909)
8	1961	100,000	400	525	(1,384)	(384)
9	1962	100,000	400	525	(984)	141
10	1963	100,000	400	525	(584)	666
11	1964	100,000	400	525	(184)	1,191
12	1965	100,000	400	525	216	1,716

* Total cash deficit 1957 to 1959: $377,000.

valuable contribution of Mr. Payne's analysis was an estimate of how much additional cash Montana would have to pour in to carry Hobson through under different sales volumes, together with an estimate of how long a period this financial subsidy would be required. The crucial point now was to decide how fast Hobson would be able to expand its future business, and which estimate would be the most realistic.

The consensus of Montana's top executives was that Hobson's sales would probably expand at a rate such as that indicated by Mr. Payne's medium optimistic estimate. Should this be the case for its actual sales, Montana's investment in Hobson obviously could not be considered as a success within the life span of its productive facility. However, Montana's top management was relieved at the knowledge that, if Hobson's sales should expand at this rate, the additional financial assistance needed from Montana would be limited to only $460,000, which would be spread over the next 4 years. Montana's financial position was strong enough to provide this continued support. Its management considered this relatively small additional investment worth spending, because Hobson might have an opportunity to expand its sales to more than 100,000 tons a year. The investment in Hobson's present productive facility and operating deficit should then be considered only as a part of Montana's cost of diversification and building up new lines of business. If Hobson's sales did expand to such a

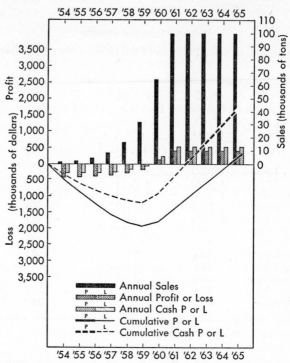

Fig. 2–4. Hobson Pigment Company. Estimates of sales, profit, and cash deficit—very optimistic—for 1954–1965.

high level as to require the construction of a second plant in the future, Montana might then be able to reap a fruitful harvest.

Montana's top management felt that, if Mr. Payne's analysis had been available in 1953, it probably would not have built Hobson's present productive facility at that time. More likely, a much smaller plant would have been built in 1953. While it recognized its own responsibility for the investment decision in Hobson, top management at Montana now realized that the original estimate of cost and profit as shown in Table 2–1 was absolutely useless if not grossly misleading in this particular case.

In order to avoid a recurrence of the same type of mistake, Montana's top management authorized Mr. Payne to develop some standard procedures for evaluating capital expenditures and to incorporate his new method of analysis in these procedures. Furthermore, in recognition of his work, the entire budgetary function at Montana, including evaluation of capital expenditures, has now been added to Mr. Payne's responsibilities.

The experience of Hobson Pigment Company is a clear example of the need for studying volume-cost relationships of a business in planning capital expenditures for a "new" product.[3] A basic defect of many conventional cost and profit analyses designed for helping management evaluate capital investment is their common failure to recognize the changing volume-cost relationships and the resultant effect upon profit caused by variations in volume of business. Too frequently, cost and profit estimates computed on the basis of maximum utilization of proposed productive facilities are accepted unequivocally by management as the guidepost to an intricate problem. At other times, a more sophisticated management will analyze its costs and profit on the basis of a certain "representative," "normal," or "average" volume of business. The optimistic pictures provided by these analyses are often accepted unhesitatingly without further examination as to whether and when the company will be able to reach the maximum or representative volume of business and, on the other hand, what will happen if it does not reach such a volume. An implicit assumption often used is that the unit cost and profit of a product will remain the same at all other levels of operation as they would at the maximum or representative volume of business. Thus, in the case of Hobson Pigment Company, it was implied in Montana's 1953 analysis that if only 4,000 tons was sold instead of 100,000 tons it would still be able to make a profit of $16,000 at the rate of $4 per ton. Obviously, this assumption was erroneous because it ignored the changing volume-cost relationships. As Montana later found out, when Hobson sold only 4,000 tons, rather than making a profit of $16,000, it suffered a loss of $368,000. Had it not been for the financial strength of Montana Metals Company and its ability to pour in substantial amounts of cash to carry Hobson through its unexpected deficit operation, one might seriously question whether Hobson would still be in existence.

Montana's recognition of the changing volume, cost, and profit relationships would necessarily have led the company to a number of searching questions basic to a realistic evaluation of proposed capital expenditures. Among these essential questions are:

1. What is the minimum sales volume a company must have in order to keep itself out of loss?
2. What is the minimum sales volume it must have to enable it to reach its profit objective?
3. Will the company be able to reach these minimum sales volumes?
4. If so, when?
5. If a deficit operation will be experienced, how much will the company lose each year and for how long a period?

[3] In addition to its use in helping management improve planning of capital expenditures, the knowledge of volume-cost relationships is also useful in assisting management to make more intelligent decisions of whether or not to discontinue operation of an unprofitable business, a subject which will be taken up separately in Chap. 4.

6. How much cash, in addition to the initial investment in plant and equipment, will be needed each year to finance this deficit operation?

7. Over the entire economic life of the proposed capital expenditures, how much of this investment can be recovered and when will it be recovered?

8. After the business is "broken in," how much profit can be expected each year and how much profit can be expected over the entire life span of the proposed investment?

Mr. Payne's analysis of Hobson's future prospects is essentially an effort to answer some of these questions. This is the type of information which should have been available to Montana's top management, but no one had explicitly raised these questions before. Thus, Montana's management was especially receptive to Mr. Payne's analysis, and it was incorporated into company procedures for evaluation of future capital expenditures.

In computing the estimated future profits of Hobson Pigment Company, Mr. Payne had made several implicit assumptions, the validity of which should be examined by Montana's management. One of his assumptions was that Hobson's future cost structure would remain the same as that experienced in 1956. This assumption requires further examination in view of the rising trend of wage rates and of the prices of many items used by Hobson. For instance, Montana has a policy of giving its employees annual salary and wage increases. Its fringe labor costs in relation to direct labor costs have also become increasingly higher through the years. Prices of a number of supplies and service items used by Hobson are likewise rising under the inflationary trend of the economy.

A second assumption by Mr. Payne requiring further examination is his projection of Hobson's cost structure experienced under an extremely low level of operation into higher levels of operation. This could be a valid assumption when Hobson's volume fluctuates within certain relatively narrow limits. However, as Hobson swings from its present low level of operation of 4,000 tons a year into operations ten or twenty times its present volume, several of its operating departments will surely have to add additional shifts or work overtime. Under such conditions, both the fixed and variable expenses of Hobson will be under upward pressure.

The future selling price of Hobson's pigment is another assumption requiring further examination. The price of a product may have an upward, stable, or downward trend, depending to a large extent upon the characteristics of the product and the nature of the industry. The validity of Mr. Payne's assumption that the future selling price of Hobson's pigment will remain at $30 per ton should, therefore, be appraised by Montana's management in accordance with its experience and reasoned judgment.

Some of these assumptions may seem to impose limitations; yet the usefulness of Mr. Payne's method of analysis need not be impaired by the presence of these assumptions. In fact, the appraisal of proposed capital expenditures can be sharpened under Mr. Payne's method of analysis if his assumptions are openly brought to the attention of management. With a full knowledge of what is involved, due allowance can be given to the interpretation of the results of Mr. Payne's computation, or a more thorough analysis can be undertaken. Under the latter approach, future wage rates and prices of other services and supplies as well as the selling price of Hobson's pigment expected by Montana's management can be spelled out before estimates of profit or loss are made. Likewise, Hobson's cost structure at higher levels of operation can be determined by more careful studies of its volume-cost relationships. The estimated minimum sales volumes required to keep the company out of loss and to reach its profit objective as well as the estimated profit or loss at different volumes in different years could then be computed, based on operating conditions expected to prevail at that time.

By recognizing the changing volume-cost-profit relationships of a business, the new approach to the evaluation of capital expenditures surpasses the conventional methods of analysis in its ability to guide management to more realistic thinking. Under this new method, management can attain a clear perception of costs, profit, and loss to be expected under actual operating conditions—not under some imaginary or deceptive situation. By learning the minimum sales volumes necessary to keep a company out of loss and to enable it to reach its profit objective, management will be forced to study whether or not and when the company will be able to reach such volumes. The knowledge of profit or loss to be expected under different sales volumes can serve as an important aid to management in studying whether or not and how much additional funds, over and above initial investment in plant and equipment, will be needed to keep the business going, that is, before it becomes self-sufficient. This knowledge of profit or loss at different volumes of business can also provide management with a convenient means of studying if and when the original investment can be recovered and how much profit in the aggregate can be expected from this investment during its life span.

While no scientific method can ever completely eliminate management's judgment in the planning and operation of a business, by dealing on an objective basis this new method provides management with a means of making sounder appraisals of the future of a capital expenditure and forces its attention on those critical areas where judgment can most effectively be used for the successful operation of a business. A proper study of volume-cost-profit relationships together with an informed application of this new method can, therefore, help management make better and more intelligent decisions on capital expenditures, a factor of vital importance not only to the business itself, but also to the community in which the business operates.

CHAPTER 3

Make-or-Buy Problems

The knowledge of cost behavior derived from volume-cost analysis may provide management with useful information in helping to decide whether a company should make or buy certain parts or products which can normally be manufactured by a business itself. Although there are a number of factors to be considered in each make-or-buy situation, cost usually plays an important role. When the cost consideration predominates, the problem may appear very simple in that all management has to do is to compare the cost of buying with the cost of making and to decide upon an alternative that will cost the company least. However, the problem is not so simple as it may seem. There are many kinds of costs and cost concepts, each of which is usually designed for certain specific purposes and may not be adapted for other uses. It is, therefore, important for management to have the proper cost information that is relevant to the particular situation when it compares the cost of buying against the cost of making. Unless this is done, management could be misled into undesirable actions without realizing that errors are being made.

The consequences of a company's lack of proper cost information and the genuine need for the knowledge of volume-cost relationships when management is confronted with certain make-or-buy problems are clearly demonstrated by the case of Sherwood Press.

Sherwood Press—A

The problem of whether certain orders should be placed with a competitor is a recurring one at Sherwood Press, which is one of the leading book publishers and manufacturers in the Middle West, with annual sales in excess of $10,000,000 and employees numbering over a thousand. The

company's manufacturing division is divided principally into four departments, i.e., composing, plate making, press (printing), and bindery. Since
the manufacturing processes of bookmaking are fairly standardized, the
company has a number of competitors, both locally and nationally.

Firmly believing in efficiency of operation and elimination of waste, the
company had established through the engineering department detailed
standards of each of its manufacturing operations. Careful control over
quality of production was maintained at all times. With the help of the management-service division of a national accounting firm, a standard cost system had been installed, and each department head was given the responsibility of earning a profit for his department as if his department constituted
a separate business within the company. To encourage internal competition,
a profit-sharing plan for divisional managers on the basis of profits earned
by the respective divisions was instituted; and the publishing divisions were
allowed to place orders with competing book manufacturers, should the
company's own manufacturing division be unable to meet competitive
costs.

In 1954, a new novel *The Great Traveler,* which soon became one of the
best sellers, was introduced by Sherwood Press. The first printing order
(100,000 copies) was placed with the company's own manufacturing division. Exclusive of paper and printing, the cost of binding *The Great Traveler*
charged by the manufacturing division against the publishing division was
58 cents a copy (see Table 3–1), which was considered high by the publishing division. Therefore, when the second printing (100,000 copies) was
being ordered, quotations were obtained from a number of competing
binderies. One competitor, Narvik Press, offered to bind the second printing
at 54 cents a copy, 4 cents cheaper than the company's own bindery price.
The binding order was therefore placed with Narvik Press. Sherwood Press'
publishing division thought that $4,000 would be saved for the company
by buying from its competitor.

When the bindery work on the second printing of *The Great Traveler* was
completed, the publishing division discovered that it had overlooked the
transportation cost of shipping printed sheet stock from Sherwood Press to
Narvik Press and the transportation cost of shipping the books back to
Sherwood Press after they had been bound. Total transportation cost on this
order amounted to approximately $4,000. Therefore, the company had not
saved the money originally expected.

Six months later, a third printing (100,000 copies) of *The Great Traveler*
was being ordered. As no savings in binding cost had been effected on the
second printing, the publishing division of Sherwood Press negotiated with
Narvik Press for a lower price. The latter was willing to take this order at
50 cents a copy. Since Sherwood Press' own bindery cost was still 58 cents
a copy, the order was again placed with Narvik Press. After allowing for

TABLE 3–1

Sherwood Press

Bindery Department
Cost Estimate

Author: Order No.

Title: *The Great Traveler*   Date:

No. of Copies: 100,000

Size:

No. of Pages:

Other Specifications:

			Cost per 100 Copies
Material:			
Material A	20 units at $0.50		$10.00
Material B	25 units at $0.20		5.00
Material C			2.00
Material D			1.90
Total Material			$18.90
Labor and Burden:			
Operation 401	1,000 hr at $4.74	$ 4,740	
Operation 402	2,800 hr at $3.99	11,172	
Operation 403	2,300 hr at $5.31	12,213	
Operation 404	1,800 hr at $4.53	8,154	
Total Labor and Burden (100,000 copies)		$36,279	
Total Labor and Burden (per 100 copies)			65.75% 36.28
Total Manufacturing Cost			$55.18
Profit to Manufacturing Department			5.1% ➝ 2.82
Cost to Publishing Department			$58.00

the transportation cost, the publishing division of Sherwood Press was certain that $4,000 would be saved for the company.

In 1955, the old manager of cost and standards at Sherwood Press retired and was replaced by Mr. George Raymond Watt. In reviewing past performances of the manufacturing division, the new manager of cost and standards noticed that, in spite of continuous efforts by the company's manufacturing division for more efficient operation and notwithstanding that a profit of 5 to 10 per cent of cost had always been allowed to the manufacturing division on every order it processed, the manufacturing division had not shown any profit in its profit and loss statement for the year 1954. There was an unfavorable burden variance of $270,000 during that year, of which two-thirds was attributed to the bindery department. This unfavorable burden variance on the profit and loss statement represented the difference from actual overhead expenses incurred by and charged against

TABLE 3–2

Sherwood Press

Bindery Expense Budget;
Standard Labor and Burden Rates
1954

| | | Bindery | | | | |
| | | Operating Center | | | | |
	Total	401	402	403	404	General
Direct labor	$ 800,000	$ 80,000	$240,000	$300,000	$180,000	
Indirect labor	$ 125,000	$ 12,000	$ 42,000	$ 50,000	$ 21,000	
Clerical	20,000	.....	.....	.....	.....	$20,000
Supervision	80,000	10,000	14,000	20,000	17,000	19,000
Overtime premium	18,000	15,000	.....	.....	.....	3,000
Night-shift premium	19,000	17,000	.....	.....	.....	2,000
Vacation and holidays	97,000	.....	.....	.....	.....	97,000
Social security taxes	36,000	.....	.....	.....	.....	36,000
Workmen's compensation insurance	10,000	.....	.....	.....	.....	10,000
Accident and sickness insurance	11,000	.....	.....	.....	.....	11,000
Operating supplies	20,000	400	5,000	8,000	6,000	600
Power	20,000	3,000	4,000	7,000	5,000	1,000
Repairs of machinery and equipment	24,000	3,000	5,000	9,000	6,000	1,000
Depreciation of machinery and equipment	50,000	5,000	11,000	18,000	14,000	2,000
Other expenses	10,000	1,600	2,000	3,000	2,000	1,400
Direct overhead	$ 540,000	$ 67,000	$ 83,000	$115,000	$ 71,000	$204,000
Paint and carpenter shop	1,000	.....	.....	.....	.....	1,000
Factory building and ground	115,000	15,000	30,000	40,000	20,000	10,000
Machine shop	24,000	3,000	6,000	9,000	6,000	
Factory general services	360,000	.....	.....	.....	.....	360,000
						$575,000
General overhead		72,000	200,000	173,000	130,000	(575,000)
Allocated overhead	$500,000					
Total overhead	$1,040,000	$157,000	$319,000	$337,000	$227,000	.....
Budgeted direct labor-hours	400,000	50,000	140,000	120,000	90,000	
Standard labor rate per direct labor-hour	$2.00	$1.60	$1.71	$2.50	$2.00	
Standard burden rate per direct labor-hour	2.60	3.14	2.28	2.81	2.53	
Standard labor and burden rate per direct labor-hour	$4.60	$4.74	$3.99	$5.31	$4.53	

Distribution of Overhead Expenses to

		Manufacturing Departments			
	Total	Compo	Plate	Press	Bindery
Direct labor	$1,295,000	$150,000	$45,000	$300,000	$ 800,000
Indirect labor		$ 30,000	$ 9,000	$ 40,000	$ 125,000
Clerical salaries		4,000	1,000	3,000	20,000
Supervision and administrative salaries		20,000	7,000	25,000	80,000
Overtime premium		1,000	1,000	21,000	18,000
Night-shift premium		1,000	...	21,000	19,000
Vacations and holidays (hourly employees)		22,000	5,000	41,000	97,000
Pension contribution		...	...	...	...
Social security taxes		7,000	1,500	13,000	36,000
Workmen's compensation insurance		1,500	500	4,000	10,000
Accident and sickness insurance		2,000	500	4,000	11,000
Operating supplies		*	6,000	25,000	20,000
Power and light		1,000	2,000	15,000	20,000
Repairs of machinery and equipment		600	800	10,000	24,000
Repairs of building and ground		...	...	...	...
Depreciation of machinery and equipment		4,000	2,000	40,000	50,000
Depreciation of building		...	...	...	...
State and local taxes		...	...	...	...
Other expenses		1,000	3,000	8,000	10,000
Departmental expenses		$ 95,100	$39,300	$270,000	$ 540,000
Distribution of expenses of nonoperating departments:					
Paint and carpenter shop		300	200	700	1,000
Factory building and ground		9,000	6,000	22,000	115,000
Machine shop		600	900	9,000	24,000
General factory services		52,000	13,000	107,000	360,000
General administrative		...	...	...	...
Total overhead expenses of manufacturing departments	$1,665,100	$157,000	$59,400	$408,700	$1,040,000
Budgeted productive hours	595,000	60,000	15,000	120,000	400,000
Standard labor rate per direct labor-hour (av)	$2.18	$2.50	$3.00	$2.50	$2.00
Standard burden rate per direct labor-hour (av)	2.80	2.61	3.96	3.41	2.60
Standard labor and burden rate per direct labor-hour	$4.98	$5.11	$6.96	$5.91	$4.60

* Included in other expenses.

28

Press

Manufacturing Departments, 1954

Paint and Carpenter Shop	Factory Building and Ground	Machine Shop	General Factory Services	General Administrative	Publishing Division	
					Dept. A	Dept. B
$20,000	$ 60,000	$38,000	$ 70,000			
...	...	...	75,000			
...	10,000	5,000	134,000	$200,000		
1,000	4,000	1,500	1,000			
...	...	...	...			
2,000	8,000	4,000	8,000			
...	...	...	60,000	18,000		
500	3,500	1,000	12,000	4,000		
200	1,000	400	1,000			
200	1,000	300	1,000			
1,000	10,000	3,000	12,000	20,000		
100	30,000	100	...	5,000		
...	5,000	100	500			
...	12,000					
...	11,000	600	1,000			
...	20,000					
...	50,000	...	24,000			
...	10,000	...	17,700	47,000		
$25,000	$235,500	$54,000	$417,200	$294,000		
(26,000)	22,800	...	...	...	$ 1,000	
1,000	(288,000)	5,000	20,000	6,000	20,000	$ 84,000
...	1,700	(59,000)	22,800			
...	28,000	...	(560,000)			
...	...	...	100,000	(300,000)	50,000	150,000
...	...	...	...	...		

.5 million allocated to
bindery from shops on
this page

the manufacturing departments after these departments had been credited for the standard cost of their production. The feeling that the company's manufacturing division was a high-cost producer in comparison with the rest of the industry prevailed among a number of executives at Sherwood Press.[1]

Further analysis by Mr. Watt revealed that the unfavorable burden variance shown on the company's profit and loss statement for 1954 was due mainly to underutilization of productive facilities rather than to inefficiency of operations. Not only was the manufacturing division, especially the bindery, not operated at full capacity, but also its manufacturing capacities were not utilized to the extent that they should have been. When the bindery orders on the second and third printing of *The Great Traveler* were lost to Narvik Press, Sherwood Press' own bindery was physically able to process such orders within the time limits desired by the publishing division. In addition to these two orders, there had been a number of similar cases where the company's publishing division decided to buy from competitors instead of the company's own manufacturing division on the ground that the company's own manufacturing cost was higher than the cost of buying from competitors.

An examination of the cost estimate of *The Great Traveler* made by Sherwood Press' bindery department (Table 3–1) shows that, of the cost of 58 cents a copy to the publishing department, 2.82 cents represents profit to the manufacturing department and 36.28 cents represents manufacturing labor and burden. On this cost-estimate form, designed by the management-service division of the accounting firm, a single combined rate for labor and burden is applied against the estimated standard hours for each operation in order to expedite computations. By referring to the standard labor and burden rates of each operation, the combined labor and burden costs of binding 100,000 copies of *The Great Traveler* can be segregated into labor and burden as follows:

Opera-tion	Standard Hours	Labor and Burden		Labor		Burden	
		Rate	Cost	Rate	Cost	Rate	Cost
401	1,000	4.74	$ 4,740	1.60	$ 1,600	3.14	$ 3,140
402	2,800	3.99	11,172	1.71	4,788	2.28	6,384
403	2,300	5.31	12,213	2.50	5,750	2.81	6,463
404	1,800	4.53	8,154	2.00	3,600	2.53	4,554
			$36,279		$15,738		$20,541

The standard labor and burden rates of each operation are established at the beginning of each year on the basis of budgeted expenses and budgeted direct labor-hours for each operation (see Table 3–2). A review of the

[1] See Chap. 6 for discussions on the use of standard cost as management's guide for control of overhead.

bindery expense budget for 1954 shows that, of the total overhead expenses ($1,040,000) budgeted for the bindery, $540,000 was direct overhead expenses of the department and $500,000 was overhead expenses allocated to the department. The bulk of the allocated overhead expenses constituted "factory building and ground" ($115,000) and "factory general services" ($360,000), none of which would be affected by any changes in volume of production in the short run. The allocation of expenses of the service and administrative departments to the bindery and other manufacturing departments is shown in Table 3–3. Of the bindery's direct overhead expenses ($540,000), $152,000 (depreciation of machinery, portion of supervision, indirect labor, and clerical salaries) would not be affected by temporary fluctuations in volume of production. On the basis of his knowledge of the

TABLE 3–4

Sherwood Press

Bindery Expense Budget
Fixed and Variable Expenses
1954

	Total	Fixed	Variable
Indirect labor	$ 125,000	$ 20,000	$105,000
Clerical	20,000	20,000	
Supervision	80,000	50,000	30,000
Overtime premium	18,000	. . .	18,000
Night-shift premium	19,000	. . .	19,000
Vacation and holidays	97,000	7,000	90,000
Social security taxes	36,000	4,000	32,000
Workmen's compensation insurance	10,000	1,000	9,000
Accident and sickness insurance	11,000	. . .	11,000
Operating supplies	20,000	. . .	20,000
Power	20,000	. . .	20,000
Repairs of machinery and equipment	24,000	. . .	24,000
Depreciation of machinery and equipment	50,000	50,000	
Other expenses	10,000	. . .	10,000
Direct overhead	$ 540,000	$152,000	$388,000
Paint and carpenter shop	$ 1,000	. . .	$ 1,000
Factory building and ground	115,000	$115,000	
Machine shop	24,000	. . .	24,000
Factory general service	360,000	360,000	
Indirect overhead	$ 500,000	$475,000	$ 25,000
Total overhead	$1,040,000	$627,000	$413,000
	100%	60%	40%

Budgeted direct labor-hours	400,000
Standard labor rate per direct labor-hour	$2.00
Standard burden rate per direct labor-hour	2.60
Standard labor and burden rate per direct labor-hour	4.60

business and experience of Sherwood Press, Mr. Watt estimated that 60 per cent of the overhead expenses budgeted for the bindery in 1954 was fixed and only 40 per cent was variable, should there be any change in the volume of production in the short run (Table 3–4).

Since the bindery department had unused capacity at the time when the second and third printings of *The Great Traveler* were ordered, the additional cost, which the company would have to incur had these two orders been placed with the company's own bindery department, was not the full 58 cents a copy or 55 cents a copy (exclusive of profit to the manufacturing department) as shown in Table 3–1, because the standard overhead rates included many expenses which would be fixed regardless of whether or not the bindery received these two orders. The additional overhead expenses that the company would have to incur were only $8,216 (40 per cent of $20,541) instead of $20,541. On this basis, a new comparison of the cost of making against the cost of buying was made by Mr. Watt as follows:

Cost of making:
Material	$18,900
Direct labor	15,738
Variable overhead	8,216
Additional expenses Sherwood Press would have incurred on each order if the orders had been placed with its own bindery	$42,854

Cost of buying:
Second printing:
Cost of binding—100,000 copies at 54¢	$54,000
Transportation cost	4,000
	$58,000

Third printing:
Cost of binding—100,000 copies at 50¢	$50,000
Transportation cost	4,000
	$54,000

Additional cost incurred by Sherwood Press by buying from Narvik Press instead of placing the orders with its own bindery:
Second printing:
Cost of buying	$58,000	
Cost of making	42,854	
		$15,146

Third printing:
Cost of buying	$54,000	
Cost of making	42,854	
		11,146

Total additional costs incurred by Sherwood Press on these two orders	$26,292

By placing the bindery orders of the second and third printing with Narvik Press, the management of Sherwood Press originally believed that it had saved $4,000 for the company. But the fact was clear that, by passing these two orders to its competitor, Sherwood Press had incurred additional expenses of more than $26,000 instead of realizing a saving of $4,000. Had these two orders alone been placed with the company's own bindery, the operating loss ($20,000) of the manufacturing division in 1954 could have been more than covered.

As the result of this study, the company's manufacturing division recaptured the bindery order on the fourth printing (100,000 copies) of *The Great Traveler* in spite of the willingness of Narvik Press to repeat the job at 50 cents a copy.[2]

The experience of Sherwood Press illustrates the genuine need for proper cost information in comparing the cost of making with the cost of buying. While it is acceptable to use full standard costs as the basis of inventory valuation and interdepartmental transfer of work, they do not necessarily represent the manufacturing cost relevant to the situation when management is confronted with the choice of whether the company should manufacture certain parts or products or buy them from an outside supplier. This is particularly important when there is unused capacity in the plant. Only through the knowledge of volume-cost relationships can proper cost information be obtained for such a situation.

Of the numerous make-or-buy problems, the experience of Sherwood Press is representative of a number of similar situations in other industries. It should be pointed out, nevertheless, that there are many other make-or-buy situations, each of which usually calls for different types of cost analysis. One such situation, for example, is whether a company should integrate backward to manufacture parts or products which it normally purchases from outside suppliers. Management, therefore, should be constantly vigilant as to whether the cost information supplied is relevant to the situation under study. Too often costs designed for the preparation of financial statements

[2] Since Sherwood Press has a profit incentive plan based on the profit of the respective divisions, bonuses to managers of publishing divisions would be adversely affected if they had to pay the manufacturing division prices higher than those of the company's competitors. To eliminate opposition by the publishing divisions to purchase from the company's manufacturing division (even though such orders should be placed with the latter if one thinks in terms of the over-all profit of the company rather than departmental profits), the manufacturing division of Sherwood Press cut down its bindery price of the fourth printing of *The Great Traveler* to 54 cents a copy, which approximated the aggregate of the price of Narvik Press (50 cents) and the transportation cost (4 cents) which the company's publishing division would have to pay. Despite a reduction of price, by accepting this order under the circumstances prevailing at that time, the manufacturing division of Sherwood Press still benefited by approximately $11,000 ($54,000 minus $42,854 yields $11,146). See discussions on Pricing to Meet Competition and the case of Sherwood Press—B in Chap. 5.

are used erroneously as the basis of deciding alternative courses of action when such figures are utterly inapplicable to the situation. When a business has unused productive capacities, and when management is considering whether it will be cheaper to purchase from outside suppliers the products or parts which can normally be made by a business itself, neither the standard cost nor the full estimated average cost is the relevant cost of manufacturing to be compared against the cost of buying. The manufacturing cost relevant in this situation is the additional cost a business would have to incur if the orders were kept in the company. Only when the volume-cost relationship of a business is known can the proper cost information be assembled and presented to management for helping it make sound decisions in such situations.

CHAPTER 4

Keeping or Dropping an "Unprofitable" Product?

What should be done with an unprofitable product is often a perplexing management problem. There is first the problem of ascertaining if the product is actually unprofitable. Not infrequently after a more careful study, the unprofitability of a product turns out to be merely an accounting "whim." In such a case, dropping this allegedly unprofitable product will decrease rather than increase the total profit of a company. Secondly, even when a product has been truly unprofitable in the past this does not necessarily mean that it should be automatically dropped. The decision of whether or not to drop a product will have to depend primarily upon management's expectation of its contribution toward the future profit of the company. In addition to this absolute profitability, management's expectation of the relative profitability of this product against that of others may, in many cases, be the controlling factor.

If management has made a conscientious study of what its costs should be and will be at various levels of operation, this seemingly complex problem of what should be done with an unprofitable product can often be simplified. Keeping or dropping a product or line of products always involves changes in the volume of operation. By studying the volume-cost relationships of a business, management can ascertain whether dropping an allegedly unprofitable product will actually increase or decrease the total profit of the company. Management of many companies with multiproduct operations has discovered that conventional accounting reports and cost analyses, while appropriate for the preparation of "certified" corporate financial statements, are often misleading as to the actual profitability of an individual product. The inadequacy of conventional cost data and the need for knowledge of volume-cost relationships to help management judge the profitability of a product and evaluate the desirability of discontinuing it are demonstrated in this chapter by the experience of Messina Plastics Company.

Knowing what a business' costs actually are, should be, and will probably be at varying levels of operation is also helpful to management in establishing a clearer perspective of the situation confronting a business with a really unprofitable product. In evaluating the future prospects of this type of product, management must know the real causes of its unsuccessful operation. There are many reasons that may cause the unprofitable operation of a product. Among them are defective materials, faulty equipment, poor workmanship, excessive spending, lack of volume, uneconomic undertakings, and so forth. The decisive cause of the unsuccessful operation of any particular business may be either one or a combination of these factors and others. Unless management has made a conscientious study of what costs should and will be, the real causes of a product's unprofitable operation can often be obscured by management's own "alibis" or misconceptions. In such case, the resulting action taken by management will naturally provide little remedy to the already unsatisfactory situation. The experience of Milbrae Mining Company illustrates the real need for studying the volume-cost relationships of a particular business in order to help management make better decisions in appraising an unprofitable situation and in evaluating future plans of action. The harm resulting from management's own misconceptions when it does not make such a study will also be brought out in this case.

Messina Plastics Company

When the financial statements for the year 1954 were presented to the board of directors of Messina Plastics Company, its members were deeply disappointed at the company's operating results. For the first time in its history, Messina Plastics Company experienced a deficit of income. Total loss for the year amounted to $98,000 (Table 4–1). Of the three lines of vinyl plastics manufactured by the company, two made profits of $37,000 and $15,000, respectively, but the other showed a loss of $150,000 (Table 4–2). Executives of the company were considering whether or not it should discontinue the manufacture of Vynel B, the line of vinyl plastics on which no profit had been made.

Messina Plastics Company is a small manufacturer of vinyl plastics in southern New England, with annual sales approximating $5,000,000. It manufactures three different types of vinyl plastics and sells them under the trade name Vynel to various industrial customers in the surrounding area.

TABLE 4-1

Messina Plastics Company

Statement of Profit and Loss
for the Year Ended December 31, 1954

		(000 omitted)
Gross sales		$4,680
Cash discount		94
Net sales		$4,586
Cost of manufacturing, excluding depreciation		3,284
Manufacturing profit		$1,302
Other expenses:		
Selling expenses	$800	
General administrative expenses	400	
Depreciation	200	1,400
Net loss for the year		($ 98)

TABLE 4-1A

Messina Plastics Company

Schedule of Manufacturing Expenses
for the Year Ended December 31, 1954

	(000 omitted)
Materials	$ 660
Direct labor	1,200
Indirect labor	400
Supplementary wage expenses	160
Supplies	57
Repairs	21
Power	34
Heat and light	16
Building service	10
Rent	600
Property taxes	66
Property insurance	60
Total manufacturing expenses	$3,284

In spite of its small size, the company has been able to capture and maintain a share of the market dominated by large chemical and plastics companies. The Messina Vynel provides better workability than most other vinyl plastics, a quality preferred by many of its customers. The company's products are sold direct to customers by its sales engineers who are paid on a straight salary basis.

At a meeting of the board of directors, the chairman of the board and several other directors recommended dropping the manufacture of Vynel B.

TABLE 4-2

Messina Plastics Company

Statement of Profit and Loss by Products
for the Year Ended December 31, 1954

	Total	Vynel					
		A		B		C	
	(000 omitted)	(000 omitted)	$ per lb	(000 omitted)	$ per lb	(000 omitted)	$ per lb
Gross sales	$4,680	$2,200	$1.100	$1,200	$1.200	$1,280	$1.280
Cash discount	94	44	0.022	24	0.024	26	0.026
Net sales	$4,586	$2,156	$1.078	$1,176	$1.176	$1,254	$1.254
Manufacturing costs:							
Materials	$ 660	$ 400	$0.200	$ 120	$0.120	$ 140	$0.140
Direct labor	1,200	510	0.255	390	0.390	300	0.300
Indirect labor	400	170	0.085	130	0.130	100	0.100
Supplementary labor expenses	160	68	0.034	52	0.052	40	0.040
Supplies	57	22	0.011	20	0.020	15	0.015
Repairs	21	8	0.004	8	0.008	5	0.005
Power	34	10	0.005	11	0.011	13	0.013
Heat and light	16	6	0.003	5	0.005	5	0.005
Building service	10	4	0.002	3	0.003	3	0.003
Rent	600	240	0.120	180	0.180	180	0.180
Property taxes	66	26	0.013	20	0.020	20	0.020
Property insurance	60	21	0.011	18	0.018	21	0.021
Total manufacturing cost, excluding depreciation	$3,284	$1,485	$0.743	$ 957	$0.957	$ 842	$0.842
Gross manufacturing profit	$1,302	$ 671	$0.335	$ 219	$0.219	$ 412	$0.412
Other expenses:							
Selling expenses	$ 800	$ 376	$0.188	$ 206	$0.206	$ 218	$0.218
General administrative expenses	400	188	0.094	103	0.103	109	0.109
Depreciation	200	70	0.035	60	0.060	70	0.070
Total other expenses	$1,400	$ 634	$0.317	$ 369	$0.369	$ 397	$0.397
Total costs and expenses	$4,684	$2,119	$1.060	$1,326	$1.326	$1,239	$1.239
Profit (loss)	($ 98)	$ 37	$0.018	($ 150)	($0.150)	$ 15	$0.015
Pounds sold	4,000,000	2,000,000		1,000,000		1,000,000	

They reasoned that on every pound of Vynel B sold the company would lose 15 cents (Table 4–2). During 1954 when 1,000,000 lb of Vynel B was sold, the company lost $150,000 on this product. Without this loss, Messina could have made a profit of $52,000. With this loss, the $52,000 profit was turned into a loss of $98,000.

The chairman of the board maintained that no business could last very long if it did not make a profit. Being a small manufacturer in the plastics industry, Messina has very little control over its selling prices. Although the Messina Vynel possesses certain superior qualities, the company has to meet the prices on similar products established by leading companies in the industry. Otherwise, the company has found it difficult to sell its products. Therefore, if the company wants to remain successful, it must manufacture and sell only those products the cost of which are low enough to yield a profit. The chairman of the board was aware that the operating management of the company had kept a very close vigilance over its costs and expenses. He did not think that Messina could cut its cost of Vynel B to a level that could make its production profitable. Hence, it appeared to him that the best solution for avoiding a repetition of the unprofitable operation experienced in 1954 would be elimination of Vynel B from the company's product lines.

After listening to the arguments in favor of discontinuance of Vynel B, Mr. James E. Perry, president of the company, stated that he could not agree with the recommendation of his colleagues. Mr. Perry is a chemical engineer himself and is personally responsible for the development of Vynel plastics manufactured by the company. With the financial support of the company's chairman of the board and several of his friends, who now serve as the directors of the company, Mr. Perry had formed the present Messina Plastics Company. Although Mr. Perry is responsible for the actual operation of the company's business, management of its financial affairs and maintenance of its books of accounts are delegated to the treasurer of the company who is a close associate of the chairman of the board of directors.

Mr. Perry told the board of directors that the profit and loss statement by products (Table 4–2), prepared by the company's accounting department and on the basis of which the chairman of the board and several other directors formed their judgment on the profitability of Vynel B, was grossly misleading in this situation. He told the directors that many of the costs and expenses charged to Vynel B (Table 4–2) would be incurred by the company regardless of whether or not the company discontinued its manufacture of Vynel B. Even if the company had not made a single pound of Vynel B in 1954, the company would have had to pay the same amount of rent, property taxes, and insurance that year. Likewise, selling and general administrative expenses, indirect labor, building service, light and heat, etc., would remain much the same. The depreciation expense charged to Vynel B could not be avoided in 1954. By producing and selling Vynel B in 1954, the only additional expenses the company had incurred were expenses such as materials, direct labor, a portion of supplementary wage expenses directly related to direct labor, supplies, repairs, and electric power. Total additional expenses incurred by the company in the manufacture of 1,000,000 lb of Vynel B in 1954 amounted to 588,000. Deducting this amount of variable expenses from the net sales proceeds of $1,176,000, Vynel B had contributed $588,000 toward the various fixed costs of the company. Mr. Perry pointed out to the directors that Messina sold all the Vynel A and Vynel C which its customers were willing to take in 1954. Therefore, had the income from Vynel B during 1954 been eliminated, the company would have lost $686,000 instead of $98,000. In his opinion, rather than being considered as causing the company a loss of $150,000, Vynel B should be credited for its contribution in reducing the company's loss by $588,000.

Mr. Perry then presented to the chairman of the board and other directors a revised statement of profit and loss by products (Table 4–3), which he himself had prepared. In this new statement of profit and loss by products, Mr. Perry showed the income from each product, the variable costs related to each product, the contribution made by each product toward fixed costs and profit, the total fixed costs of the company, and finally the net profit or loss of the company. For the year 1954, each of the three Vynel products had contributed the following amount toward the various fixed costs of the company: $1,155,000 from 2,000,000 lb of Vynel A, $588,000 from 1,000,000 lb of Vynel B, and $751,000 from 1,000,000 lb of Vynel C. The total contribution of these three products toward fixed costs aggregated $2,494,000. Since the total fixed cost of the company amounted to $2,592,-000, a loss of $98,000 was sustained.

Mr. Perry explained to the board of directors that the main reason Messina Plastics Company had suffered a loss in 1954 was that the company experienced a price reduction of 10 cents a pound on Vynel A during that year. Supplies of Vynel A type plastics had become increasingly more abundant as more companies entered this field in recent years. Consequently, the price of this product had been reduced several times during the last few years. Had the price of Vynel A been 10 cents higher in 1954, Messina Plastics Company would have made a profit of $98,000 [1] instead of a loss of $98,000.

Because of this keener competition on Vynel A type plastics and the resultant downward pressure on its prices, Mr. Perry told the board of directors that Messina Plastics Company had been stressing the development of newer and better plastics to keep itself abreast of the competitors.

---

[1] (2,000,000 lb. × $0.098 per lb *) − $98,000 = $98,000.

* 10 cents per pound less 2 per cent cash discount.

TABLE 4-3

Messina Plastics Company

Revised Statement of Profit and Loss by Products
for the Year Ended December 31, 1954

	Total	A		Vynel B		C	
	(000 omitted)	(000 omitted)	$ per lb	(000 omitted)	$ per lb	(000 omitted)	$ per lb
Gross sales	$4,680	$2,200	$1.100	$1,200	$1.200	$1,280	$1.280
Cash discount	94	44	0.022	24	0.024	26	0.026
Net sales	$4,586	$2,156	$1.078	$1,176	$1.176	$1,254	$1.254
Variable costs:							
Materials	$ 660	$ 400	$0.200	$ 120	$0.120	$ 140	$0.140
Direct labor	1,200	510	0.255	390	0.390	300	0.300
Supplementary wage expenses	120	51	0.025	39	0.039	30	0.030
Supplies	57	22	0.011	20	0.020	15	0.015
Repairs	21	8	0.004	8	0.008	5	0.005
Power	34	10	0.005	11	0.011	13	0.013
Total variable costs	$2,092	$1,001 _220_	$0.500	$ 588 _204_	$0.588	$ 503 _254_	$0.503
Contribution to fixed costs and profit	$2,494	$1,155	$0.578	$ 588	$0.588	$ 751	$0.751
Fixed costs:							
Indirect labor	$ 400						
Supplementary wage expenses	40						
Rent	600						
Building service	10						
Heat and light	16						
Property taxes	66						
Property insurance	60						
Fixed manufacturing costs	$1,192						
Selling expenses	800						
General administrative expenses	400						
Depreciation	200						
Total fixed costs	$2,592						
Profit (loss)	($ 98)						
Pounds sold	4,000,000	2,000,000		1,000,000		1,000,000	

Both Vynel B and Vynel C were recent additions to the Messina plastics. They had been warmly received by the company's customers in 1954 and could be expected to become good profit makers for the company. Mr. Perry estimated that sales of Vynel B and Vynel C in 1955 would be at least 10 to 20 per cent higher than those of 1954, while sales of Vynel A would probably remain on the same level as 1954. He predicted that, barring other changes of economic conditions, prices of Vynel B and Vynel C would hold at their present levels for the next two or three years, but the price of Vynel A might experience another decline during the second half of 1955. On the basis of his estimate, Mr. Perry forecasted that the company would make a profit of $48,000 before taxes during the first six months of 1955. A summary of his forecast is shown in Table 4–4.

Using his forecast as an example, Mr. Perry demonstrated to the board of directors that, by increasing the sales of Vynel B and Vynel C, the company could make a profit of $48,000 during the first six months of 1955. Whereas, if the manufacture of Vynel B were discontinued, Messina Plastics would probably lose $305,000 during this period,[2] because it would lose an income of $353,000 which could otherwise be earned by the company. For the benefit of Messina Plastics Company, Mr. Perry told the board of directors that he could not agree with the recommendation to discontinue the manufacture of Vynel B.

Mr. Perry's analysis and presentation of the situation confronted by Messina Plastics Company were so thorough and revealing that all members of the board of directors were convinced of the soundness of his judgment. They authorized him to proceed with his plans and voted him their full support. Actual operating results of Messina Plastics Company for the first six months of 1955 turned out even better than Mr. Perry's expectation. The company sold 700,000 lb of Vynel B, 600,000 lb of Vynel C, and 1,000,000 lb of Vynel A. Actual profit for this period amounted to $144,000 (Table 4–5).

The experience of Messina Plastics Company clearly demonstrates the inadequacy of cost analysis under the conventional accounting method and the need of knowing a business' volume-cost relationships in order to help management judge the profitability or unprofitability of an individual product. If the president of this company had not had any knowledge of its volume-cost relationships, the recommendation by its chairman for discontinuing the manufacture of Vynel B would have been put through. Such things do happen in other companies. Then, after the allegedly unprofitable product had been discontinued, management would find, much to its dismay, a deterioration instead of an improvement in the over-all profit of the company. If Messina Plastics Company had discontinued its manufacture

[2] $353,000 – $48,000 = $305,000.

TABLE 4-4

Messina Plastics Company

Forecast of Profit and Loss by Products
For the Six Months Ended June 30, 1955

	Total (000 omitted)	A (000 omitted)	A $ per lb	Vynel B (000 omitted)	B $ per lb	C (000 omitted)	C $ per lb
Gross sales	$2,524	$1,100	$1,100	$ 720	$1.200	$ 704	$1.280
Cash discount	50	22	0.022	14	0.024	14	0.026
Net sales	$2,474	$1,078	$1,078	$ 706	$1.176	$ 690	$1.254
Variable costs	1,130	500	0.500	353	0.588	277	0.503
Contribution to fixed costs and profit	$1,344	$ 578	$0.578	$ 353	$0.588	$ 413	$0.751
Fixed costs	$1,296						
Profit before taxes	$ 48						
Pounds forecasted	2,150,000	1,000,000		600,000		550,000	

TABLE 4–5

Messina Plastics Company

Statement of Profit and Loss by Products
for the Six Months Ended June 30, 1955

	Total	Vynel					
		A		B		C	
	(000 omitted)	(000 omitted)	$ per lb	(000 omitted)	$ per lb	(000 omitted)	$ per lb
Gross sales	$2,708	$1,100	$1.100	$ 840	$1.200	$ 768	$1.280
Cash discount	54	22	0.022	17	0.024	15	0.026
Net sales	$2,654	$1,078	$1.078	$ 823	$1.176	$ 753	$1.254
Variable costs:							
Materials	$ 368	$ 200	$0.200	$ 84	$0.120	$ 84	$0.140
Direct labor *	778	280	0.280	300	0.429	198	0.330
Supplies	34	11	0.011	14	0.020	9	0.015
Repairs	13	4	0.004	6	0.008	3	0.005
Power	21	5	0.005	8	0.011	8	0.013
Total variable costs	$1,214	$ 500	$0.500	$ 412	$0.588	$ 302	$0.503
Contribution to fixed costs and profit	$1,440	$ 578	$0.578	$ 411	$0.588	$ 451	$0.751
Fixed costs:							
Indirect labor *	$ 220						
Rent	300						
Building service	5						
Heat and light	8						
Property taxes	33						
Property insurance	30						
Total fixed manufacturing costs	$ 596						
Selling expenses	400						
General administrative expenses	200						
Depreciation	100						
Total fixed costs	$1,296						
Profit before taxes	$ 144						
Pounds sold	2,300,000	1,000,000		700,000		600,000	
Pounds forecasted	2,150,000	1,000,000		600,000		550,000	

* Includes supplementary wage expenses (approximately 10 per cent of direct wages and salaries.)

44

of Vynel B in 1955, it would have lost $267,000 during the first six months instead of making a profit of $144,000 for that period.

Through his knowledge of the volume-cost relationships of the business, the president of Messina Plastics Company ascertained those costs which would have been saved if the manufacture of Vynel B were discontinued. He also segregated those costs which were currently charged to Vynel B but would remain with the company even if the manufacture of this product were discontinued. On the basis of this analysis, Mr. Perry showed that the revenue from each of the three products manufactured by Messina far exceeded the respective variable costs of these products. However, in 1954 the aggregate contribution of these products toward fixed costs was not sufficient to cover the total fixed costs of the company, resulting in a loss of $98,000 for the entire company. The cause of this loss was attributed by Mr. Perry to the decline in the price of Vynel A during that year rather than to the unprofitable operation of Vynel B. Mr. Perry's remedy was to intensify the sales efforts on Vynel B and Vynel C instead of dropping the manufacture of Vynel B. Subsequent events proved the soundness of Mr. Perry's diagnosis of the situation confronting Messina as well as the wisdom of his prescription for solving its problems.

In weighing whether or not a certain product should be discontinued, the importance of recognizing the circumstances surrounding the business at that particular moment should not be overlooked. In the case of Messina Plastics Company, its productive capacities were more than its sales capacities in 1954 and 1955. By discontinuing the manufacture of any of its three products, a study of the company's volume-cost relationships would reveal that the resultant loss of revenue would far exceed the corresponding savings in variable costs. In the meantime, the fixed costs of the company would remain unchanged. Therefore, it would be economically undesirable to drop any of the three products in 1954 and 1955 even though the total cost assigned to a particular product might be more than the total revenue from that product.

Under a different set of circumstances, Messina Plastics Company might find it desirable to discontinue the manufacture of one of its products even though the total revenue from that product exceeds its variable cost or even its total cost. For instance, sales of Vynel B and Vynel C might expand to a level where the demand for such products from Messina's customers could be met only by expanding the company's productive capacities or by cutting down the production of Vynel A. Or, the company might have developed a new product Vynel D which could be manufactured with the existing productive facilities but could be marketed more profitably than Vynel A. If, in the judgment of the management of Messina Plastics Company, future economic conditions do not warrant an immediate expansion of its productive facilities, and if Vynel A experiences another price reduction as expected by the president of the company, it might be more advantageous to cut down the production of Vynel A. Depending upon the circumstances prevailing at the time, it might even become desirable to drop the manufacture of Vynel A entirely and to subcontract its production to competitors.

It should also be noted that, in the case of Messina Plastics Company, the fixed costs charged to Vynel B would remain fixed if the manufacture of this product were discontinued. In another case, such as that of Milbrae Mining Company to be presented later in this chapter, its fixed costs could be eliminated when its unprofitable operation was discontinued. Consequently, although the total revenues from both unprofitable products exceeded their respective variable costs, one company found it more advantageous to retain its "unprofitable" product, whereas another company found it more advisable to discontinue its unprofitable product.

It is, therefore, the duty of management to use its own intelligence to size up the situation confronting it and to select the proper cost information for evaluating different alternatives. Since dropping, adding, and pushing a line of product always involves changes in the volume of operation, management must know how the cost of its business will respond to such contemplated changes in volume of business and what its costs and expenses should be and will be under different sets of circumstances.

To demonstrate further the definite need of a true knowledge of volume-cost relationships for helping management make better decisions on keeping or dropping an unprofitable product and to illustrate more clearly that such decisions must take into consideration the circumstances under which a business operates, the experience of Milbrae Mining Company will be presented as a contrast to that of Messina Plastics Company.

Milbrae Mining Company

Milbrae Mining Company, a subsidiary of San Rafael Sulphur Company, mines and processes paper filler clays in the southwestern United States. It was acquired by the parent company in 1952 under its diversification program. At the time of acquisition, management of San Rafael expected that, by applying the talents of the engineering and sales organizations of the parent company, the existing business of this newly acquired subsidiary could be expanded. It was further hoped that through improved processes paper coating clays could be produced from the same raw materials used for the manufacture of paper filler clays. The market price of paper coating clays is approximately 40 per cent higher than that of paper filler clays. It appeared to the management of San Rafael Sulphur Company that its investment in Milbrae Mining Company would be a highly successful one.

However, in spite of the high expectations envisaged by the management of San Rafael Sulphur Company, the operating results of Milbrae Mining

Company were disappointing. Approximately a third of a million dollars was spent by Milbrae Mining Company for new and improved processing facilities. Nevertheless, the company was neither able to produce any paper coating clays nor able to make any profit on paper filler clays. During the first 16 months of operation, a total loss of $270,000 was sustained. The management of the parent company reported to its stockholders in the 1953 annual report as follows:

"Profits have not been realized from the clay operations of Milbrae Mining Company. Capital additions are being held at modest levels pending further evaluation of the best opportunities in this field."

While the management of San Rafael Sulphur Company was evaluating the future of Milbrae Mining Company, operations of the subsidiary remained much the same throughout 1954. In spite of an increase of sales of paper filler clays, the operating loss kept mounting. For the entire year of 1954, the total loss approximated $266,000. The following message was conveyed from the management of San Rafael Sulphur Company to its stockholders in the 1954 annual report:

"Although dollar sales of clay, mined and processed by Milbrae Mining Company, advanced 33 per cent over the past year, operating losses continued. We are still in the process of evaluating our prospects in this business, but no final decisions have yet been reached."

Table 4–6 shows the statement of income and expenses of Milbrae Mining Company for the year 1954.

Mr. Harry C. Krieg, controller of San Rafael Sulphur Company, like many of its other executives was very much concerned over the situation at Milbrae and felt that drastic actions were needed there. When he brought up this matter at the executive meeting of San Rafael, the executive responsible for the investment in Milbrae claimed that a new company, such as Milbrae Mining Company, would always require a "break-in" period before it started to earn a profit. This executive maintained that it would take time to build up a business. At this early stage of the game, profit had not been earned because volume was low. When Milbrae's volume reached a satisfactory level, San Rafael could expect good profit from this investment. However, Mr. Krieg felt that the difficulty of Milbrae Mining Company was not any lack of volume of business. In fact, based upon its experience of the past 28 months, the more clay Milbrae sold, the higher would be its loss. The company was simply engaged in an uneconomic operation, a fact which should be clearly brought to the attention of top management at San Rafael.

Operating reports of each division or plant within the San Rafael organization were prepared at regular periodic intervals and presented to its top

TABLE 4–6

Milbrae Mining Company

Statement of Income and Expenses
for the Year Ended December 31, 1954

Gross sales	$361,185
Less: Commissions and discounts	42,017
Net sales	$319,168
Manufacturing cost of goods sold:	
Inventory at beginning	None
Manufacturing expenses:	
Royalties	$ 15,000
Operating labor	89,650
Indirect labor	55,350
Fringe benefits	14,500
Supplies and expenses	294,100
Power and water	23,000
Fixed charges:	
Depreciation	42,000
Depletion	100
Insurance	3,700
Property taxes	2,200
Total manufacturing expenses	$539,600
	$539,600
Inventory at end	1,523
Cost of goods sold	$538,077
Operating profit (loss)	($218,909)
General expenses:	
Clay prospecting	$ 42,000
Other general expenses	5,000
Total general expenses	$ 47,000
Net profit (loss) before Federal taxes	($265,909)
Estimated Federal income taxes	None
Net profit (loss) to surplus	($265,909)
Operating statistics:	
(In tons)	
Inventory at beginning	None
Production	33,000
Sales	32,835
Inventory at end	165
(In dollars per ton)	
Manufacturing cost *	$16.35
Gross average price received	11.00
Commissions and discounts	1.28
Net average price received	9.72
Cost of sales *	16.39
Gross operating profit (loss) *	(6.67)

* Exclude clay prospecting expenses.

management. In addition to the statement of income and expenses, as shown in Table 4–6, top executives of San Rafael received also an analysis of costs and expenses of each operating unit (Table 4–7, Analysis of Manufacturing Expenses, Milbrae Mining Company, 1954). Mr. Krieg was afraid that the significance of the figures contained in the operating reports of Milbrae Mining Company could easily be buried under the voluminous reports received by the top executives of San Rafael Sulphur Company.[3] Furthermore, the disappointing operating results of Milbrae Mining Company were overshadowed by the size and successful operation of the entire San Rafael organization.[4]

In order to bring the uneconomic operations at Milbrae more forcibly to the attention of San Rafael's top management, a new report was prepared by Mr. Krieg. In this revised analysis of cost and expenses (Table 4–8), all expenses of Milbrae Mining Company incurred during 1954 were grouped under two major classifications: (1) variable expenses and (2) fixed expenses. Included in the variable expenses were those expenses directly related to (a) mining and processing operations, such as royalties, hauling, operating labor, and supplies; and (b) packing and shipping operations. The fixed expenses were divided into two subgroups: (a) those fixed expenses which would require additional cash outlays during the year and (b) those fixed expenses which would not require cash outlays. Included in the "cash fixed costs" were maintenance and administrative labor, supervisory salaries, property taxes and insurance, clay prospecting, etc. Included in the "non-cash fixed costs" were depreciation and depletion of properties and equipment and amortization of "overburden removal." [5]

Table 4–8 shows that total variable expenses for the year 1954 amounted to $398,770, averaging $12.08 per ton of finished clay. The net average selling price realized by Milbrae during 1954 was only $9.72 per ton. For a total production of 33,000 tons, total variable costs of $398,770 exceeded total net sales value of production of $320,772 by $77,998. After including cash fixed costs of $113,730 and non-cash fixed costs of $74,100, total cash loss for the year became 191,728 and total book loss $265,828,[6] respec-

[3] San Rafael Sulphur Company had 6 operating subsidiaries which were comprised of 12 operating divisions and over 30 manufacturing plants in 1954.

[4] Consolidated net sales of San Rafael Sulphur Company were in excess of $50,000,000 in 1954.

[5] "Overburden" is a term used in the mining industry, denoting the top soil lying above any minerals, coal, or "clays."

[6] The slight difference of this total loss of $265,828 computed by Mr. Krieg and the total loss of $265,909 per Milbrae's statement of income and expense (Table 4–6) is due to the fact that, in Mr. Krieg's revised computation, the entire production of 1954 was considered sold, while in the actual statement of income and expense, 165 tons of 1954 production was added to Milbrae's inventory. This 165 tons was valued at the net average selling price realized less an allowance for administrative expenses amounting to 5 per cent of net average selling price.

TABLE 4–7

Milbrae Mining Company

Analysis of Manufacturing Expenses
1954

Royalties	$ 15,000
Operating labor:	
Mining	$ 6,750
Hauling	
Milling	46,500
Quality control	3,400
Packing and shipping	33,000
Total operating labor	$ 89,650
Indirect labor:	
Supervision:	
Mining	
Hauling	
Milling	$ 4,800
Quality control	
Packing and shipping	1,700
Maintenance:	
Mining	4,800
Hauling	
Milling	24,000
Quality control	
Packing and shipping	50
General administrative	
Administrative:	
General administrative	$ 20,000
Total indirect labor	$ 55,350
Fringe benefits *	$ 14,500
Supplies and expenses:	
Operating:	
Mining	$ 7,500
Hauling	
Milling	57,000
Quality control	3,000
Factory general	5,400
Packing and shipping	49,500
General administrative	23,300
Maintenance:	
Mining	16,500
Hauling	
Milling	40,500
Quality control	50
Factory general	600
Packing and shipping	100
General administrative	1,200

* Payroll taxes, workmen's compansation insurance, group insurance, employees' welfare expense (details omitted here).

TABLE 4–7 (continued)

Expendable tools:	
Mining	100
Hauling	
Milling	1,100
Quality control	
Packing and shipping	
Contract hauling:	
Hauling	56,250
Overburden removal:	
Mining	32,000
Total supplies and expenses	$294,100
Power and water:	
Factory general	$ 23,000
Total power and water	$ 23,000
Fixed charges:	
Depreciation	$ 42,000
Depletion	100
Insurance	3,700
Property taxes	2,200
Total fixed charges	$ 48,000
Total manufacturing cost including packing and shipping expenses	$539,600
Production, tons	33,000

tively. Since the total variable expense of $12.08 per ton exceeded the net average selling price realized of $9.72 by $2.36 per ton, it was obvious that the more clay Milbrae sold, the more staggering would be its loss. A volume-cost-loss diagram (Fig. 4–1) was prepared by Mr. Krieg to show pictorially the hopeless situation of the Milbrae Mining Company in 1954. A simplified diagram showing only the relationship between volume and loss is given in Fig. 4–2. By glancing at either chart, one can easily see that, should the operating conditions of 1954 persist, there would never be a "break-even" volume for Milbrae Mining Company, regardless of how much more clay the company could sell.

The revised analysis of Milbrae's expenses in 1954 and the charts showing its volume-cost-loss relationships were presented to San Rafael's top management at the next executive meeting. By showing these charts and his analysis, Mr. Krieg convinced top management at San Rafael that, unless some corrective actions were taken immediately, the situation at Milbrae was really hopeless.

During the course of discussions at the executive meeting, it was noted that the actual yield of finished clays during 1954 (and prior years) was only 44 per cent of the wet clay mined and processed by Milbrae (Table

TABLE 4–8

Milbrae Mining Company

Revised Analysis of Cost and Expenses
1954

	Total	Per Ton of Clay Processed	Per Ton of Finished Clay
Variable expenses:			
Royalties	$ 15,000	$0.20	
Hauling	56,250	0.75	
Operating labor * (mining, milling, and quality control)	62,315	0.83	
Operating supplies (mining, milling, and quality control)	68,700	0.91	
Power and water	23,000	0.31	
Maintenance supplies †	57,050	0.76	
General supplies	30,500	0.41	
	$312,815	$4.17	$ 9.48
Packing and shipping labor *	36,355		1.10
Packing and shipping supplies	49,600		1.50
Total variable expenses	$398,770		$12.08
Fixed expenses:			
Cash expenditures needed:			
Maintenance labor *	$ 31,680		
Administrative labor *	22,000		
Supervision *	7,150		
Property insurance and taxes	5,900		
Clay prospecting, etc.	47,000		
	$113,730		
Cash expenditures not needed:			
Depreciation and depletion	$ 42,100		
Overburden removal	32,000		
	$ 74,000		
Total fixed expenses	$187,830		
Total cost and expenses	$586,600		
Total production	33,000 tons		
Net average price received per ton	$9.7204		
Net sales value of production	$320,772		
Clay mined and processed	75,000 tons		
Yield	44%		

* Include 10 per cent fringe labor expenses.
† Exclude packing, shipping, and general supplies.

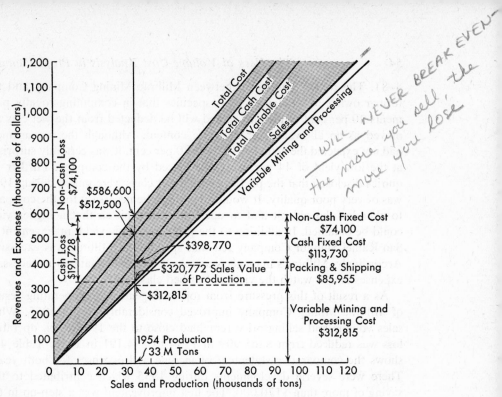

Fig. 4–1. Milbrae Mining Company. Volume-cost-loss diagram for 1954.

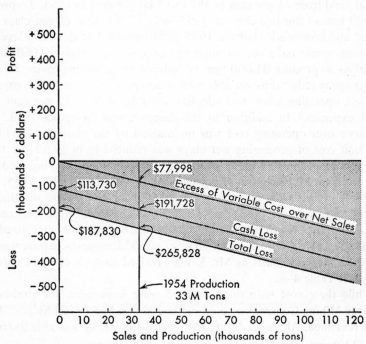

Fig. 4–2. Milbrae Mining Company. Volume-loss diagram for 1954.

4–8). The royalty agreement between Milbrae Mining Company and the former owner of its clay reserves specifies that in computing royalty payments 20 per cent of the clay mined will be deducted from the wet clay removed as an allowance for moisture content. Although the management had not expected the actual yield to be 80 per cent, it was certainly surprised at the low yield of 44 per cent experienced by the company. Further inquiries disclosed that the pit from which wet clays were mined during 1954 was of very poor quality. It would, therefore, be necessary for the company to abandon the old pit and to open up a new pit so that a higher yield could be obtained. In addition to the problem of low yield, management of San Rafael Sulphur Company felt that spending at Milbrae was excessive. Accordingly, Milbrae's manager was requested to eliminate all unnecessary expenses and to watch the yield of finished clays more closely.

As a result of this pressure from top management, the operating results of Milbrae Mining Company improved considerably during 1955. While sales volume and selling price remained close to the 1954 level, operating loss was reduced from $265,909 in 1954 to $94,191 in 1955. Table 4–9 shows the comparative statement of income and expenses for both years. There were several developments during 1955 which contributed to this saving of more than $170,000. The first improvement was a step-up in the yield of finished clays. By closing down old pits, the company raised its actual yield from 44 per cent in 1954 to 54.4 per cent in 1955. To produce 31,000 tons of finished clays in 1955, only 57,000 tons of wet clays were mined and processed. Had the 1955 yield remained at the 1954 level, the company would have had to mine and process more than 70,000 tons of wet clays to produce 31,000 tons of finished clays. By improving its yield, the company reduced its variable mining and processing cost (i.e., royalties, hauling, operating labor, and supplies, etc.) by at least 19 per cent of its 1954 expenses.[7] In addition to this improvement in actual yield, close vigilance over operating cost was maintained by the manager at Milbrae. The unit cost of processing wet clays was reduced from $4.17 per ton of clay processed in 1954 to $3.40 in 1955. Packing and shipping labor was reduced from $1.10 per ton of finished clay in 1954 to $0.82 in 1955. Considerable savings were also effected in fixed-labor and clay-prospecting expenses. Furthermore, total non-cash fixed expenses were reduced by $27,000 as the "overburden removal" account became fully amortized during 1955. Table 4–10 shows an analysis of 1955 expenses, which was prepared on the same basis as Mr. Krieg's revised analysis of 1954 expenses shown in Table 4–8.

While these cost reductions in 1955 were impressive, the problem of Milbrae Mining Company as a financial drain on San Rafael Sulphur Company remained. Although during that year the company was able to recover

[7] (70,500 tons − 57,000 tons) ÷ 70,500 tons = 19.2 per cent.

TABLE 4–9

Milbrae Mining Company

Statement of Income and Expenses
for the Years Ended December 31, 1955 and 1954

	1955	1954
Gross sales	$348,300	$361,185
Less: Commissions and discounts	40,403	42,017
Net sales	$307,897	$319,168
Manufacturing cost of goods sold:		
Inventory at beginning	$ 1,523	None
Manufacturing expenses:		
Royalties	$ 11,400	$ 15,000
Operating labor	66,200	89,650
Indirect labor	42,800	55,350
Fringe benefits	10,900	14,500
Supplies and expenses	163,100	294,100
Power and water	21,500	23,000
Fixed charges:		
Depreciation	45,000	42,000
Depletion	100	100
Insurance	3,300	3,700
Property taxes	2,300	2,200
Total manufacturing expenses	$366,660	$539,600
	$368,123	$539,600
Inventory at end	1,935	1,523
Cost of goods sold	$366,188	$538,077
Operating profit (loss)	($ 58,291)	($218,909)
General expenses:		
Clay prospecting	$ 33,000	$ 42,000
Other general expenses	2,900	5,000
Total general expenses	$ 35,900	$ 47,000
Net profit (loss) before Federal taxes	($ 94,191)	($265,909)
Estimated Federal income taxes	None	None
Net profit (loss) to surplus	($ 94,191)	($265,909)
Operating statistics:		
(In tons)		
Inventory at beginning	165	None
Production	31,000	33,000
Sales	30,960	32,835
Inventory at end	205	165
(In dollars per ton)		
Manufacturing cost *	$11.83	$16.35
Gross average price received	11.25	11.00
Commission and discount	1.31	1.28
Net average price received	9.94	9.72
Cost of sales *	11.83	16.39
Gross operating profit (loss) *	(1.89)	(6.67)

* Exclude clay prospecting expenses.

TABLE 4–10

Milbrae Mining Company

Analysis of Cost and Expenses
1955

	Total	Per Ton of Clay Processed	Per Ton of Finished Clay
Variable expenses:			
Royalties	$ 11,400	$0.20	
Hauling	42,750	0.75	
Operating labor * (mining, milling, and quality control)	47,575	0.83	
Operating supplies (mining, milling, and quality control)	28,490	0.50	
Power and water	21,500	0.38	
Maintenance supplies †	28,920	0.51	
General supplies	12,920	0.23	
	$193,555	$3.40	$6.24
Packing and shipping labor *	25,245		0.82
Packing and shipping supplies	48,020		1.55
Total variable expenses	$266,820		$8.61
Fixed expenses:			
Additional cash expenditures needed:			
Maintenance labor *	$ 24,750		
Administrative labor *	14,850		
Supervision *	7,480		
Property insurance and taxes	5,600		
Clay prospecting, etc.	35,900		
	$ 88,580		
No additional cash expenditures needed:			
Depreciation and depletion	$ 45,100		
Overburden removal	2,000		
	$ 47,100		
Total fixed expenses	$135,680		
Total cost and expenses	$402,500		
Total production	31,000 tons		
Net average price received (per ton)	$9.94		
Net sales value of production	$308,140		
Clay mined and processed	57,000 tons		
Yield	54.4%		

* Include 10 per cent fringe labor expenses.
† Exclude packing, shipping, and general supplies.

its variable costs ($8.61 per ton) from the net average selling price realized ($9.94), it still suffered a cash loss of approximately $47,000 and a total book loss of over $94,000. On the basis of its 1955 operations, Mr. Krieg estimated that Milbrae Mining Company would have to sell approximately 66,500 tons of finished clays before it could recover its out-of-pocket cash expenditures and would have to sell 101,800 tons before it could start to earn any money on its investment. Figure 4–3 shows the volume-cost-profit

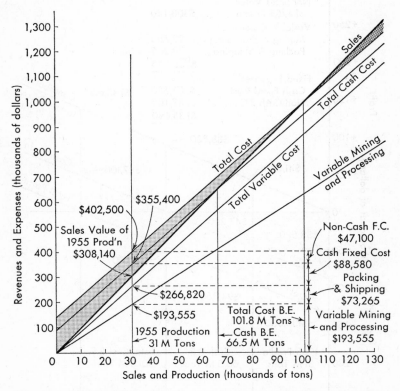

Fig. 4–3. Milbrae Mining Company. Volume-cost-profit diagram for 1955.

diagram of Milbrae Mining Company for the year 1955; Fig. 4–4 shows the volume-profit-loss diagram of the company for the same year.

Since operating costs of Milbrae Mining Company had already been cut down to the bone, it appeared that further cost savings could be achieved only through mining better clays. If, by better prospecting and closer quality control, the yield of finished clays could be brought up from 54.4 per cent to 60 per cent, only 51,700 tons of wet clays would be needed to produce 31,000 tons of finished clays. The cost of mining and processing could therefore be reduced from $193,555 to $175,490 on the basis of 1955

experience. Assuming that the company could attain a yield of 60 per cent
and that all operating costs would remain on the same levels as 1955, Mr.
Krieg estimated that Milbrae Mining Company would have to sell approximately 46,200 tons of finished clays before it could recover its out-of-pocket
cash outlays and would have to sell 70,800 tons before it could begin to

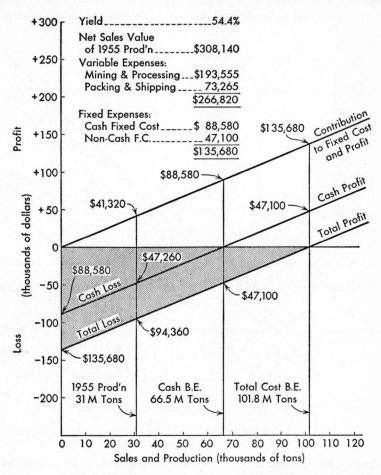

Fig. 4–4. Milbrae Mining Company. Volume-profit-loss diagram for 1955.

earn any return on its investment. Figure 4–5 shows the volume-profit-loss
relationship of Milbrae Mining Company on the assumption that the yield
could be raised to 60 per cent.

Mr. Krieg's analysis of Milbrae's situation as it stood at the end of 1955
was presented to the top management of San Rafael Sulphur Company.
After careful deliberations of the problems involved, management of San

Rafael Sulphur Company decided that the investment in Milbrae Mining Company was a failure and summed up its size-up of Milbrae's situation as follows: There was little prospect that the price of paper filler clay would go up in the foreseeable future. Under the prevailing market conditions, it

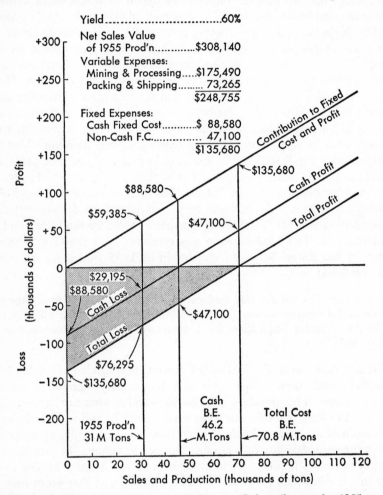

Fig. 4–5. Milbrae Mining Company. Volume-profit-loss diagram for 1955, assuming yield at 60 per cent.

would be impossible for the company to sell 100,000 tons of finished clay in any year, the volume needed to break even on its cost. Mr. Krieg had estimated that, if the yield could be brought up to 60 per cent, the break-even volume could be reduced to approximately 70,000 tons a year. From the experience of the past 40 months, management of San Rafael Sulphur

Company became convinced that the prospects of both raising the yield to 60 per cent with existing equipment and increasing the sales to 70,000 tons were very bleak. Operating cost had already been reduced to the minimum in 1955, and no further cost saving could be expected from operations. There were only two possible methods by means of which Milbrae might be able to stand on its own feet. The first method was to develop a process whereby higher-priced paper coating clays could be produced. However, after years of experiment, the company had not been successful in this respect. The second method was to invest an additional $1,700,000 worth of new equipment to step up further the actual yield of the company. However, such money was badly needed by San Rafael's other expanding businesses, which could provide a far better profit opportunity to the company than would Milbrae. If Milbrae Mining Company were liquidated, both the proceeds from its liquidation and the valuable time and attention which top management of San Rafael had to devote to its problems could be profitably diverted to more promising ventures. The workers at Milbrae could be transferred to other divisions of San Rafael. Therefore, hardships on employees, if Milbrae were closed down, could be minimized. All these reasons led to the conclusion that Milbrae Mining Company should be liquidated and its properties sold. This final decision was contained in a message to stockholders of San Rafael Sulphur Company in its 1955 annual report, which read as follows:

"We now intend to sell our clay business as the only alternative to a large and dubious added investment. Our Milbrae Mining Company's filler clay reserves can be an attractive acquisition for a company with an established line of coating clays."

The experience of Milbrae Mining Company is a striking example of the damaging result from a management's fragmentary knowledge of the volume-cost-profit relationships of its business and of what can happen when it does not make a real effort to learn what should be and will be the costs of its business at different levels of operation. Too frequently, management blames the unprofitability of a business on lack of volume. In certain cases this may be true. The concept held by the executive of Milbrae Mining Company that it takes time to break in a new business and that profit may be expected when its volume reaches a satisfactory level certainly applies to many other companies. However, in this particular situation, Milbrae Mining Company was simply engaging in an uneconomic operation. For 2 years and 4 months, the more clay Milbrae sold, the more serious became its loss. If this executive had not been indifferent to the operating reports prepared by the controller's department and if he had made any conscientious study of the company's costs and expenses, he would have discovered the problems of low yield and excessive spending long before the controller of

San Rafael brought up the issue with its top management. Instead, he let himself be trapped by his own misconceptions, and he believed that its loss was caused by low volume of business.

Furthermore, when any executive, such as the one at Milbrae Mining Company, expects his business to become profitable by expanding the volume, he should ask himself what volume the company needs before it can start to earn any money. He should also ask himself what the possibility is of the company's reaching that volume. Naturally, no executive can answer these questions until he has studied what should be and will be the costs and expenses of his company at different levels of operation. If the executive of Milbrae had made any such studies, he would have discovered 2 years before the controller of San Rafael brought up the issue with its top management that the operation at Milbrae would never break in as he had expected. He would have also discovered that even under improved operating conditions, such as those experienced by the company in 1955, the chance that Milbrae would reach a profitable volume of business would be very bleak. Much of Milbrae's loss could have been saved if these questions had been raised earlier and a study of its costs and expenses made. Therefore, to have only a fragmentary concept of volume-cost-profit relationships of business in general without any real knowledge of what the costs and expenses of a particular business should be and will be at different levels of operation can be as harmful as not having any such concept.

CHAPTER 5

Pricing Decisions

Pricing a product is one of the most important and delicate of management's problems. Sound pricing decisions together with other marketing strategy can frequently determine the success or failure of a business. Among other factors [1] that management must consider in its pricing decisions, cost is one that cannot be overlooked. Consistently selling below cost is the surest way to bankruptcy. If a business is to survive and be successful, it must try to recover from its sales not only its cost and expenses but also a profit adequate to maintain the incentive for its continued operation.

The interplay of cost and price differs from company to company and from occasion to occasion, depending to a large extent upon whether the company is a "price follower" or "price setter" under the particular circumstances. A price follower is one who follows the prices of his competitors or competing products. An example of this type of pricing practice is that used by Messina Plastics Company and Milbrae Mining Company, discussed in the previous chapter. The price follower usually studies his price-cost relationship by comparing the expected income he may receive under prevailing selling prices with his expected costs and expenses. He often selects those products which he thinks he can produce and sell at a profit. If his cost is too high to yield a profit, he will have to find ways and means to reduce his cost to a satisfactory level; or short of this, he may find it to his advantage to sell, or discontinue either temporarily or permanently, the unprofitable part of his business, if by so doing, his over-all profit position can be improved. To the price follower, cost is, therefore, a resistance point to the extent that it forces him to be selective with respect to the goods he produces and sells under given market prices.

---

[1] Included in these other factors are business conditions, consumer demand, product characteristics, methods of distribution, intensity of competition, available financial resources, and so forth.

In contrast to the price follower, a price setter is, of course, one who endeavors to establish prices by himself. Included in this group are companies which try to be "price leaders" of their industry, those which refuse to follow the price leaders, those which make built-to-order products, and those which make new products with nothing comparable in the market. To the price setter, cost is often the starting point in establishing the selling price. "Mark-up" pricing is, therefore, a common practice among price setters,[2] though, of course, the final selling price of any product will be influenced by many other non-cost factors previously mentioned. Regardless of the extent of adjustment for these non-cost factors, however, it is desirable for management to have first a framework upon which it can make such adjustment. The cost of producing and selling a product provides management with this needed framework in its pricing decisions.

Of particular importance to management in the use of the cost estimate as a basis in its pricing decisions is a knowledge of the volume-cost relationship of its business. Owing to the fact that not all costs and expenses will vary in direct proportion to changes in volume of operation, the unit cost of any product depends, among other things, upon the volume of business that may be realized. The use of any unit cost without knowing the volume on the basis of which such cost is computed and without examining the reasonableness of the underlying assumptions can often lead management into unsound pricing decisions. The need and value of this knowledge of volume-cost relationships in pricing a new product will be shown by the experience of the Olympia Manufacturing Company, to be discussed in detail later in this chapter.

At times when competition becomes keener, and sales have dropped as a result, price cutting has often been used as a means to stimulate demand and to improve profit. Whether or not profit can be improved depends not only upon the additional volume that can be generated by the price reduction but also upon the volume-cost structure of the particular business. More intelligent decisions on price reductions can be made if the price cutter studies in advance the minimum increase of sales volume needed to accompany any price reduction in order to make such price cutting worthwhile. If management knows its volume-cost relationships, the minimum increase of sales volume required to accompany any price reduction can be easily ascertained by the use of the new formula, table, or charts developed by the author and presented later in this chapter in the section Evaluating Price Reductions.

Another pricing problem frequently confronted by management is whether or not it should accept a "custom-tailored" order at a price desired by a customer but lower than the company would normally like to charge.

---

[2] Under "mark-up" pricing, selling price is established by adding to the unit cost of product a profit desired by management.

Sometimes the price demanded by the customer may not even cover the full unit cost of the product compiled under the regular pricing and costing procedure of a business. If the customer is unwilling to pay a price higher than the one being sought, management has to decide whether to accept the price demanded or lose the order. The experience of Sherwood Press—B discussed in the section Pricing Below "Cost"? in this chapter illustrates that on certain occasions management can increase the over-all profit of a company by accepting an order at a "loss" from estimated full unit cost. However, to ascertain whether or not the over-all profit can be improved by accepting an order at a loss, management again must study the volume-cost relationship of its business.

PRICING A NEW PRODUCT

Olympia Manufacturing Company

Olympia Manufacturing Company was one of the leading manufacturers in the vacuum-cleaner industry. The introduction of its new roll-around canister-type Clean-O-Matic vacuum cleaner was scheduled for the fall of 1955. According to the judgment of an independent testing agency and the controlled experience of a group of selected housewives, this new vacuum cleaner was far superior to any other make in the market, not only for its operating efficiency but also for its style and color. During the summer of 1955, management of Olympia was confronted with the problem of deciding the retail and factory prices for this new vacuum cleaner which would soon be introduced to the public.

The manufacturing facilities at Olympia were considered to be among the most modern and efficient in the vacuum-cleaner industry. Over two and one half million dollars had been spent for the construction of a new plant in which the Clean-O-Matic vacuum cleaners would be manufactured. Laborsaving and high-speed machinery had been purchased and installed. Straight line production was achieved through carefully studied and ingeniously designed plant layout. Material handling was reduced to a minimum by the installation of an extensive conveyor system. With this new and efficient plant, Olympia would be able to manufacture products not only of high quality but also at costs much lower than previously achieved.

On the basis of engineering estimates, the accounting department of Olympia had submitted to its top management a summarized cost estimate of the new Clean-O-Matic vacuum cleaners as shown in Table 5–1.

Until the introduction of Olympia's Clean-O-Matic, most vacuum cleaners with comparable features were being sold at a retail price of approximately $100 each. A customary margin of 33⅓ per cent was allowed to the dealer, bringing the factory sales price to $66.67 each. Since it should cost only $30 to produce and sell the Clean-O-Matic, Olympia would make

TABLE 5–1

Olympia Manufacturing Company

Cost estimate of Clean-O-Matic

	Per Vacuum Cleaner
Direct material	$10.00
Direct labor	5.00
Manufacturing overhead	
(150% of direct labor)	7.50
Total manufacturing cost	$22.50
Selling and administrative	
(33⅓% of manufacturing cost)	7.50
Total cost	$30,000

a profit of $36.67 per vacuum cleaner if it followed the prevailing selling prices. However, management of Olympia believed that the only sound foundation on which a business could build its future lay in its ability to supply the consuming public with high-quality products that must either fill a need not provided otherwise or be offered at prices lower than those of comparable items currently available in the market. The motto at Olympia was *better products for a higher standard of living at the lowest possible cost.* Since the acquisition of the new plant would bring tremendous cost savings in the manufacture of Clean-O-Matic, management of Olympia decided to share this operating economy with its customers by selling Clean-O-Matic at prices lower than those of competing makes.

Satisfied with an after-tax profit of 20 per cent of its costs, which would be the equivalent of approximately 14 per cent of sales at the tax rate of 50 per cent of profit, management of Olympia arrived at a factory selling price of $42 as follows:

	Per Vacuum Cleaner	*% of Cost*	*% of Sales*
Cost	$30	100	72
Profit after taxes	6	20	14
	$36	120	86
Income taxes	6	20	14
Factory selling price	$42	140	100

After having established the factory selling price, management of Olympia considered whether or not its dealers should be given the customary margin of 33⅓ per cent of retail. If the customary margin were given, Clean-O-Matic would be retailed at $63 each, $37 cheaper than the retail price of most comparable makes. However, the merchandising manager of Olympia feared that, if only the customary margin were granted, such a high reduction in retail price would cause dealer antipathy because of the accompanying reduction of the dealer's profit for the same number of vacuum cleaners he could sell. In order to encourage its dealers in pushing Clean-O-Matic over competing brands, management of Olympia decided to raise the dealer's margin to 40 per cent of retail. The contemplated retail price of Clean-O-Matic was then raised from $67 to $70 as follows:

	Per Vacuum Cleaner	*% of Retail*
Retail price	$70	100
Dealer's margin	28	40
Factory price	$42	60

With this increased margin, management of Olympia was confident of the support of its dealers for the Clean-O-Matic. At the same time, it felt pleased with its ability to provide the consuming public a $30 saving if it purchased a Clean-O-Matic instead of a vacuum cleaner of any other competing brand.

The Clean-O-Matic was introduced to the public in the fall of 1955 at $70 each. Olympia's advertising and promotional campaign emphasized both the superior quality of Clean-O-Matic and its savings to the housewife. Response to this new vacuum cleaner was enthusiastic. For the fiscal year ended September 30, 1956, the company sold 100,000 Clean-O-Matics, 25 per cent more than its original expectation.

In spite of this success in selling Clean-O-Matic to dealers and the consuming public, management of Olympia was disappointed with the meager profit made by the company during this period. Out of total sales of $4,200,000, pre-tax profit amounted to only $200,000, less than 5 per cent of its net sales. This was a disturbingly poor performance in comparison with the original estimate of 28 per cent of net sales. Olympia's profit and loss statement for the year ended September 30, 1956, is shown in Table 5–2.

At a total cost of $4,000,000, the cost per vacuum cleaner produced and sold during 1956 averaged $40 each. Management of Olympia felt that either the company's cost had been out of control in 1956 or the original estimate of $30 per vacuum cleaner must be erroneous. An investigation was thus ordered.

A comparison of Olympia's actual cost with its estimated cost disclosed that, although actual direct material and direct labor costs were identical with the original estimate, actual manufacturing overhead and actual selling and administrative expenses had greatly exceeded the original estimates. Actual manufacturing overhead amounted to 200 per cent of direct labor against an original estimate of 150 per cent. Actual selling and administrative expenses of $15 per unit were 100 per cent more than the original estimate of $7.50 per unit.

TABLE 5–2

Olympia Manufacturing Company

Profit and Loss Statement

			Per Vacuum Cleaner	
		Year Ended 9-30-56	Actual	Estimate
Sales		$4,200,000	$42.00	$42.00
Manufacturing cost of sales:				
Material	$1,000,000		$10.00	$10.00
Direct labor	500,000		5.00	5.00
Manufacturing overhead	1,000,000		10.00	7.50
Total manufacturing cost		2,500,000	$25.00	$22.50
Gross margin over manufacturing cost		$1,700,000	$17.00	$19.50
Selling and advertising	$ 900,000			
Administrative and general	600,000			
Total selling and administrative		1,500,000	15.00	7.50
Net profit before taxes		$ 200,000	$ 2.00	$12.00

Careful examination of these overhead expenses was then made by the management of Olympia. However, no excessive spending was found, and the operation of the company in the past year could be considered as under good control. On the other hand, in re-examining the original cost estimate, it was discovered that the estimated manufacturing overhead expenses of $7.50 per vacuum cleaner was based upon a "normal production" of 200,-000 units a year. The new Clean-O-Matic plant had a practical annual capacity of 250,000 units. The accountant had assumed that 80 per cent of its practical capacity should be the normal capacity of the company and had therefore estimated the unit cost of Clean-O-Matic on that basis. It was found that, if the company had produced and sold 200,000 units in 1956, its manufacturing overhead expenses would have averaged $7.50 per unit. Likewise, at this volume the average selling and administrative expenses would have been $7.50 instead of $15 per unit.

By this time, management of Olympia began to realize that the unit cost of Clean-O-Matic would change at different volumes of operation. This was due to the fact that while some costs, such as direct material and direct labor, would vary (in total) with changes in the volume of operation, many of the overhead expenses, including supervision, selling and advertising, administrative expenses, depreciation, and the like, would remain fixed (in total) during an accounting period regardless of the number of vacuum cleaners produced and sold by the company. The consequence was that the higher the volume of business, the lower would be the unit cost. Conversely, the lower the volume of business, the higher would be the unit cost. Although it would be appropriate to consider manufacturing overhead as 150 per cent of direct labor and selling and administrative as 33⅓ per cent of manufacturing cost at the volume of 200,000 vacuum cleaners a year, it would be grossly erroneous to use the same percentages for any other volume. Therefore, if management had estimated a sales volume of 100,000 units, the estimated cost would be $40 per vacuum cleaner rather than $30 each.

During the fall of 1956, retail prices of all other brands of vacuum cleaners had been reduced to $70 to meet the competition of Clean-O-Matic. Inventories of Clean-O-Matics in dealers' hands had been gradually accumulating, and Olympia's sales had been slowed down. Under these circumstances it would be difficult for the company to repeat its record sales of 1956 (fiscal) in the near future. Management of Olympia began to show concern about the future profitability of the company.

The experience of Olympia Manufacturing Company is a clear illustration of the need for knowledge of the volume-cost relationships of a business when cost is used as the basis of setting the price of a product. The unit cost of a product depends upon the number of units produced and sold. This is due to the fact that different types of cost respond differently to changes in volume of operation. Some will vary (in total) in direct proportion to changes in volume of business. Others will remain fixed during an accounting period regardless of changes in volume. Still others will respond only in part to these changes. Consequently, the unit cost of a product at a particular volume differs from that at any other volume. Within the practical capacity of a business, the higher its volume, the lower will be the unit cost. The lower its volume, the higher will be the unit cost. To accept any unit product cost without knowing the basis of computing such cost and questioning the reasonableness of the underlying assumptions can frequently be one of the major causes leading management, such as that of Olympia, to uneconomic pricing decisions which later develop into disturbing and disastrous situations.

The concern as to Olympia's future profitability was a serious one. Although the company did make a meager pre-tax profit of $200,000 in 1956 as the result of record sales of 100,000 vacuum cleaners, the company had not made a profit in three of the five preceding years. The keener competition resulting from its competitors' actions in the fall of 1956 to meet the price of Clean-O-Matic created growing doubt as to Olympia's ability to repeat its 1956 (fiscal) performance. According to the most optimistic estimate, the company would fare well if it could maintain within the next few years an annual sales volume of 80,000 Clean-O-Matics. At this level, the company would face a possible annual deficit of $240,000 under its recently ascertained price-volume-cost structure. The volume-cost-profit relationships of the company in 1956 were summarized by its management as follows:

		Per Vacuum Cleaner
Variable costs:		
	Direct material	$10.00
	Direct labor	5.00
		$15.00
Variable manufacturing overhead		5.00
	Total variable costs	$20.00

		Total
Fixed costs:		
	Fixed manufacturing overhead	$ 500,000
	Selling and advertising	900,000
	Administrative and general	600,000
	Total fixed costs	$2,000,000

With retail and factory prices at $70 and $42, respectively, sales of 80,000 Clean-O-Matics would bring Olympia a total revenue of $3,360,000 against a total cost of $3,600,000, resulting in a net loss of $240,000. A graphical presentation of Olympia's volume-cost-profit relationships is shown in Fig. 5–1.

The disappointing profit in 1956 and the grim situation lying ahead of Olympia must be attributed to the use of improper cost information and the ignorance of volume-cost relationships by its management in establishing the prices of Clean-O-Matic in 1955. Had the management of Olympia realized at that time that the unit cost of a product would be different at different operating volumes and questioned the basis on which the estimated unit cost of $30 per vacuum cleaner had been computed, it would never have started to tag the Clean-O-Matic at its present low prices of $70 (retail) and $42 (factory). Top management of Olympia had never expected its annual sales volume to reach 200,000 units. Although 100,000 units were actually sold in 1956 (fiscal), expected sales had been only 80,000 units. At this expected volume, the average unit cost of Clean-O-Matic would have amounted to $45 and the company would have lost $240,000.[3] Only the successful sales campaign which pushed its sales to 100,000 units had saved the company from this loss.

The disturbing situation confronting Olympia in the fall of 1956 could have been avoided if a more intelligent approach to its pricing problem had

---

[3] At the rate of $12 per unit, Olympia's management had originally expected a pre-tax profit of $960,000 on a sales volume of 80,000 units.

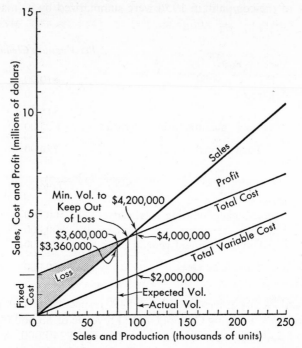

Fig. 5–1. Olympia Manufacturing Company. Volume-cost-profit diagram for 1956.

been used by its management in 1955. Instead of using the customary mark-up formula of:

	Per Unit of Product
Direct material	$xxx
Direct labor	xxx
Manufacturing overhead (% of direct labor)	xxx
Total manufacturing cost	$xxx
Selling and administrative (% of manufacturing cost)	xxx
Total cost	$xxx
Profit (% of total cost)	xxx
Selling price	$xxx

which was extremely misleading in this case, a more logical approach could be achieved by a careful study of the company's volume-cost relationships, followed by an examination of the sales volumes necessary under different proposed prices to keep it out of loss and to enable it to reach its profit objective. The economic wisdom of any proposed price could then be judged by comparing these minimum required sales volumes with the sales volumes that might be reasonably expected under such a price.

The minimum sales volumes necessary under any price to keep a company out of loss and to enable it to reach its profit objective can be determined by the application of the following commonly used formulas, if the volume-cost relationships, such as that shown in Fig. 5–1, have been ascertained and the profit objective has already been established:

$$V_m = \frac{F}{s_f - v} \qquad (5\text{–}1)$$

$$V'_m = \frac{F + P}{s_f - v} \qquad (5\text{–}2)$$

where V_m = minimum volume necessary to keep a company out of loss
  V'_m = minimum volume necessary to enable a company to reach its profit objective
  F = total fixed cost in dollars
  v = variable cost per unit of product
  P = pre-tax profit objective in dollars
  s_f = factory selling price

The total fixed cost F of Olympia in 1956 was $2,000,000. Its variable cost per unit of product v was $20 per Clean-O-Matic. A return of 10 per cent of investment after taxes was considered necessary by its management. With a total investment of $5,000,000 and a tax rate of 50 per cent of profit, the pre-tax profit objective P was set at $1,000,000.[4]

The first prices to be selected for study should be the prices of competitors or competing products. In the fall of 1955, most competing brands of Clean-O-Matic were being sold at a retail price of $100. With a customary dealer's margin of 33⅓ per cent of retail, the factory selling price would be $66.67. Substituting in formulas (5–1) and (5–2) the known values of F, v, and P and the factory selling price s_f selected for study, the minimum sales volumes necessary to keep the company out of loss, on the one hand, and to enable it to reach its profit objective, on the other, would be 42,700 and 64,000 units, respectively.

According to the best estimate of Olympia's management, a reasonable sales expectation would range from a low of 70,000 units to a high of 90,000 units annually. The medium sales volume expected over a period of years would be 80,000 units. With these sales expectations, it would appear very unlikely that the company would lose money if its operation were kept under proper control, because the expected low sales volume of 70,000 units

---

[4] Included in the total investment of $5,000,000 was $2,500,000 of plant and equipment.

a year would provide a safe margin of 27,300 units over the minimum sales volume of 42,700 units necessary for keeping the company out of loss.

Furthermore, with these sales expectations, the company could expect to make more than the necessary profit because not only the expected medium sales volume (80,000 units) but also the expected low sales volume (70,000 units) would be above the minimum volume (64,000 units) necessary to enable the company to reach its profit objective ($1,000,000). At a sales volume of 70,000 units, the expected profit would be $1,266,900. At a sales volume of 80,000 units, the expected profit would be $1,733,600. Since these profits would be more than those considered necessary, under Olympia's policy of sharing its operating economy with the consuming public, it would appear desirable to price the Clean-O-Matic at some level lower than the prevailing price of competing brands.

Assume that the next price to be studied was $70 retail and that the dealer's margin was set at 40 per cent of retail, thereby bringing the factory selling price to $42 per unit. Substituting in formulas (5–1) and (5–2) this new factory selling price, the minimum sales volumes necessary for keeping the company out of loss and for reaching the profit objective would become 90,500 units and 136,000 units, respectively. If the company had expected to sell only 70,000 to 90,000 units a year, the most optimistic sales estimate (90,000 units) would have fallen short of the minimum volume necessary for keeping the company out of loss.[5] It would, therefore, be obvious that, at the retail price of $70 with the dealer's margin raised to 40 per cent of retail, the company would face financial catastrophe if its sales should turn out to be the volume expected. To avoid this, the company would have to increase its annual sales to 90,500 units or more. Even at this increased volume of 90,500 units, its costs would barely be covered by its sales revenue and no profit would be made. To reach its profit objective, the company would have to increase its annual sales to 136,000 units and sustain that volume for a period of years. In the judgment of Olympia's management it would be impossible to reach such a high volume of sales under foreseeable circumstances. The price of $70 retail with a dealer's margin at 40 per cent would, therefore, be economically undesirable to the company.

Since the price of $100 retail with a dealer's margin of 33⅓ per cent would be too high and the price of $70 with a dealer's margin of 40 per cent would be too low, the desirable price would have to fall between these two extremes. By moving the selected price up and down and substituting it in formulas (5–1) and (5–2), the minimum sales volumes under different selected prices necessary to keep the company out of loss and to enable it to reach its profit objective can be computed and tabulated as follows:

---

[5] Although actual sales in 1956 turned out to be better than expected when the company sold 100,000 units, this volume was still 36,000 units below the minimum volume necessary for its reaching the profit objective.

Retail Price	Factory Selling Price	Minimum Volume to Keep Out of Loss	Minimum Volume to Reach Profit Objective	Factory Selling Price	Minimum Volume to Keep Out of Loss	Minimum Volume to Reach Profit Objective
		Dealer's Margin at 33⅓ % of Retail			Dealer's Margin at 40% of Retail	
$100	$66.67	42,700	64,000	$60	50,000	75,000
95	63.33	46,200	69,000	57	54,000	81,000
90	60.00	50,000	75,000	54	58,000	88,000
89	59.33	50,800	76,200			
85	56.67	54,400	81,800	51	64,400	96,800
70	46.67	75,000	112,500	42	90,500	136,000

The economic wisdom of any of these selected prices should be judged by whether or not Olympia could achieve the minimum sales volumes required under this price. If the sales expectation under any price would fall short of the minimum sales volume required to keep the company out of loss, a deficit would have to be anticipated. In order to reach the profit objective of the company, the sales volume expected to be sustained over a period of years must be more than or close to the minimum sales volume required to enable it to reach that objective.

With annual sales volumes expected to range from 70,000 to 90,000 units over a period of years under circumstances foreseeable by Olympia's management, the group of prices that might be considered desirable would be $85 to $90 retail with a dealer's margin of 33⅓ per cent, or $95 to $100 if the dealer's margin were raised to 40 percent. At these prices, Olympia's medium sales expectation of 80,000 units a year would be either above or close to the minimum sales necessary to enable it to reach its profit objective. At the same time, the low sales expectation would be sufficiently above the minimum sales necessary to keep the company out of loss. Therefore, even if sales volume should run low, the company could still expect to maintain its profitable position under these prices. Although expected profits at these low sales volumes would fall short of the objective, they would be compensated for by better profits at high levels of activities. Therefore, over a period of years, if the company were able to sustain on the average its medium sales expectation, its average profit under these prices could be expected to be close to the established objective.

It should be pointed out here that in an intelligent pricing decision more is involved than the pure mathematics of product costing. However, the use of volume-cost-profit analyses in approaching pricing problems as discussed here helps management make the policy and judgment decisions more effectively. For instance, while retail prices of $95 to $100 with the dealer's margin raised to 40 per cent of retail might be considered acceptable from the point of view of maintaining its financial strength and reaching its profit objective, such prices would be little or no different from those of the competing brands. Since it was the purpose of Olympia's management to share its operating economy with the consuming public, it would not be considered desirable under this business philosophy to set the retail prices of Clean-O-Matics at $95 or $100 and to short-circuit, at the dealer's level, the benefits intended for the ultimate consumers.

The exclusion of these prices would now narrow the choice of the desirable prices of Clean-O-Matic to a range of $85 to $90 retail, with a dealer's margin at the customary level of 33⅓ per cent of retail. Assume that $89 was selected for further study. At this price, Olympia's profit at different volumes of sales ranging from 60,000 to 100,000 units would be as follows:

Sales	Pre-tax Profit
60,000 units	$ 319,800
70,000	753,100
80,000	1,146,400
90,000	1,539,700
100,000	1,933,000

The pre-tax profits shown here are computed by the use of the following formula:

$$P = (s_f - v)V - F \qquad (5\text{--}3)$$

where P = pre-tax profit

s_f = factory selling price which is the equivalent of $s_r (1 - m_a)$, in which s_r is the retail selling price and m_a is the dealer's margin (in decimal)

v = variable cost per unit of product

V = sales volume in units

F = total fixed cost in dollars

Management of Olympia could clearly see from these figures that, under this price of $89, even if sales should drop to a level of 60,000 units a year, it would still be in a comfortably safe position. Although such profit would be less than the established objective, better-than-objective profit could be made during years of high activity. Over a period of years, if the company could sustain an average sales volume of 80,000 units a year, the average profit during this period could be close to the objective.

In addition to the desirability from the point of view of maintaining the financial strength and achieving the profit objective, this price would also provide Olympia an opportunity to supply its consuming public not only with a better product (in 1955 and 1956), but also with one at a cost more than $10 below that of competing brands.

To Olympia's dealers, the better quality and work-saving features provided by Clean-O-Matics, its lower selling prices, and the aggressive advertising and promotional campaigns could mean faster turnover and reduced investment in inventory, both of which could bring in increased profits.

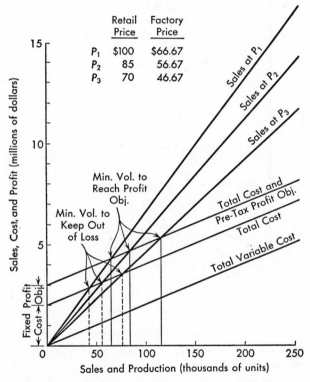

Fig. 5–2. Olympia Manufacturing Company. Volume-cost-price-profit diagram at selected prices with dealers' margin at 33⅓ per cent.

With an effective sales organization, Olympia most likely should be able to gain the support of its dealers at a retail price of $89, even though the retail dealer's margin was kept at 33⅓ per cent.

If Olympia had priced its Clean-O-Matics at $89 with a dealer's margin of 33⅓ per cent, the company would have made a pre-tax profit of $1,933,000 during 1956 (fiscal) on a sales volume of 100,000 units. Even on a reduced volume of 90,000 units, its pre-tax profit could amount to $1,539,700. In a competitive market such as the one in which Olympia operated, one could be sure that any price cutting would be shortly met by one's competitors. The higher-than-objective profit made during years of successful sales campaigns would provide the company with the necessary financial strength to meet the more difficult competition lying ahead. When Olympia's competitors began to cut their prices to meet that of Clean-O-Matics, Olympia's management would need worry little over its profit position even if its sales were slowed down from 100,000 units to 80,000

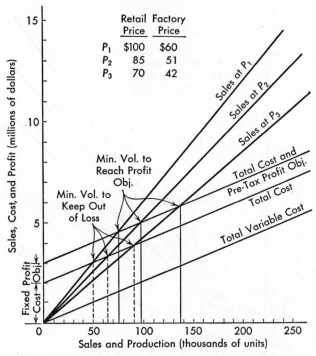

Fig. 5–3. Olympia Manufacturing Company. Volume-cost-price-profit diagram with dealers' margin at 40 per cent.

units or even to 60,000 units. Whereas, under its present price structure, Olympia was heading for a loss even at a volume of 90,000 units.

In the preceding analysis, the minimum sales volumes necessary under any selected prices to keep a company out of loss and to enable it to reach its profit objective are calculated by the use of formulas (5–1) and (5–2). Instead of using the formulas, these minimum sales volumes can be obtained graphically by the construction of volume-cost-price-profit diagrams such as those shown in Figs. 5–2, 5–3, and 5–4. In these diagrams, the same volume-cost relationships shown in Fig. 5–1 are used. By drawing the sales-revenue line of any price selected for study, the profit or loss at any particu-

lar volume under this price could be measured as the vertical distance between the sales-revenue line and the total-cost line. The volume at which
the sales-revenue line intersects the total-cost line is the minimum sales
volume necessary for keeping the company out of loss under this price.

The (pre-tax) profit objective can be added above the total-cost line by
drawing a line parallel to the total-cost line at a vertical distance equivalent
to the (pre-tax) profit objective. This line of total cost and (pre-tax) profit

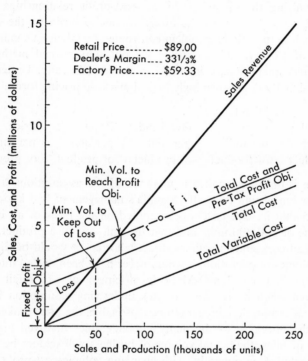

Fig. 5–4. Olympia Manufacturing Company. Volume-cost-profit diagram at retail
price of $89.

objective represents the amount of money which management would like to
recover from its operations. Whether or not its wish would be fulfilled would
depend upon the price as well as the volume attained. The minimum sales
volume necessary under any price to enable the company to reach this profit
objective is the volume at which the line of total cost and profit objective
intersects the sales-revenue line under this price. At any volume below this
minimum sales volume, the expected profit would be less than the established objective by an amount equivalent to the vertical distance by which
the sales-revenue line falls below the line of total cost and profit objective.
At any volume above this minimum sales volume, the expected profit would

exceed the profit objective by the vertical distance by which the sales-revenue line rises above the line of total cost and profit objective.

Figure 5–2 shows the volume-cost-profit relationships under three selected retail prices of $100, $85, and $70, with the dealer's margin set at 33⅓ per cent. Figure 5–3 shows the volume-cost-price-profit relationships under the same selected retail prices, but with the dealer's margin raised to 40 per cent. Figure 5–4 shows the volume-cost-price-profit relationships under the selected retail price of $89, with the dealer's margin at 33⅓ per cent.

By recognizing the changing volume-cost-profit relationships and the difficulty of predicting exactly the future volume of business, the suggested new approach to the pricing problem confronted by Olympia's management in the fall of 1955 greatly surpasses the old conventional method in its ability to guide management in thinking more realistically. Under the old conventional method, the seemingly logical mark-up pricing formula of

Direct material per unit of product	+	Direct labor per unit of product	+	Overhead per unit of product	+	Profit per unit of product	=	Price per unit of product

is deceptive if the price maker is unaware of the assumptions underlying the computation of unit costs. If Olympia's management had known in the fall of 1955 that its unit cost was computed on the basis of an imaginary sales volume of 200,000 units and that the unit cost of a product, particularly overhead cost, and sometimes direct labor cost,[6] would be different at different volumes of operation, it would never have been misled into expecting a $12 profit per Clean-O-Matic by pricing it at $70 retail and $42 factory. Even when he is aware of this underlying assumption and even when such an assumption appears to be reasonable, the price maker still has to realize that, because of the many imponderables involved in the consummation of sales, the actual volume of business will seldom be the same as that expected. Consequently, with changing volume-cost-profit relationships, the profit to be realized under actual operating conditions will most likely (except in rare instances) differ from the planned profit shown in the mark-up pricing formula.

Even if it causes no harm, the conventional method is, therefore, of little value to Olympia's management in helping it make intelligent pricing decisions. The suggested new approach to Olympia's pricing problem is better because, under the new method, management would be forced to recognize the changing volume-cost-profit relationships of its business and the difficulty of predicting exactly its future sales volume. The new method provides management with an objective analysis from a cost point of view by showing

[6] See Menlo Chemical Company case in Appendix C.

the minimum sales volume necessary under any proposed price to keep the company out of loss and to enable it to reach its profit objective. It also alerts management to the dangers of not achieving the desired sales volume.

Unlike the elements in the conventional mark-up pricing formula, the elements making up the formulas of

$$V_m = \frac{F}{s_f - v} \qquad \qquad (5\text{--}1)$$

$$V'_m = \frac{F + P}{s_f - v} \qquad \qquad (5\text{--}2)$$

for computing these minimum required sales volumes can be expected to hold true under actual operating conditions, if the cost structure remains unchanged and operations are kept under proper control. The new method also tells management that the actual profit under any price will depend upon how successfully the company is able to produce and sell its products to the satisfaction of its customers. Should the company be able to sell more than the minimum volume necessary to reach the profit objective, a higher-than-objective profit can be expected, and vice versa. The expected profit (or loss) at different sales volumes under any proposed price could be studied by the use of the third formula:

$$P = (s_f - v)V - F \qquad \qquad (5\text{--}3)$$

As pointed out earlier, none of the suggestions here implies that management's judgment is no longer needed; its role is as vital as always. But this new method eliminates deception, deals with real facts, and assures that management's judgment will be focused on a crucial area where skilled judgment is most needed for the successful operation of a business.

EVALUATING PRICE REDUCTIONS

One of the pricing problems frequently confronted by a price setter is whether or not he should reduce the price of his products to stimulate demand, thereby reducing his unit cost through spreading overhead over more units of product and thus increasing profit. Whether or not profit can be increased after the price reduction will depend upon two major factors, viz.: (1) the additional volume that can be generated by the price reduction and (2) the volume-cost structure of the *particular* business. For instance, if no increase of sales volume is expected to follow a contemplated price reduction, it is obvious that the company will be worse off after the price reduction. However, if an increase of 100 per cent in volume can be expected with a price reduction of 30 per cent, will the company be better off? No proper answer can be given unless management has learned the volume-cost relationships of its business. Later in this section it will be shown that, if the variable cost of a product constitutes 40 per cent of the selling price before price reduction, a 100 per cent increase in volume accompanying a 30 per cent price reduction merely enables a company to maintain its profit position before the price reduction. If its variable cost is more than 40 per cent of the selling price before reduction, the company will more likely be worse off; if the variable cost is less than 40 per cent of the selling price before reduction, the company will more likely be better off. Therefore, ignorance of either the volume-cost structure of a business or the additional volume that can possibly be generated by the price reduction can mislead management into unsound pricing decisions.

If the volume-cost relationships of a business have been ascertained, the new method suggested for the price selection of new products discussed in the preceding section can be equally useful to management in helping it make better decisions on any proposed price reductions. Under this method, the minimum sales volumes necessary under any contemplated reduced price to keep a company out of loss and to enable it to reach its profit objective can be determined either graphically or by the use of the two previously suggested formulas:

$$V_m = \frac{F}{s_f - v} \tag{5-1}$$

and
$$V'_m = \frac{F + P}{s_f - v} \tag{5-2}$$

The most likely profit or loss at different levels of operation under the contemplated reduced price could likewise be determined either graphically or by the use of the formula

$$P = (s_f - v)V - F \tag{5-3}$$

By comparing these minimum sales volumes with the volumes the company will likely achieve under its reduced price and by studying the possible profit or loss at varying volumes under the reduced price, more intelligent evaluation of the effect of the contemplated price reduction upon the financial strength and profit of the company can thus be made.

Instead of computing the minimum sales volumes necessary to keep a company out of loss and to enable it to reach its profit objective, an alternative method of evaluating price reduction may sometimes be used when a company is making a satisfactory profit under the present price and management wants to know only the minimum increase of sales volume necessary to accompany the contemplated price reduction in order to maintain its present profit position. If its volume-cost relationships have already been ascertained, this minimum increase of sales volume required can be computed by the use of the following formula developed by the author:

$$\Delta V_\% = \frac{\Delta s_\%}{(100 - v_{\%s_1}) - \Delta s_\%} \times 100 \qquad (5\text{--}4)^{[7]}$$

where $\Delta V_\%$ = minimum increase of sales volume (expressed in percentage of V_1) required to accompany a price reduction of $\Delta s_\%$, if the profit, which could otherwise be obtained under the old price-volume combination of s_1 and V_1, is to be maintained

V_1 = sales volume before price reduction

s_1 = selling price before price reduction

$\Delta s_\%$ = reduction in selling price (expressed in percentage of s_1)

v = variable cost per unit of product

$v_{\%s_1}$ = variable cost (expressed in percentage) in relation to selling price before reduction

To illustrate the use of this formula, assume that Olympia Manufacturing Company is making a satisfactory profit by selling its Clean-O-Matics at prices of $90 retail and $60 factory. A 30 per cent reduction of selling price has been suggested. Management wants to know the minimum increase in sales volume necessary to accompany the proposed price reduction if its present profit position is to be maintained. Assume also that the variable cost of Clean-O-Matics is $20 per unit or 33⅓ per cent of the present factory selling price and that Olympia's cost structure will remain unchanged. Substituting the known values of the proposed price reduction (30 per cent)

[7] Formula (5–4) is derived from

$$V_1 = \frac{F + P}{s_1 - v} \qquad V_2 = \frac{F + P}{s_2 - v}$$

$$V_1(s_1 - v) = F + P \qquad V_2(s_2 - v) = F + P$$

$$V_1(s_1 - v) = V_2(s_2 - v)$$

$$\frac{V_2}{V_1} = \frac{s_1 - v}{s_2 - v} \qquad \frac{V_2}{V_1} - 1 = \frac{s_1 - v}{s_2 - v} - 1$$

$$\frac{V_2 - V_1}{V_1} = \frac{s_1 - v - s_2 + v}{s_2 - v}$$

Substitute, $\Delta V = V_2 - V_1$, $\Delta s = s_1 - s_2$, and $s_2 = s_1 - \Delta s$

then
$$\frac{\Delta V}{V_1} = \frac{\Delta s}{s_1 - \Delta s - v}$$

$$= \frac{\Delta s / s_1}{\dfrac{s_1 - \Delta s - v}{s_1}} = \frac{\Delta s / s_1}{1 - v/s_1 - \Delta s / s_1}$$

$$\frac{\Delta V}{V_1} \times 100 = \frac{100 \times \Delta s / s_1}{100 (1 - v/s_1) - 100 \times \Delta s / s_1} \times 100$$

$$\Delta V_\% = \frac{\Delta s_\%}{(100 - v_{\%s_1}) - \Delta s_\%} \times 100 \qquad (5\text{--}4)$$

where F = total fixed cost in dollars

P = pre-tax profit in dollars under the old price-volume combination of s_1 and V_1

s_2 = reduced selling price

V_2 = minimum sales volume to maintain a profit of P when price is reduced to s_2

and the relationship between the variable cost and the present selling price
(33⅓ per cent) into formula (5–4), the minimum increase of sales volume
required will be

$$\Delta V_\% = \frac{30}{(100 - 33.33) - 30} \times 100 = 82\%$$

that is, 82 per cent of its present volume. If the present volume is 75,000
units, the new minimum sales volume, which Olympia must achieve to
maintain its present profit position, will be 136,000 units (75,000 units
$\times 1.82 = 136,000$ units).

To check the result obtained under this alternative method, assume that
Olympia's present pre-tax profit is $1,000,000 and that its total fixed cost
is $2,000,000. A 30 per cent price reduction will bring Clean-O-Matic's
factory selling price down to $42. The minimum sales volume necessary to
enable Olympia to reach a profit objective of $1,000,000 under the reduced
factory selling price of $42 per unit, computed by the use of formula (5–2),
will be

$$V'_m = \frac{2,000,000 + 1,000,000}{42 - 20} = 136,000$$

that is, 136,000 units, which corresponds to the result obtained under the
alternative method.

By using formula (5–4), the minimum increase of sales volume required
to accompany certain selected price reductions ranging from 1 to 90 per
cent for different businesses with different selected cost structures has been
computed. The results of these computations are shown in Table 5–3 and
Figs. 5–5 and 5–6.

Table 5–3 and Figs. 5–5 and 5–6 can be of value to management in at
least two different ways. First, reference to the author's table and charts
provides management with a short-cut method of determining the minimum
increase of sales volume necessary to make any price reduction worthwhile.
For instance, earlier in this section it has been questioned whether or not a
company will be better off with a 30 per cent reduction of selling price if
such price reduction can increase its sales volume 100 per cent. By referring
to Table 5–3 or Fig. 5–6, it can be noted that, when the variable cost
constitutes 40 per cent of the present selling price, in order to maintain its
profit position, a company needs to increase its sales at least 100 per cent
to accompany a price reduction of 30 per cent. If the variable cost is 50 per
cent of the present selling price, a minimum increase of 150 per cent of sales
volume will be required. If the variable cost is 30 per cent of the present
selling price, then the minimum increase of sales volume will only be
75 per cent. In other words, the company can be better off profitwise only if
the increase in sales volume exceeds the minimum required by its volume-

TABLE 5–3

Tse's Table for Finding the Minimum Increase of Sales Volume Required to Accompany Selected Price Reductions to Maintain the Profit Position before Price Reduction under Selected Cost-Price Structures

Price Reduction $\Delta s_\%$	Per Cent Increase Required in Sales, $\Delta V_\%$ *								
	Variable Cost in Per Cent of Selling Price before Price Reduction ($v_{\% s_1}$)								
	10%	20%	30%	40%	50%	60%	70%	80%	90%
1	1.12	1.27	1.45	1.95	2.04	2.56	3.45	5.26	11.12
2½	2.86	3.23	3.71	4.34	5.27	6.67	9.08	14.28	33.33
5	5.88	6.67	7.69	9.08	11.11	14.28	20.00	33.33	100.00
7½	9.08	10.34	12.00	14.30	17.65	23.08	33.33	60.00	300.00
9	11.11	12.69	14.76	17.67	21.95	29.05	42.85	81.80	900.00
10	12.50	14.29	16.67	20.00	25.00	33.33	50.00	100.00	Loss
12½	16.10	18.50	21.70	26.30	33.33	45.40	71.40	166.67	
15	20.00	23.08	27.24	33.33	42.80	60.00	100.00	300.00	
17½	24.10	28.00	33.33	41.20	53.80	77.80	140.00	700.00	
18	25.00	29.05	34.60	42.80	56.20	81.80	150.00	900.00	
20	28.58	33.33	40.00	50.00	66.67	100.00	200.00	Loss	
25	38.50	45.40	55.50	71.40	100.00	166.67	500.00		
27	42.90	50.90	62.80	81.80	117.40	207.50	900.00		
30	50.00	60.00	75.00	100.00	150.00	300.00	Loss		
33.33	58.70	71.20	90.80	125.00	200.00	500.00			
35	63.60	77.70	100.00	140.00	233.33	700.00			
36	66.67	81.80	105.90	150.00	257.00	900.00			
40	80.00	100.00	133.33	200.00	400.00	Loss			
45	100.00	128.50	180.00	300.00	900.00				
50	125.00	166.67	250.00	500.00	Loss				
54	150.00	207.50	337.00	900.00					
55	157.60	220.00	366.67	1,100.00					
60	200.00	300.00	600.00	Loss					
63	233.00	370.00	900.00						
65	260.00	433.33	1,300.00						
66.67	286.00	500.00	2,000.00						
70	350.00	700.00	Loss						
72	400.00	900.00							
75	500.00	1,500.00							
80	800.00	Loss							
81	900.00								
85	1,700.00								
90	Loss								

Formula (5–4) not applicable.

NO LONGER WILL INCREASE OF SALES VOLUMES BE HELPFUL; BY REDUCING SELLING PRICE TO A LEVEL BELOW VARIABLE COST, THE MORE ONE SELLS, THE MORE WILL BE HIS LOSS. (THIS NOTATION REFERS TO ALL THE "LOSS" COLUMNS.)

$$*\Delta V_\% = \frac{\Delta s_\%}{(100 - v_{\% s_1}) - \Delta s_\%} \times 100 \qquad (5\text{–}4)$$

cost structure. Otherwise, it will more likely be worse off under the reduced price.

A second contribution of the author's table and charts is that they point out to the reader how important it is for management to study the volume-cost relationships of *its own particular business.* From preceding discussions, one can easily gather that, for the same percentage reduction of selling price, a company with a higher variable cost in relation to selling price will

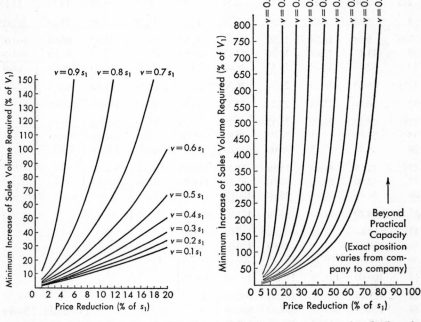

Fig. 5–5. Tse's chart for finding the minimum increase of sales volume required to accompany any price reduction to maintain the profit position before price reduction under selected cost-price structures.

Fig. 5–6. Tse's chart for finding the minimum increase of sales volume required to accompany any price reduction to maintain the profit position before price reduction under selected cost-price structures.

need a higher increase of sales volumes to maintain the profit position before price reduction than the company with a lower variable cost (in relation to selling price). Furthermore, one can readily see from the table and charts that this rate of increase of required minimum sales volume rises faster as the variable cost becomes an increasingly higher proportion of the selling price. For instance, with a 15 per cent reduction of selling price, the minimum required increase of sales volume rises from 23.08 per cent to 27.24 per cent when the variable cost rises from 20 per cent to 30 per cent of the selling price. Yet, for the same percentage reduction of selling price, the minimum required increase of sales volume rises from 100 per cent to 300 per cent, when the variable cost rise from 70 per cent to 80 per cent of selling price (before price reduction).

One may also note from the author's table and charts that, even under the same cost structure, the required minimum increase of sales volume rises at a rate faster than the rate at which prices are reduced. For instance, with the variable cost at 40 per cent of the selling price before price reduction, a 5 per cent price reduction requires a minimum increase of only 9.08 per cent of sales volume, a 30 per cent price reduction will raise the minimum required increase of sales volume to 100 per cent, and a 45 per cent price reduction will raise the minimum required increase of sales volume even higher to 300 per cent.

The author's table and charts also indicate that, depending upon the cost structure of a business, certain price reductions will require a company to increase its sales volume far beyond its practical capacity. For instance, if a company is operating at 80 per cent of its capacity, it will obviously be impossible to increase its sales 300 per cent without reaching the top limit of its productive capacity or changing the entire cost structure, even assuming that much more product could be sold.

Also shown by the author's table and charts is that, even with a compensating increase of sales volume, the variable cost of a product sets a lower limit on the price reduction any company can afford. One will find that any price reduction beyond this lower limit will place the company in a position where the more it sells, the more it will lose. Increase of sales volume will be of little help under such circumstances.

To sum up, if price reduction is to be used as a means to stimulate demand and to increase profit, management must study not only the additional volume that can be generated by the contemplated price reduction but also the volume-cost relationships of its particular business. If the volume-cost relationships have been determined, the formula, table, and charts developed by the author in this section can provide management with a valuable framework in evaluating whether the proposed price reduction will be worthwhile.

PRICING BELOW "COST"?

Another pricing problem frequently confronted by management is whether or not it should accept a "custom-tailored" order at a price desired by a customer but lower than the company would normally like to charge. Sometimes the price demanded by the customer may not even cover the "full (unit) cost" of this product computed under the regular pricing and costing procedure of a business. If the customer is unwilling to pay a price higher than the one being sought, management has to choose between accepting such an order at a "loss" (from full estimated unit cost) or losing the order. There are, however, occasions when management, by accepting such an order, may be able to increase the over-all profit of the company. Whether or not this can be done depends upon the additional revenue and the additional expenses that would be incurred by accepting a particular order, even though the price the customer is willing to pay may be less than the "fully allocated" unit cost of the product. If there are unused productive capacities at the time, the fully allocated unit cost computed under the regular costing procedure of most companies does not represent the additional cost the company would incur under the circumstances. Many of the costs and expenses included in the cost estimate compiled under such a costing procedure would be incurred by the business regardless of whether or not this order is accepted. To ascertain the additional costs that a business would have to incur by accepting the order, management must know the volume-cost relationships of its business. When management does not possess this needed knowledge of volume-cost relationships, it can easily be misled into taking economically undesirable actions on the basis of improper cost information. The importance of this knowledge of volume-cost relationships toward helping management make more profitable decisions in pricing problems of this kind can be illustrated by examination of a pricing problem which confronted executives of Sherwood Press.

Sherwood Press—B [8]

The manufacturing division of Sherwood Press is one of the largest among book manufacturers in this country. In addition to the manufacture of books for the publishing division of Sherwood Press, printing and binding orders from outside publishers are actively solicited and accepted. For establishing the price of any such "manufacturing sales order," the followlowing formula is used by the company:

(Direct material + labor and overhead)
     + profit to manufacturing department
        = price (per book) to customer

The direct material cost in this formula is the aggregate of the quantity of each of the different materials needed for the particular order on the basis of specifications from the customer, multiplied by the respective standard (expected actual) prices of the materials to be used. The labor and burden cost represents the aggregate of the standard time of each of the manufacturing operations needed for the particular order as established by the

[8] See Sherwood Press—A in Chap. 3 for additional description of the company.

engineering department of the company, multiplied by the respective stand-ard labor and burden rates of these operations.

In 1955 Sherwood Press was asked if it would accept an order to bind 10,000 copies of *Who's Who in Neptune* at 61 cents a copy. After studying detailed specifications of this book, the company estimated that the bindery cost of this order would amount to 67.09 cents a copy (see Table 5–4). Ordinarily, a profit of approximately 10 per cent of the sales price is added

TABLE 5–4

Sherwood Press
Bindery Cost Estimate

Author:			Order No.	
Title:	*Who's Who in Neptune*			
No. of Copies:	10,000		Date:	
Size:				
No. of Pages:				
Other Specifications:				

			Per 100 copies
Material:			
Material A	20 units at $0.60	$12.00	
Material B	30 units at $0.20	6.00	
Material C		3.00	
Material D		2.00	
Total material			$23.00
Labor and Burden:			
Operation 401	120 hr at $4.74	$ 569	
Operation 402	340 hr at $3.99	1,356	
Operation 403	280 hr at $5.31	1,487	
Operation 404	220 hr at $4.55	997	
Labor and Burden (10,000 copies)		$4,409	
Labor and Burden (per 100 copies)			44.09
Total Manufacturing Cost			$67.09
Profit Objective			7.91
Price Objective			$75.00
	Actual price billed		$61.00
	Manufacturing cost		67.09
	Manufacturing profit (loss)		($ 6.09)
	Approved by: _____		

to the manufacturing cost to arrive at the selling price of a "manufacturing sales order." In this case, the desired selling price would be 75 cents a copy (Table 5–4). Since the customer was willing to pay only 61 cents a copy, it seemed that not only Sherwood Press would not be able to make any profit, but it would lose $609 if the order were accepted.

Before Mr. George Raymond Watt became the manager of cost and standards at Sherwood Press, all orders that could not yield a profit on this basis were declined by management. At the time the binding order of *Who's Who in Neptune* was being considered by Sherwood Press, Mr. Watt knew that its bindery had unused productive capacities which would remain idle should this order be refused. Realizing the volume-cost relationship of this company, Mr. Watt was aware that the additional cost the company would incur by accepting this order was not 67 cents a copy as shown on the company's cost estimate, because the standard labor and burden rates used in this estimate (Table 5–4) included many overhead expenses which the company would incur regardless of whether or not this order was accepted. By using the applicable labor and burden rates to each manufacturing operation, Mr. Watt segregated the combined labor and burden cost shown on the cost-estimate sheet into labor and burden as follows:

Opera-tion	Standard Hours	Labor and Burden		Labor		Burden	
		Rate	Cost	Rate	Cost	Rate	Cost
401	120	4.74	$ 569	1.60	$ 192	3.14	$ 377
402	340	3.99	1,356	1.71	581	2.28	775
403	280	5.31	1,487	2.50	700	2.81	787
404	220	4.53	997	2.00	440	2.53	557
Total			$4,409		$1,913		$2,496

The standard labor and burden rates of each manufacturing operation at Sherwood Press are established at the beginning of each year on the basis of budgeted expenses and budgeted direct labor-hours for each operation (see Table 5–5). Of the total budgeted overhead expenses ($1,040,000) of the bindery department, $540,000 was direct overhead expenses of the department and $500,000 was overhead expenses allocated to the department. The bulk of the overhead expenses allocated to the bindery consists of "factory building and ground" ($115,000) and "factory general service" ($360,000), none of which would be affected by any short-term change in the volume of production. The allocation of expenses of various service and administrative departments to manufacturing departments is shown in Table 5–6). Of the bindery's direct overhead expenses ($540,000), $152,000 would remain fixed whether or not the company accepted the order. These fixed expenses included depreciation of machinery and a portion of super-

TABLE 5–5

Sherwood Press

Bindery Expense Budget;
Standard Labor and Burden Rates
1955

	Total	Bindery Operating Center				General
		401	402	403	404	
Direct labor	$ 800,000	$ 80,000	$240,000	$300,000	$180,000	
Indirect labor	$ 125,000	$ 12,000	$ 42,000	$ 50,000	$ 21,000	
Clerical	20,000	.....	.....	.....	.....	$20,000
Supervision	80,000	10,000	14,000	20,000	17,000	19,000
Overtime premium	18,000	15,000	.....	.....	.....	3,000
Night-shift premium	19,000	17,000	.....	.....	.....	2,000
Vacation and holidays	97,000	.....	.....	.....	.....	97,000
Social security taxes	36,000	.....	.....	.....	.....	36,000
Workmen's compensation insurance	10,000	.....	.....	.....	.....	10,000
Accident and sickness insurance	11,000	.....	.....	.....	.....	11,000
Operating supplies	20,000	400	5,000	8,000	6,000	600
Power	20,000	3,000	4,000	7,000	5,000	1,000
Repairs of machinery and equipment	24,000	3,000	5,000	9,000	6,000	1,000
Depreciation of machinery and equipment	50,000	5,000	11,000	18,000	14,000	2,000
Other expenses	10,000	1,600	2,000	3,000	2,000	1,400
Direct overhead	$ 540,000	$ 67,000	$ 83,000	$115,000	$ 71,000	$204,000
Paint and carpenter shop	$ 1,000	.....	.....	.....	.....	1,000
Factory building and ground	115,000	15,000	30,000	40,000	20,000	10,000
Machine shop	24,000	3,000	6,000	9,000	6,000	.....
Factory general services	360,000	.....	.....	.....	.....	360,000
						$575,000
General overhead		72,000	200,000	173,000	130,000	(575,000)
Allocated overhead	$500,000					
Total overhead	$1,040,000	$157,000	$319,000	$337,000	$227,000	.....
Budgeted direct labor-hours	400,000	50,000	140,000	120,000	90,000	
Standard labor rate per direct labor-hour	$2.00	$1.60	$1.71	$2.50	$2.00	
Standard burden rate per direct labor-hour	2.60	3.14	2.28	2.81	2.53	
Standard labor and burden rate per direct labor-hour	$4.60	$4.74	$3.99	$5.31	$4.53	

		Manufacturing Departments			
	Total	*Compo*	*Plate*	*Press*	*Bindery*
Direct labor	$1,295,000	$150,000	$45,000	$300,000	$ 800,000
Indirect labor		$ 30,000	$ 9,000	$ 40,000	$ 125,000
Clerical salaries		4,000	1,000	3,000	20,000
Supervision and administrative salaries		20,000	7,000	25,000	80,000
Overtime premium		1,000	1,000	21,000	18,000
Night-shift premium		1,000	...	21,000	19,000
Vacations and holidays (hourly employees)		22,000	5,000	41,000	97,000
Pension contribution		...	...	...	...
Social security taxes		7,000	1,500	13,000	36,000
Workmen's compensation insurance		1,500	500	4,000	10,000
Accident and sickness insurance		2,000	500	4,000	11,000
Operating supplies		*	6,000	25,000	20,000
Power and light		1,000	2,000	15,000	20,000
Repairs of machinery and equipment		600	800	10,000	24,000
Repairs of building and ground		...	...	...	...
Depreciation of machinery and equipment		4,000	2,000	40,000	50,000
Depreciation of building		...	...	...	...
State and local taxes		...	...	...	...
Other expenses		1,000	3,000	8,000	10,000
Departmental expenses		$ 95,100	$39,300	$270,000	$ 540,000
Distribution of expenses of nonoperating departments:					
Paint and carpenter shop		300	200	700	1,000
Factory building and ground		9,000	6,000	22,000	115,000
Machine shop		600	900	9,000	24,000
General factory services		52,000	13,000	107,000	360,000
General administrative		...	...	...	...
Total overhead expenses of manufacturing departments	$1,665,100	$157,000	$59,400	$408,700	$1,040,000
Budgeted productive hours	595,000	60,000	15,000	120,000	400,000
Standard labor rate per direct labor-hour (av)	$2.18	$2.50	$3.00	$2.50	$2.00
Standard burden rate per direct labor-hour (av)	2.80	2.61	3.96	3.41	2.60
Standard labor and burden rate per direct labor-hour	$4.98	$5.11	$6.96	$5.91	$4.60

* Included in other expenses.

Press

Manufacturing Departments, 1955

Paint and Carpenter Shop	Factory Building and Ground	Machine Shop	General Factory Services	General Administrative	Publishing Division	
					Dept. A	Dept. B
$20,000	$ 60,000	$38,000	$ 70,000			
...	...	...	75,000			
...	10,000	5,000	134,000	$200,000		
1,000	4,000	1,500	1,000			
...	...	...	...			
2,000	8,000	4,000	8,000			
...	...	...	60,000	18,000		
500	3,500	1,000	12,000	4,000		
200	1,000	400	1,000			
200	1,000	300	1,000			
1,000	10,000	3,000	12,000	20,000		
100	30,000	100	...	5,000		
...	5,000	100	500			
...	12,000					
...	11,000	600	1,000			
...	20,000					
...	50,000	...	24,000			
...	10,000	...	17,700	47,000		
$25,000	$235,500	$54,000	$417,200	$294,000		
(26,000)	22,800	...	...	...	$ 1,000	
1,000	(288,000)	5,000	20,000	6,000	20,000	$ 84,000
...	1,700	(59,000)	22,800			
...	28,000	...	(560,000)			
...	...	...	100,000	(300,000)	50,000	150,000
...	...	...	...	...		

visory, indirect labor, and clerical salaries. On the basis of his knowledge of the business and experience of Sherwood Press, Mr. Watt estimated that 60 per cent of the overhead expenses budgeted for the bindery department in 1955 was fixed and only 40 per cent was variable (see Table 5–7).

TABLE 5–7

Sherwood Press

Bindery Expense Budget
Fixed and Variable Expenses
1955

	Total	*Fixed*	*Variable*
Indirect labor	$ 125,000	$ 20,000	$105,000
Clerical	20,000	20,000	
Supervision	80,000	50,000	30,000
Overtime premium	18,000	. . .	18,000
Night-shift premium	19,000	. . .	19,000
Vacation and holidays	97,000	7,000	90,000
Social security taxes	36,000	4,000	32,000
Workmen's compensation insurance	10,000	1,000	9,000
Accident and sickness insurance	11,000	. . .	11,000
Operating supplies	20,000	. . .	20,000
Power	20,000	. . .	20,000
Repairs of machinery and equipment	24,000	. . .	24,000
Depreciation of machinery and equipment	50,000	50,000	
Other expenses	10,000	. . .	10,000
Direct overhead	$ 540,000	$152,000	$388,000
Paint and carpenter shop	$ 1,000	. . .	$ 1,000
Factory building and ground	115,000	$115,000	
Machine shop	24,000	. . .	24,000
Factory general service	360,000	360,000	
Indirect overhead	$ 500,000	$475,000	$ 25,000
Total overhead	$1,040,000	$627,000	$413,000
	100%	60%	40%

Budgeted direct labor-hours	400,000
Standard labor rate per direct labor-hour	$2.00
Standard burden rate per direct labor-hour	2.60
Standard labor and burden rate per direct labor-hour	4.60

Since the company's bindery department had unused productive capacities at that time, Mr. Watt figured that the additional overhead expenses the company would have to incur by taking on this order was, therefore, not $2,496 but $998 (40 per cent of $2,496). On this basis, a new estimate of the additional cost which the company would have to incur by accepting this order was made as follows:

Material	$2,300
Direct labor	1,913
Variable overhead	998
Additional expenses Sherwood Press would have to incur should the order be accepted	$5,211

The additional revenue of $6,100 (10,000 copies at 61 cents) the company could obtain by accepting this order now exceeds the additional cost which the company would incur on this order by $889 ($6,100 − $5,211). This means that, if the manufacturing division of Sherwood Press was making money at the time, its profit would be increased by $889. If the manufacturing division was losing money at the time, by accepting this order its loss would be reduced by this amount. In contrast to an estimated loss of $609 from the first estimate compiled under the company's regular costing and pricing procedure, Mr. Watt's revised estimate showed a completely different result. Since Mr. Watt's analysis clearly presents a more truthful picture of the company's situation at the time, the order to bind 10,000 copies of *Who's Who in Neptune* at 61 cents a copy was accepted by the manufacturing division of Sherwood Press.

During the same year Sherwood Press accepted a number of manufacturing orders at a "loss" (from standard cost) to spread its overhead. The total operating profit of its manufacturing division for 1955 came close to $100,000. Whereas, in 1954 every order accepted by the manufacturing division showed a profit, the operating result for the entire year was a loss of $20,000. The main reason for this improvement of operating results in 1955 was an increase in volume of business and a reduction of idle productive capacities at the manufacturing division. By introducing a knowledge of the volume-cost relationships of the business, Mr. Watt enabled Sherwood Press to capture a number of orders for the manufacturing division which would otherwise have been lost to competitors while the company was physically able to turn out such products and to increase its over-all profit at the same time.

The experience of Sherwood Press illustrates again the need of proper cost information to help management solve business problems. In a "job-order" company, such as Sherwood Press, "mark-up pricing" on the basis of full standard or estimated cost is a common practice. Although the procedure may be useful in the normal course of operation in this type of business, strict adherence to such a method in certain situations, as the case shows, may bring damaging results unsuspected and unanticipated by management. One of the situations that calls for a departure from such procedure is whether or not a business should accept an order at a price desired by the customer but less than the company would normally charge. If there were unused productive capacities which would remain idle should the order be refused, it might be advantageous for the company to accept such an order even if the price was less than the full standard cost. Whether the acceptance of such an order under the prevailing circumstances would result in increased over-all profit to the company depends primarily upon the relationship between the additional revenue from this order and the additional cost which the company would incur for this order. There is no other way management can ascertain the additional cost which the business would incur for such an order except through a knowledge of the volume-cost relationships of its business.

It should be pointed out that, while the concept of "spreading overhead" is familiar to many executives, such a concept can be misleading unless management really knows the volume-cost relationships of the business. For instance, suppose that Sherwood Press' customer was willing to pay only 47 cents a copy on the bindery order of 10,000 copies of *Who's Who in Neptune*. Should the management of Sherwood Press accept such an order? Some people might say so on the assumption that the price of 47 cents a copy is still 4.87 cents more than the aggregate of direct material (23 cents) and direct labor (19.13 cents) costs. These people would contend that there would be a contribution of $487 to "spread the company's overhead." However, from Mr. Watt's analysis one can easily see that the additional overhead expenses the company would incur by taking on this order would average 9.98 cents a copy. Should the company accept this order at the price of 47 cents a copy, there would be a drain on the company's financial resources amounting to $511. The company should naturally refuse the order in such a case. The additional expense (translated into an average cost per unit of product) the company would incur by accepting this order hence becomes the "floor" of prices acceptable to the company.[9] That is to say, under the prevailing circumstances, any price above the floor will yield an additional over-all profit to the company. Any price below the floor will cause a financial loss to the company. Before management can ascertain the floor of acceptable prices, it must possess a knowledge of the volume-cost relationships of its business.

In addition to the presence of unused productive capacities, a second condition, equally important, must also be present so that this concept of matching additional cost against additional revenue can be used advantageously. This second condition is that the decision to accept this specific order at a price lower than the full cost should not affect the general price structure of a business. In arriving at the conclusion that Sherwood Press can increase its profit by $889 through accepting the order on *Who's Who*

[9] The floor of acceptable prices of 10,000 copies of *Who's Who in Neptune* was 52.11 cents a copy in 1955.

in Neptune at a price less than standard cost, an implicit assumption was made by Mr. Watt that this decision would not have any material effect upon other revenues of the company.[10] Should the acceptance of this order at 61 cents a copy lead to a general decrease of selling prices on all other orders, the increased revenue for this particular order may be more than offset by the decrease in revenue from other orders. Mr. Watt's analysis will, therefore, no longer apply to the situation, since this would represent a change in the general price structure of the business. Discussions on the use of knowledge of volume-cost relationships in helping management evaluate such changes in the general price structure have been presented in earlier sections of this chapter.

[10] Orders from Sherwood Press' publishing division make up the bulk of sales of its manufacturing division.

CHAPTER 6

Cost Control

After World War II, conditions of declining sales and profits led a number of companies into the use of volume-cost analysis for helping management keep costs under better control. The cessation of war had left these companies with a serious shrinkage in their volume of business and while revenues dropped, costs and expenses failed to come down proportionately. The result was that the profit position of these companies deteriorated even more than the decline in volume of business. For example, with respect to some of the companies considered in connection with this study, sales of Lafayette Brass Company dropped to $52,900,000 in 1945 from the wartime peak of $67,500,000 in 1943. Although the decline in sales during this 2-year period amounted to only 22 per cent, the drop in net profits before taxes was more severe. The company earned only $3,100,000 before taxes in 1945 in comparison with $7,600,000 in 1943, a drop of 59 per cent. At Menlo Chemical Company, while its sales dropped 30 per cent from $37,000,000 in 1945 to $26,000,000 in 1946, its net income before taxes declined from $4,200,000 to $1,300,000, a drop of 69 per cent. Sales of Otterbein Corporation dropped more than 50 per cent in 1946 as compared with the preceding year. For the first time since 1938 the company suffered an operating loss, although its net earnings after taxes were still in the black because of an income-tax adjustment. At Burlingame Manufacturing Company a severe decline in sales and profits was also experienced because of the end of the war and the termination of the immediate postwar boom.

Confronted with this problem of declining sales and profits, executives of these companies decided that a tighter control over their costs must be exercised. However, in their efforts to keep manufacturing costs under better control, they found that their cost systems as then used were inadequate and did not provide them with the information necessary to serve as a basis for intelligent action.

Among the various types of control devices used at these companies prior to the introduction of volume-cost analysis is the system which can be categorized as *comparison of actual cost with that of the preceding period.* Menlo Chemical Company had used such a system prior to 1946. It had been customary for the company to compare its actual costs of the current period with the actual costs of the preceding period to find any item that appeared to be out of line and required management's special attention. The same control system is still used by many other business enterprises today.

The main trouble with this type of control system is that what has been spent during the preceding period does not necessarily tell what should be spent for the current period. The operating conditions of the two periods may be entirely different. This is especially so when the volume of business changes from one period to another. An implicit assumption in comparing the actual expenditure of the current period with that of the preceding period under such a situation is that a cost is either completely fixed or will vary in direct proportion to changes in volume of operation. While this may be true for certain items, the assumption has no validity either for the manufacturing expenses as an aggregate or for many of the items making up such manufacturing expenses. Because of the nature of these expenses, they will neither remain stable at two different volumes of operation, nor will they fluctuate in direct proportion to changes in volume of business.

In its efforts to pinpoint the real causes of its deteriorating profit situation and to plan for a constructive future course of action, Menlo Chemical Company found it difficult to determine whether its decaying profit situation was due merely to the decline in volume of business, to inefficiency of operation, or to a combination of both. Because of the nonuniform response of different manufacturing expenses to changes in volume of business, the company discovered that it could no longer rely upon what had been spent during a preceding period to make an intelligent appraisal and analysis of the situation confronting the company.

Its management was told that if a volume-cost analysis had been made by the company, it would have been able to make an intelligent appraisal of the situation with which it was confronted and would have had the proper information to keep its future costs and expenses under close control. The company would be able to know not only what its costs should have been at the actual volume of business during any given period, but also what its costs should be at different levels of operation. Upon the recommendations of a well-known management-consulting firm, a formal system of volume-cost analysis was installed at Menlo Chemical Company. This system is more commonly known as variable budgeting or flexible budgeting, a term which will be used hereafter in this book to mean volume-cost analysis for cost-control purposes.

A second device for control of manufacturig overhead, often used prior to the introduction of variable budgeting, is the *standard cost* system. Both Lafayette Brass Company and Burlingame Manufacturing Company had used such a system before the adoption of their variable budget systems. The standard cost system at Lafayette Brass Company was installed during World War II. Until 1942 the company had used an actual process cost system. As the company's business expanded from $31,000,000 in 1940 to $61,000,000 in 1942, its top executives began to feel that the company's actual cost system was unable to provide them with "sufficient and timely information," not only for proper pricing, product costing, and inventory valuation, but also for cost control. A standard cost system, therefore, was designed and installed to meet the new needs of management.

Although the standard cost system at Lafayette Brass Company seemed to have worked well during World War II, the company later discovered that it was still inadequate to serve as management's guide for the control of manufacturing overhead. As the company's volume of sales and production declined, its actual overhead expenses were found to have greatly exceeded their standards. In its efforts to control this "excessive spending," the company realized that many of its overhead expenses were fixed and would not drop proportionately with declines in the level of activity. Some of its overhead expenses were partly fixed and partly variable in relation to changes in volume of business. Under the standard cost system, manufacturing overhead was absorbed by products at standard rates, and thus the total standard costs varied from period to period directly in proportion to changes in the volume of production. Because of the inability of its standard cost system to take into consideration the different nature of various manufacturing expenses in their response to changes in volume of business, Lafayette Brass Company found it difficult to ascertain whether its "unfavorable overhead variance" after World War II was caused by the decline in volume of business, by inefficiency of operation, or by both in combination.

The same dissatisfaction with its standard cost system was experienced by Burlingame Manufacturing Company. The standard cost system used by this company was similar to the one at Lafayette Brass Company, except in the method of computing standard overhead rates. While Lafayette Brass Company based the computation of standard overhead rates upon its normal volume of production, Burlingame Manufacturing Company based its computation upon the volume of business expected for the ensuing year. Through its own experience, the company later found that its actual volume of business would seldom be the same as that expected. During a period of high level of activity when the actual volume of operation was higher than the expected volume of business, the actual manufacturing expenses tended to be less than the overhead absorbed into the costs of products at standard rate. Little concern was shown then because the variance "looked favorable" to the company. However, when the actual volume of business was less than the expected one, actual manufacturing overhead tended to exceed the standard overhead absorbed into the costs of products. As the company's sales and profits declined after World War II, its management found that a sizable amount of manufacturing overhead was left underabsorbed. In its efforts to reduce this unfavorable variance, the company, like Lafayette Brass Company, found that not all its manufacturing expenses would fluctuate with changes in production volume. Some expenses would remain fixed at all levels of operation, while others might be partly fixed and partly variable. Its standard cost system was thus found unsatisfactory as a means of helping management judge the efficiency of operation in relation to manufacturing overhead expenses, because no consideration was given to the different nature of each expense in its response to changes in production volume.

Since variable budgeting takes into account the differing characteristics of expenses in relation to fluctuating volume, both Lafayette Brass Company and Burlingame Manufacturing Company decided to install this system. This would enable them to determine whether the company had spent more money than it should have and would help keep manufacturing overhead expenses under close control in the future. It should be noted that variable budgeting is used by these companies as a supplement to their standard cost systems, which are still useful for other purposes.

Another control device which often proves unsatisfactory in control of manufacturing overhead is the *fixed budget* system. Otterbein Corporation had used such a system prior to World War II. The company was prompted into the use of budgetary control by a severe decline in sales and profits in 1938. Its fixed budgets were expected to assist management in planning the future course of business and controlling the company's costs and expenses. These fixed budgets were in the form of a projected profit and loss statement based upon management's sales forecasts for the period covered.

However, subsequent experience at Otterbein Corporation showed that, if its actual sales and production differed from its forecast sales and production, fixed budgets could not serve as adequate guides to management for judging the company's efficiency of operation. Under this system, all costs and expenses are regarded as fixed for the period under consideration. However, actual experience shows that, although some expenses might be fixed for the period, others would fluctuate with changes in volume of business. Therefore, when the actual volume of operation is less than the expected volume of operation, actual expenditures are often found to be less than their corresponding fixed budget allowances. On the other hand, when the actual volume of business is higher than that expected, fixed budget allowances are often found to be unreasonably tight as related to what should have been spent. The expansion of its sales during World War II, a change in top management, and the lack of clerical help during the war resulted in abandonment of the fixed budget system at Otterbein Corporation.

When the budgetary system was restored by a new management after the end of World War II as an aid to meeting the problem of declining sales and profits, the company decided that fixed budgets, though useful in helping management in planning its operation, should not again be used as management's guides for controlling manufacturing overhead.[1] Instead, measurement of actual performance of these expenses should be based upon the company's expected expenditures at its actual level of operation, not at its forecast level of operation. This is variable budgeting.

The case of Wabash Manufacturing Company provides an example of the operation of variable budgeting in relation to other inadequate noncomprehensive systems. In this illustration, variable budgeting is confined to its use in helping management meet problems of controlling manufacturing overhead.

Wabash Manufacturing Company, a manufacturer of product X, has used a variable budgeting system for a number of years. Its budgetary system is considered by its management as one of the most useful tools in helping to keep manufacturing expenses under good control. The controller of this company frequently delivers speeches to professional groups and contributes extensively to accounting literature as to the satisfactory experience which his company has had with its variable budgeting system. An illustration frequently used by this controller follows:

Assume that in January, 1955, Wabash Manufacturing Company produced and sold 1,300,000 lb of product X. Its manufacturing overhead incurred during this month amounted to $24,000. During the following month, the company produced and sold 900,000 lb of product X, and its manufacturing overhead amounted to $18,000. In order that more intelligent action could be taken in the future, management of this company wanted to know whether it had done a better or worse job in February than in January in controlling its manufacturing overhead.

If the company had used the type of cost analysis based upon comparison of the actual cost of the current period with that of the preceding period, it would have found that, while production and sales dropped 31 per cent, from 1,300,000 lb in January to 900,000 lb in February, its manufacturing overhead dropped only 25 per cent, from $24,000 to $18,000. It would appear that the company was less efficient in February than in January in controlling its manufacturing overhead and should, therefore, find ways and means to prevent a repetition of its poor February performance.

However, Wabash Manufacturing Company had long learned that its

---

[1] This is not to say that fixed budgets are entirely eliminated under variable budgeting. If the nature of the expense is fixed (e.g., depreciation) in relation to volume, of course the budget allowance will also be fixed within a given period.

manufacturing overhead was a semivariable expense, i.e., one with some elements that were fixed in relation to changes in volume of business and with other elements that would vary with changes in volume of operation. Under the variable budgeting system used by the company, it had made careful studies of its volume-cost relationships and had established what it should spend for each of its manufacturing expenses at different levels of operation. The budget estimates of its manufacturing overhead established by its management for the year 1955 are as follows:

Monthly Production	Manufacturing Overhead *
500,000 lb	$16,000
600,000	16,800
700,000	17,600
800,000	18,400
900,000	19,200
1,000,000	20,000
1,100,000	20,800
1,200,000	21,600
1,300,000	22,400
1,400,000	23,200
1,500,000	24,000

* Budget estimates.

Since the company knew what it should spend for its different expenses at various levels of operation, actual expenditures of each month were compared against the budget estimates for the actual volume of business realized during this period, instead of against the expenditures incurred during the preceding month or the same month of the last year. By comparing its actual manufacturing overhead with the corresponding budget estimates, actual expenditures of $24,000 during January were found to be $1,600 more than what the company would normally spend ($22,400) for the production of 1,300,000 lb during this period. Actual expenditures of $18,000 during February were $1,200 less than what the company would normally spend ($19,200) for the production of 900,000 lb. The unfavorable result experienced during January made the operating supervisors of this company more cost conscious in the following months. Ways and means to cut down unnecessary expenditures were sought and put into effect. As a result of these measures, a saving of $1,200 from what the company would have normally spent was attained during February. With its variable budget analysis, the operating management could see that it had been more efficient in controlling the company's manufacturing overhead during February than in January. If it had applied the old customary method of comparing this month's expenditure with that of the preceding month, management might have erroneously believed that its January operation was more efficient than its February operation. The facts, however, were just the reverse.

Had the company used a standard cost system as its guide for control of manufacturing overhead, how would the variable-budget analysis differ from the standard cost analysis? Assume that January, 1955, was a month of unusually high activity and that the normal volume of production at Wabash Manufacturing Company was 1,000,000 lb per month. With an estimated manufacturing overhead of $20,000 at the normal volume of production, standard manufacturing overhead would be set at the rate of $2 per 100 lb of product X produced. For a total production of 1,300,000 lb in January, the standard manufacturing overhead would then become $26,000. An actual expenditure of $24,000 would, therefore, be $2,000 less than the standard cost of products manufactured. Under such a standard cost system, management could mistakenly believe that the company had spent $2,000 less than it should and that good cost control had been achieved in January. Instead, the variable budget analysis presented earlier shows that the company had actually spent $1,600 more on its manufacturing overhead than it would normally have done for a production of 1,300,000 lb.

Now assume that the company's sales and production continued to decline after February and reached a low of 700,000 lb in March. Actual manufacturing overhead for that month amounted to $15,700. At the rate of $2 per 100 lb, the company's standard manufacturing overhead would be $14,000 for that month. Therefore, the company had spent $1,700 more than its standard manufacturing cost. In a period of declining sales and profits, management would naturally be concerned about such substandard operation. Without the variable budget analysis, management would think that excessive manufacturing overhead had been incurred in March and that corrective action would be necessary in the future. What actually happened in March was that the operating people had already done a good job in keeping this cost under proper control. From the company's variable budget estimates, its manufacturing overhead at a production level of 700,000 lb would normally be $17,600. Its actual expenditure of $15,700 during March was therefore $1,900 less than it would normally have to spend. This was made possible because the excessive spending in January disclosed by the variable budget analysis had especially pointed out to the operating supervisors the need of keeping manufacturing overhead under better control. They had undertaken the necessary measures in the following month to cut down any excessive or unwarranted spending.

The reason the variable budget analysis presents a more truthful picture than the standard cost analysis in the preceding illustration is that, under a standard cost system, all costs are treated as ones that would vary in direct proportion with changes in volume of production, whereas under a variable budgeting system, due consideration is given to the different nature of different expenses in their response to changes in volume of business.

Again, it should be emphasized that variable budgeting indicates what expenses are proper at *actual volume*. On the other hand, standard costs cannot show the correct cost of manufacturing overhead at any volume other than the one on the basis of which the standard was established.

If Wabash Manufacturing Company had used a fixed budget system, how would its analysis of manufacturing overhead differ from that under a variable budget system? Assume that the company had expected to produce and sell 1,000,000 lb of product X and that it had estimated it would need to spend $20,000 on manufacturing overhead each month. Assume also that during April, 1955, the company's sales and production reached 1,300,000 lb and that $21,100 was spent on manufacturing overhead. Under a fixed budget system, the budget allowance of its manufacturing overhead for each month would be $20,000. Its actual spending of $21,100 during April would, therefore, be $1,100 more than the (fixed) budget allowance. Under such circumstances, management might think that the operating supervisors had been inefficient in keeping the company's manufacturing overhead within bounds. What had actually happened was just the opposite, as the variable budget analysis will show. According to the volume-cost studies made by the company, its manufacturing overhead at a production volume of 1,300,000 lb would normally be $22,400. Therefore, actual spending of $21,100 during April, 1955, was $1,300 less than the company would normally have to spend.

As previously indicated, the reason the variable budget analysis differs from the fixed budget analysis in the preceding illustration is that, under a fixed budgeting system, all costs are regarded as fixed for the period under consideration, whereas under a variable budgeting system, due allowance is made for the variation of different costs in relation to changes in volume. Except for completely fixed expenses (e.g., depreciation) it can easily be seen that a fixed budget would be valid only if the actual volume of business did not differ from the one expected, a condition which very seldom exists. On the other hand, a variable budgeting system takes into consideration not only that some costs can be fixed, but also that others act differently with changes in volume.

Only by acquiring a full knowledge of how each cost and expense responds to changes in volume of business can management effectively know what its costs should be at any anticipated volume of business and what its cost should have been at its actual volume of business. Thus, variable budgeting or volume-cost analysis provides management with a powerful tool in keeping manufacturing expenses under close control and, thereby, bringing the company one step nearer its profit goal.

Part II

*MAKING YOUR
IMPROVED BUDGETARY
SYSTEM WORK*

CHAPTER 7

Some Fundamental Considerations

In the preceding chapters it has been shown that, in order to make intelligent decisions and plans for the future, management needs to know the volume-cost relationships of its particular business for a variety of decisions. These decisions include planning of capital expenditures, make or buy, product selection, pricing, cost control, and so forth. In the author's judgment, all the concepts of achieving better profit planning through volume-cost analysis which are discussed in this book are within practical reach of most companies. In fact, the smaller the company, the easier will be the application of these concepts. In small companies, the organization structure is usually simple, and top management, if alert and capable, is generally in a position to have fairly detailed knowledge of the various phases of their operations. Once they have been initiated to the use of volume-cost analysis, this intimate knowledge of their operations makes relatively easy the job of analyzing the changing relationships between volume and costs in their particular companies. The preceding statement, however, is less applicable to many large companies. In a large industrial organization, activities are generally carried on by the joint effort of hundreds and thousands of people. Its organizational structure is more complex, and multilevel management is invariably used. Under these circumstances, it is usually difficult for a single individual to be thoroughly familiar with every phase of its operations or to have an intimate knowledge of its operations at all levels. Studies of volume-cost relationships in these large companies therefore require a more formal approach than do those of most small companies.

The formal system of volume-cost analysis is generally known as variable budgeting or flexible budgeting. In early stages, the main objective of variable budgeting systems in most companies studied was that of helping management control costs and expenses, particularly in the area of overhead costs. This is due mainly to the fact that overhead costs consist of a conglomeration of expenses, each of which behave differently in relation to changes in volume of business, and also because they have become an increasingly high proportion of the total cost of many businesses. Furthermore, "cutting costs" is usually one of the most easily sold rationalizations of a new tool or device since it appears that cutting cost should increase profit.

Knowledge of volume-cost relationships of a business, as found in variable budgeting, however, has much broader managerial implications and uses than simply helping management to keep its costs and expenses under better control. It has been shown in earlier chapters that management needs to know the volume-cost relationships of its business in many other areas, including pricing, make or buy, keeping or dropping a line of product, and so forth. When an intelligently designed and properly administered variable budgeting system has been in use, it is a relatively simple matter even for the large companies to assemble this needed knowledge of volume-cost relationships for helping management make better decisions in areas beyond cost control, because the basic data would already be in an orderly and readily available form.[1]

Through the years, an increasing number of companies have adopted variable budgeting, and it is believed that more companies will adopt this new system in the future. The experience of companies that have experimented with variable budgeting, however, is not universal. Some have had very satisfactory experience and consider variable budgeting as one of the basic tools of management. On the other hand, there are also a few claiming, after a short trial, that variable budgeting is not applicable to their particular business.

Analyses of the experience of several companies studied by the author reveal that, in order to make this new budgetary system work, there are several fundamental factors which management must take into consideration. A primary factor necessary for the successful application of variable budgeting is that, in a large modern industrial enterprise, management must orient itself toward a sound philosophy as to how this large company should be organized and operated. As defined previously, in a large industrial enterprise the activities are carried on by the joint effort of hundreds and thousands of people. In this large industrial enterprise, management policies and operating plans are usually formulated by the executives at the top. The actual execution of such plans are usually delegated to people all the way down the line. Top management and accounting people in such large industrial enterprises have to recognize that the foremen, who are the people at

---

[1] An example of the evolution of volume-cost analysis into uses other than cost control is shown in the case of Lafayette Brass Company in Appendix A.

the lowest end of this chain of authority, are a part of the entire operating management. The responsibilities of this lower management are not limited only to jobs assigned to them, but should also include the costs and expenses related to their work.

If variable budgeting is to achieve what it could purportedly do for management in keeping cost under proper control and in providing better information for profit planning, there should certainly be present this basic management philosophy which has just been described. Under this philosophy, it would be necessary to compile and report a business' costs and expense on the basis of managerial responsibilities. Each departmental manager or foreman should set up standards for his department as to what its costs and expenses should be at various levels of operation. The accounting and financial department should provide these departmental managers with all necessary information, not only to help them set up proper standards, but also to help them evaluate and improve their operations.

A second important factor responsible for the successful application of variable budgeting is that the person who initiates and administers the variable-budgeting system in the business organization must be able to deal with people and get things done through people. It is human nature that most people do not like to change from what they have been used to doing. The person who is going to introduce variable budgeting has therefore first to sell his idea to top management and obtain its full support. He will then have to sell his idea to operating management and overcome its suspicion. He has to convince the operating management that variable budgeting is a tool designed to help it to do a better job, not something designed to be used as a whip over its shoulder. He will have to be careful in seeing that the budget standards are set up by the operating people themselves and that operating reports are properly made to management. It is a job which requires a lot of patience, diplomacy, and tactfulness, and one where human skill is as important as technical skills.

A third determinant in the successful application of variable budgeting is the reliability of budget estimates as to what the costs should be in the period ahead and what the costs should have been in the period just ended. The reliability of budget estimates, in turn, hinges upon how carefully these budget estimates have been set up. While this may seem overly elementary, nevertheless, preposterous budget estimates have usually been a fundamental cause for the failure of a number of variable budgeting systems.

From the procedures used by companies where variable budgeting has been successful, it appears that the establishment of reliable budget estimates requires (1) proper understanding of the behavior of each of the various costs and expenses in relation to changes in level of activity *in the particular business* and (2) a full knowledge of the operating conditions *in the particular business*. In a large industrial organization where a multitude of activities are carried on by the joint effort of hundreds and thousands of people, the job of establishing reliable budgets necessarily calls for the concerted effort of a great many persons within the organization. This includes definition of policies and objectives by top executives and careful consideration by lower-level supervisors of the particular nature and problems of their respective departments. In addition, the accounting and controller's department will have to provide the necessary information in usable and comprehensive form. Major departures from this tested procedure may result in unreliable budget estimates and consequent discredit of the entire budgetary system.

Selecting a proper measure of the level of activity as the basis for setting up budget allowances of variable manufacturing expenses is another crucial factor which determines whether or not the variable budget can be relied upon by operating management for such purposes as (1) ascertaining what should have been spent by any department for the period just ended, (2) determining who should be held responsible for the variation of actual expenditure from expected expenditure and to what extent he should be held responsible, and (3) discovering the causes of such variation so that proper courses of action can be taken for the future. Although a wide variety of measures are open to the choice of management, not all measures are equally suitable. One measure may be perfectly appropriate for one purpose but may not be adequate for another. Even for the same purpose, different sets of circumstances may call for the use of different measures.

Another factor which should not be overlooked in the practical application of variable budgeting is the role of the time element in establishing the volume-cost relationships of manufacturing expenses. Different manufacturing expenses require different minimum time periods to bring out their volume-cost relationships. Since the length of the budget period usually conforms to the length of the reported period selected by management, the time intervals needed by some manufacturing expenses to "bring out" their volume-cost relationships may be longer than the budget period. Under such circumstances, judgment must be exercised in the comparison of actual expenditures against budget allowances as to whether a long enough period has elapsed to make such comparisons meaningful. Failure to understand the operating conditions of the particular business and to appreciate the role of the time element in volume-cost relationships of different manufacturing expenses, together with the use of improperly selected budget periods, were found to be among the basic reasons leading to alleged failures of variable budgeting.

Effective use of volume-cost analysis for profit planning requires a proper understanding of the nature of profit forecasting and several other related factors. Volume, of course, is not the sole determinant of the revenue, cost, and profit of a business. The final profit of a business is also dependent upon other factors such as selling price, product mix, cost structure, operating efficiency, and so forth. At companies where such studies have been properly and successfully used, all these other factors are taken into consideration in formulating and evaluating management's operating plans.

As pointed out earlier, a main purpose of volume-cost-profit studies is to help management choose the most desirable and most reasonable operating plans for the achievement of its profit objectives. These plans have to be selected under circumstances foreseeable at the time when a decision has to be made by management. Admittedly, the operating conditions which will actually occur in the future may differ from those foreseeable at the present, and the present operating plans may have to be revised to meet the new operating conditions, resulting in a variation of actual profits from those which are predicted *today*. But this variation should not be taken as an impairment of the value of properly established volume-cost-profit studies. Their value has to be judged from their purposes. If the volume-cost-profit studies failed to provide management with reliable cost and profit information for the specific operating plan under the specific operating conditions which it has in mind, they would certainly be useless. On the other hand, if volume-cost-profit studies do provide management with reliable cost and profit information for the operating plan and operating conditions which it has in mind, such studies are found of immeasurable value whenever cost and/or profit is used as the criterion for weighing future operating plans, even though conditions may later change.

Like many other management tools, variable budgeting can be and has been misused. When variable budgeting is properly used, however, it is one of the most valuable aids to management in planning and controlling business operations. In the following chapters, some of the more important factors underlying the successful application of variable budgeting will be discussed in detail. As pointed out in the Preface, it is not intended that this study will cover all the possible uses of volume-cost relationships and all the factors that one should take into consideration in the practical application of variable budgeting. It is limited to a few most important aspects which, in the author's opinion, have not been recognized by most people. If, however, this study stimulates management's awareness of the need for and potentiality of volume-cost studies, if it promotes a deeper understanding of the factors underlying the successful and unsuccessful application of variable budgeting, and if, thereby, volume-cost analysis and variable budgeting are made better tools of management as an aid in the formulation of wiser business decisions and a healthier economy, the objectives of this book will have been accomplished.

CHAPTER 8

Preparing
Budget Estimates

A cardinal principle in the successful application of variable budgeting for cost control is that budget estimates must be reliable as to what the costs should be in the period ahead and what the costs should have been in the period just ended. The reliability of budget estimates, in turn, depends to a large extent upon how carefully these budget estimates have been set up. This may seem overly elementary; nevertheless, the fact is that preposterous budget estimates have usually been a fundamental cause for the disrepute into which a number of variable budgeting systems have fallen.

One of the reasons advanced by Menlo Chemical Company for the failure of its old flexible budget system was that under this system all its labor expenses had been treated as though they varied in direct proportion to changes in volume of business; it was later found that:

"Its labor expenses in many producing centers were more or less fixed. Within certain limits, the company could not decrease or increase the number of persons in a crew even if the volume of production changed. Only when the plant's operation was changed from a one-shift operation to a two- or three-shift operation, or vice versa, would its labor expenses undergo significant changes. At such time, an entire crew had to be added or dropped from operation." [1]

The old flexible budget system of Menlo Chemical Company together with the budget estimates of various manufacturing expenses under this system were the product of the consulting firm engaged by the company to look over its problem of declining sales and profit. In establishing the budget

[1] See Menlo Chemical Company case in Appendix C.

estimates of different costs and expenses, this management consultant was hampered by the lack of orderly accounting records of various manufacturing expenses for each operating center, because the company had not in the past accumulated cost figures on a departmental basis.[2] Instead of searching the company's accounting records for factual information as to how each of the different manufacturing expenses had actually responded to changes in volume of business at various operating centers, this management consultant proceeded to set up budget estimates for Menlo Chemical Company solely on the basis of his "experience" and judgment and the opinion of the operating foremen with whom he had talked.

The seemingly logical approach used by this management consultant is fallacious for two reasons. First, if cost information had been withheld from lower-level supervisors, and if the accounting department had not in the past departmentalized costs and expenses, the opinion given by the lower-level supervisors to this management consultant as to what the various costs and expenses should be at different volumes of operation would have been obviously unreliable. This is due to the fact that, despite the responsibility of a foreman for the origination of various expenses of his department, it is beyond the normal human capacity to memorize various expenses at different volumes of business over any length of time even if one knew what the cost of each item was. Since the foremen had not had even a fragmentary knowledge of the real costs of their departments, how would the management consultant be able to obtain any reliable cost data from these people?

Secondly, unless the management consultant of Menlo Chemical Company had obtained concrete evidence of the cost behavior of each of these expenses at its various operating centers, he could never set up proper budget estimates for the different manufacturing expenses of this company. This is true regardless of how good the expert in management counseling is and regardless of how much experience he has accumulated from working with other businesses. Because of inevitable variations in the operating nature of different businesses, the cost behavior of a great many expenses in one business will differ from those with identical or similar names in another business. A conscientious study of the actual cost behavior of different expenses at the particular business is, therefore, indispensable for the establishment of reliable budget estimates.

Whenever a person tries to copy what might have worked in another business without giving careful consideration to the operating conditions and the cost behavior of the various expenses at the particular business, his

[2] An operating center at Menlo Chemical Company is one of the several departments within a plant wherein the foreman or manager of each department would be charged with the responsibility of keeping his expenses under proper control. These were developed under the new management philosophy recommended by the management consultant and adopted by the company after World War II.

budget system is destined for trouble even before it is installed. This was exactly the procedure used by the management consultant of Menlo Chemical Company in establishing the budget estimates of its various costs and expenses. Because of his failure to appreciate the particular operating conditions of his client and his failure to make a real effort to study the cost behavior of the various expenses of his client, the budget estimates of Menlo Chemical Company under its old flexible budgeting system simply reflect the imagination of this management consultant. The labor expense cited earlier is only an example of the unreliability of his budget estimates. Naturally, after this system had been put in, the company would find that its budget estimates were completely out of line with what its costs should be and should have been.

In contrast to the method used by the management consultant of Menlo Chemical Company for setting up its budget estimates, a completely different approach was used by other companies, such as Lafayette Brass Company and Otterbein Corporation, where variable budgeting has been successfully used. These companies found that the most efficacious means of obtaining a dependable basis for setting up reliable budget estimates was to study first the behavior of different costs and expenses *actually experienced* by each of their numerous departments or operating centers. Statistical techniques of correlation, including the use of scatter diagrams and regression lines, were invariably used by these companies in studying their past volume-cost relationships. The following description is typical of the procedures they used as a first step in establishing their budget estimates.

Actual expenditures of various costs and expenses spent by each department over a period of time are gathered from the accounting records and tabulated against its level of activity for the corresponding period. The expenditures actually experienced at different volumes of business are then plotted on a chart (statistically called a scatter diagram), with the horizontal axis representing the volume of business and the vertical axis the amount of expenditure. Each dot on the scatter diagram represents the amount of actual expenditure at the production volume experienced during any given period. After a sufficient number of dots (experience) have been plotted on the scatter diagram, the volume-cost relationship of the particular expense under study can be determined by an examination of the dispersion of these dots on the scatter diagram. If any definite relation exists between the volume of business and the amount of expenditures, most of the dots will cluster along a band or line. A regression line can thus be drawn, indicating the central tendency of the past volume-cost relationship of the particular expense under study.[3] Figures 8–1 and 8–2 illustrate the volume-cost relationships of monthly operating supplies and supervisory salaries

[3] The regression line can also be fitted mathematically by the method of least squares.

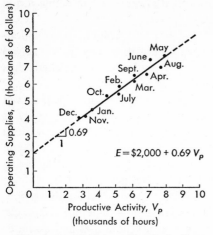

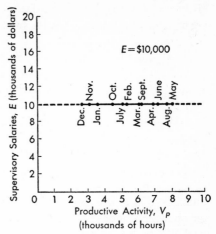

Fig. 8–1. Waltham Chemical Company, Department A. Scatter diagram showing correlation between monthly operating supplies and productive activity for 1955. SOURCE: Table 8–1.

Fig. 8–2. Waltham Chemical Company, Department A. Scatter diagram showing correlation between monthly supervisory salaries and productive activity for 1955. SOURCE: Table 8–1.

experienced by Department A of Waltham Chemical Company during 1955.

The chief advantage of the preceding method used by Lafayette Brass Company and Otterbein Corporation is that, by studying how each of the different expenses has actually responded to changes in volume or level of activity in the particular department, a realistic basis is obtained for setting up the budget estimates of such expense for the period ahead. This is espe-

TABLE 8–1

Waltham Chemical Company—Department A

Monthly Productive Activity, Operating Supplies, and Supervisory Salaries—1955

	Productive Activity	Operating Supplies	Supervisory Salaries
January	3,650 hr	$4,500	$10,000
February	5,380	5,760	10,000
March	6,150	6,200	10,000
April	6,990	6,550	10,000
May	8,040	7,560	10,000
June	7,200	7,300	10,000
July	5,180	5,440	10,000
August	7,740	6,950	10,000
September	6,220	6,450	10,000
October	4,560	5,240	10,000
November	3,220	4,100	10,000
December	2,730	4,000	10,000

cially true if the operating conditions prevailed during the preceding period are expected to continue into the future.[4]

Furthermore, through this objective study of past volume-cost relationships of different expenses at the particular business, any preconceived misconception of the behavior of a cost can be effectually dispelled, thus greatly reducing the danger of having an unrealistic budget.

If Menlo Chemical Company or its management consultant had delved into the company's accounting records and had made an intelligent study of the volume-cost relationships of the different costs and expenses at various cost centers in the same manner as Otterbein Corporation and Lafayette Brass Company had done, the correct behavior of its various manufacturing expenses in relation to changes in volume of business could have been established at the very beginning of its budgetary system. As an illustration, the operating labor in relation to monthly production volume in Department B of Waltham Chemical Company is tabulated in Table 8–2 and a scatter

TABLE 8–2

Waltham Chemical Company—Department B

Monthly Production and Operating Labor
1955

	Monthly Production	Operating Labor	No. of Shifts
January	86,500 tons	$97,500	3
February	77,500	97,500	3
March	58,400	65,000	2
April	52,700	65,000	2
May	50,200	65,000	2
June	24,300	32,500	1
July *	10,000	17,000	1
August	29,900	32,500	1
September	27,200	32,500	1
October	56,000	65,000	2
November	80,100	97,500	3
December	84,000	97,500	3

* Plant shut down 2 weeks for vacation.

diagram such as that shown in Fig. 8–3 is constructed. From this statistical study of actual experience, it can be readily seen that the operating labor of this department is fixed within certain ranges of production volume and steps up or down only when an additional shift is added or dropped from operation. By making a similar study of its volume-cost relationships, Menlo Chemical Company could have discovered from the outset that its operating

[4] Infra, p. 119.

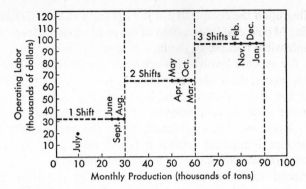

Fig. 8–3. Waltham Chemical Company, Department B. Scatter diagram of operating labor in relation to monthly production volume for 1955.

labor and a number of other expenses would not have behaved in the same manner as that expected by its management consultant.

It might be argued that, at the time when this management consultant set up the flexible budget system for Menlo Chemical Company, departmental cost information was not readily available, since, as mentioned before, the company had not in the past compiled cost information on this basis in its books of account. To a person unfamiliar with the actual operation of accounting systems, this argument might appear reasonable. However, the fact is that it is always possible to dig into subsidiary records and to reconstruct cost and accounting information to suit management's needs, even though such information had not been suitably compiled in the past and had not been recorded as such in the books of account. With few exceptions, most companies, including Lafayette Brass Company and Otterbein Corporation, had not departmentalized their costs prior to the introduction of their variable budgeting systems. Yet, by digging into accounting records, they were all able to assemble the necessary cost information for each operating center in order to obtain a reliable basis in setting up their budget estimates.

The reason Lafayette Brass Company and Otterbein Corporation could accomplish what appeared to be impossible at Menlo Chemical Company is that the installation of variable budgeting systems at the former companies was placed in the hands of their own accounting executives who knew how and where the necessary cost information could be located. At Menlo Chemical Company, the management consultant had been trusted with the design and installation of the entire system, including the establishment of budget estimates for each department. His unfamiliarity with the company's accounting records and routines, together with what seems a lack of resourcefulness, had made the job of reassembling a set of useful cost information appear insurmountable.

Depending upon the complexity of the situation at a particular company, reassembling of past cost information at lower supervisory levels may sometimes be unfeasible because of the lack of qualified personnel to do the job or because the expense involved in such work would be too "costly." Under such circumstances, the alternative would be to revise a company's accounting routine first and to postpone the installation of expense budgets (for 6 to 12 months) until the cost behavior of different expenses at those lower supervisory levels could be established. While this process may appear too slow to produce immediate results, it is not necessarily slower than the reconstruction of past cost figures in a complex situation.

When careful studies of volume-cost relationships of different expenses at lower supervisory levels are made, the following varieties of cost behavior can usually be found:

1. The particular expense will fluctuate in direct proportion with changes in volume of business [Fig. 8–4(*a*)].

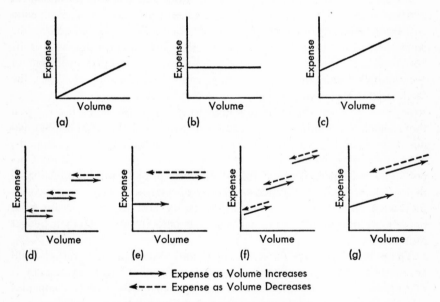

Fig. 8–4.   Variations in cost behavior.

2. The particular expense will remain fixed within the practical productive capacity of a department regardless of changes in volume of business [Fig. 8–4(*b*)].

3. The particular expense will contain both fixed and variable elements, and its volume-cost relationships can be represented by a straight line [Fig. 8–4(*c*)].

4. The particular expense is fixed within a certain range of volume of business; it will step up or down to another level when the volume of business rises above or falls below a certain level [Fig. 8–4(*d*)].

5. The particular expense is similar to 4 when the volume of business is rising, but will not step down when the volume of business recedes [Fig. 8–4(*e*)].

6. The particular expense has both fixed and variable elements and is thus similar to 3 within a certain range of volume of business. However, its fixed element will step up or down when the volume of business rises above or falls below certain levels [Fig. 8–4(*f*)].

7. The particular expense is similar to 6 when the volume of business is rising, but its fixed element will not step down when the volume of business recedes [Fig. 8–4(*g*)].

From the wide variety of cost behavior shown here, one can again appreciate the importance of studying first the volume-cost relationships of various expenses at the particular business, if the budget estimates are to be reliable.

After the volume-cost relationships of different costs and expenses have been ascertained, the operating conditions expected to prevail in the period ahead should then be taken into consideration and the budget estimates of various expenses established. At companies where variable budgeting has been successfully used, studies of past volume-cost relationships of each expense constitute only a first step in establishing budget estimates. Because of the likely changes in the operating conditions in the period ahead from that experienced in the past, the cost at different volumes of business in the period ahead may not necessarily be the same as that experienced in the past. Changes are likely to occur in prices of materials and supplies, wage rates, manufacturing methods, machinery and equipment, plant layout, working conditions, organization, range and direction of fluctuations in volume of business. Owing to the existence of these changes, the past volume-cost relationships can serve only as a general framework or starting point in setting up budget estmates. Therefore, operating conditions expected to prevail in the period ahead must be taken into account in the establishment of budget estimates of various costs and expenses.

With a proper understanding of the cost behavior of different expenses at various operating centers and with the expected operating conditions clearly defined by management, the budget estimates of each of these expenses for different volumes of business can then be properly established. The following procedure is illustrative of the method of establishing budget estimates at a number of companies where variable budgeting has been successfully used. First, the probable range of level of activity at any department for the period ahead is determined by management. The expenditures for each expense at the anticipated high and low levels of operation under the operating conditions expected to prevail are then estimated. If the volume-cost relationship of the particular expense is one that can be represented by a straight line, its budget estimates at any volume between the anticipated high and low levels can then be determined by the use of the following formula:

$$E = a + bV$$

where
$$b = \frac{E_2 - E_1}{V_2 - V_1}$$

and
$$a = E_2 - bV_2 \qquad \text{or} \qquad a = E_1 - bV_1$$

in which E = budget estimate at any volume V between V_1 and V_2
$\quad\quad E_1$ = estimated expense at V_1
$\quad\quad E_2$ = estimated expense at V_2
$\quad\quad V$ = volume of business or level of activity between V_1 and V_2
$\quad\quad V_1$ = probable low level of activity
$\quad\quad V_2$ = probable high level of activity

In place of the mathematical method of determining the two constants a and b in the formula $E = a + bV$, they can also be determined graphically, as shown in Fig. 8–5.

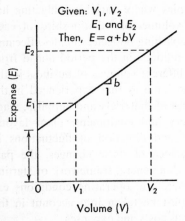

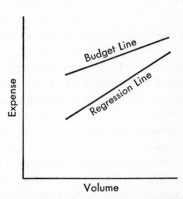

Fig. 8–5. Graphic method to determine the budget line of a semivariable expense with a straight-line volume-cost relationship.

Fig. 8–6. Illustration of possible variation of a budget line for the period ahead from the regression line of volume-cost relationships experienced in the past.

It should be noted that the budget line such as that shown in Fig. 8–5 may not be the same as the regression line of the volume-cost relationships of the same expense experienced in the past, although the two lines may look very much alike. Only when there is no change in operating conditions is it possible for these two lines to become identical. Otherwise, by plotting them in one diagram, they will be two distinct separate lines such as those shown in Fig. 8–6, with the regression line representing the volume-cost relationships under the operating conditions experienced in the past and the budget line representing the volume-cost relationships under the operating conditions expected to prevail in the period ahead. The budget estimate, as previously pointed out, is established on the basis of both the volume-cost relationship (as represented by the regression line) experienced by an operating center and the operating conditions anticipated by management for the period ahead. The budget line may, therefore, be regarded as an "adjusted regression line" after the expected operating conditions in the budget period have been taken into account.

The application of the preceding method of setting up budget estimates is not limited to semivariable expenses with straight-line volume-cost relationships [Fig. 8–4(c)]. It can also be applied to completely variable costs [Fig. 8–4(a)] and to completely fixed costs [Fig. 8–4(b)]. If the expense is one that will vary in direct proportion with changes in volume of operation, the constant a in the formula $E = a + bV$ will be found to equal zero. Under such circumstances, the formula for the budgeted expenditure at any volume between the anticipated high and low levels of activity will become $E = bV$. If the expense is a completely fixed expense, the estimated expenditure E_1 at the expected low level of activity V_1 will be the same as that E_2 at the high level of activity V_2, and the constant b in the formula $E = a + bV$ will be found to equal zero. Under such circumstances, the formula of budgeted expense at any volume of business between V_1 and V_2 will become $E = a$, in which the fixed constant a is equivalent to E_1 or E_2.

With some slight modifications the preceding method can also be applied to those expenses with "stepped-line" volume-cost relationships [Fig. 8–4 (d) to (g)]. Basically, the volume-cost relationships of these expenses are represented by a straight line within each step, although over a wider range of level of activity they become a series of steps. If the range of high and low levels of activity expected for the period ahead falls within the range covered by a single step, the budget formula $E = a + bV$, discussed earlier, for the estimated expenditure at any volume within this anticipated range is equally applicable under such circumstances. However, both the person setting up the budget estimates and the person making use of such estimates must caution himself against applying this budget formula or against extending the budget line represented by this formula beyond the expected range of level of activity. If, for any reason, it becomes necessary to determine what should be the cost at a certain volume either above or below this expected range, the applicability of the original budget formula to this particular volume must be examined with care. If this volume falls into another "step," a second budget formula, applicable to that particular step, will have to be determined. The procedure described here is essentially the one currently used by Otterbein Corporation and has provided satisfactory results.

If the expected range of level of activity is so wide as to cover more than one step, for the purpose of setting up a reliable budget estimate, it will be necessary to determine two or more budget formulas, one for each step. Management must first determine the volume or volumes of business at which the "stepping" up or down of the particular expense will occur, such as the addition or dropping of a shift. The formula of budgeted expense at different volumes of business within each step can then be determined in the same manner as that for an expense with a straight-line volume-cost relationship.

Since the budget estimates for the period ahead are based upon the operating conditions expected by management, it will obviously be necessary to revise the budget estimates if there is any significant change in operating conditions, when such change makes the original budget estimates no longer representative of what the cost should be under the new operating conditions. Ordinarily, budget estimates are revised at least once a year, and the new budgets are established on the basis of operating conditions expected to prevail in the new year.

Whether or not the "expense budgets" should be revised within a year depends to a large extent upon the changes in operating conditions within this period and the significance of the effect of such changes upon the representativeness of the original budget estimates under the new operating conditions.

In the normal course of business, the likelihood of major changes in operating conditions from that expected are much less within a "relatively short period immediately ahead" than over a longer period of time. For instance, if wage rates are covered by collective bargaining and the labor contract will remain effective for 12 months, they will, of course, be fairly stable within this period. Another example is that, under the pricing practices of most manufacturers of industrial products, prices are revised only at periodic intervals. Hence, the prices of most supplies are fairly stable within a certain period. Likewise, changes in manufacturing methods and organization structure at a particular business seldom occur every day or every month. All these factors tend to make it relatively less complex to forecast accurately the operating conditions and, hence, the budget estimates in the period immediately ahead.

However, the presence of these stable factors in many instances does not necessarily preclude the possibility of any major changes in operating conditions at other times. For instance, new wage contracts may be signed, prices of raw materials and supplies may be increased, new machinery may be installed, and so forth. When such changes do occur, the budget estimates will, of course, have to be revised.

Sometimes certain changes in operating conditions during the next budget year can be anticipated in advance. Changes in manufacturing methods and organizational structure are typical examples. Under such circumstances, it is, of course, possible to set up several sets of budget estimates, each being applicable to the operating conditions expected to prevail during a specific period within the next year.[5]

From the procedures employed by companies where variable budgeting has been successfully used, it can be readily seen that the establishment of reliable budget estimates under such a system requires (1) a proper under-standing of the behavior of each of the various costs and expenses in rela-tion to changes in the level of activity at the particular business and (2) a full knowledge of the operating conditions at this particular business. In a large industrial organization where a multitude of activities are carried on by the joint endeavor of hundreds and thousands of people, the job of estab-lishing reliable budget estimates as a guide to management necessarily calls for the concerted effort of a great many persons within the organization. This includes definition of policies and objectives by top executives and careful consideration by lower-level supervisors of the particular nature and problems of their respective departments. In addition, the accounting or controller's department will have to provide the necessary information in usable and comprehensible form. Any departure from this tested procedure will easily result in unreliable budget estimates and consequent discredit of the entire budgetary system.

[5] See Otterbein Corporation case in Appendix B.

CHAPTER 9

Measuring Production
and Sales Volume

Selecting a proper measure of level of activity as the basis for setting up budget allowances of variable manufacturing expenses is one of the crucial factors which determines whether or not the variable budget can be relied upon by operating management: to ascertain what should have been spent by any department for the period just ended, to conclude who should be held responsible for the variation of actual expenditures from what should have been spent and to what extent he should be held responsible, and to discover the causes of such variation so that proper courses of action can be taken for the future.

Although a wide variety of measures are open to the choice of management, it must nevertheless be recognized that not all measures are equally suitable. One measure may be perfectly appropriate for one purpose but hardly fit for another. Even for the same purpose, different sets of circumstances may call for the use of different measures. The proper selection can thus be achieved only when the person responsible for the design, installation, and administration of a variable budgeting system understands the implications involved in the use of different measures and in the cost behavior of various types of expenses of the particular business. Failure to recognize the importance of this problem and to understand the volume-cost relationships of the particular business often leads to the use of improper measures of level of activity, resulting in unreliable budget allowances and consequent discredit of the budgetary system.

DOES PRODUCT MIX CONSTITUTE
A REAL OBSTACLE IN THE PRACTICAL
APPLICATION OF VARIABLE BUDGETING?

Another reason advanced by the budget director of Menlo Chemical Company for the unsuccessful experience with its variable budgeting system is the complication arising from the presence of product mix.[1] The company had experienced considerable difficulty with its variable budgets in those departments where a multitude of products were handled. Under its flexible budget system, the company had treated the cost of handling an equal tonnage of two different products as being the same. It was later discovered that the actual cost of handling two different products could be entirely different.

If this problem of product mix constitutes a real difficulty in the practical application of variable budgeting, then it would be a universal problem at all multi-product companies using variable budgeting, including those which have had successful experience with this managerial tool. In fact, such a problem would be more severe at Lafayette Brass Company or Otterbein Corporation, because at every producing center of these two companies a multitude of products are manufactured. Why then is product mix not considered by Lafayette Brass Company and Otterbein Corporation as a hindrance to the successful application of variable budgeting, whereas Menlo Chemical Company, which has a far less complex problem of product mix, regards this as an obstruction to its practical application?

Actually it was not product mix per se that had contributed to the unsatisfactory experience at Menlo Chemical Company and had made variable budgeting unsuitable for this company. Instead, the crux of the problem lies in the indiscriminate use by the company of physical units of output, i.e., tons of chemicals, as the basis for setting up its budget allowances, and in its failure to understand the implications involved in the use of different measures of level of activity. The problem of product mix at Menlo Chemical Company could be easily solved by replacing physical units of output with productive time as the measure of manufacturing activity for setting up its variable budgets. The difference arising from the use of these two different measures in a multiproduct department is shown by the following illustration of Delta Manufacturing Company:

Assume that only two types of wires, viz., $\frac{1}{8}$ in. and $\frac{1}{16}$ in., are manufactured by the extrusion department of Delta Manufacturing Company. Its output is customarily expressed in terms of pounds of wire extruded. In February, 1955, this department produced a total of 1,000,000 lb of wire. In March, 1955, it produced a total of 900,000 lb. If pounds of output

[1] See Menlo Chemical Company case in Appendix C.

had been used as the measure of level of activity for manufacturing expenses, it might be thought that the extrusion department had been operated at a higher level of production in February (1,000,000 lb) than in March (900,000 lb). The management of Delta Manufacturing Company, however, was fully conversant with the company's cost behavior and was careful in the selection of a proper measure of level of activity in establishing the budget allowances of its manufacturing expenses. It knew that, for an equal tonnage of these two products, more time and expense would have to be spent for the extrusion of $\frac{1}{16}$-in. wire than $\frac{1}{8}$-in. wire. For example, to produce 100,000 lb of $\frac{1}{16}$-in. wire would take the extrusion department 20 hr with a crew of 20 persons. To produce 100,000 lb. of $\frac{1}{8}$-in. wire would take the same crew only 10 hr. Of the 1,000,000 lb produced during February, 500,000 lb was $\frac{1}{8}$-in. wire and 500,000 lb was $\frac{1}{16}$-in. wire. Of the 900,000 lb produced during March, 700,000 lb was $\frac{1}{16}$-in. wire and 200,000 lb was $\frac{1}{8}$-in. wire. Therefore, the extrusion department would have needed 160 crew-hours or 3,200 man-hours during March to produce a total of 900,000 lb whereas it needed only 150 crew-hours or 3,000 man-hours during February to produce a total of 1,000,000 lb. Since variable manufacturing expenses at this department are dependent upon its production activity, it would obviously be erroneous to use pounds of output as the measure of such activity. Instead, productive time in terms of direct labor-hours is found to be more representative of its production activity and is thus used by Delta Manufacturing Company as the basis for setting up budget allowances of manufacturing expenses at its extrusion department.

The preceding illustration of Delta Manufacturing Company shows how important it is for a company to know the operating conditions of its particular business and to select a proper measure of level of activity for setting up the variable budgets of its manufacturing expenses. Had the management of Delta Manufacturing Company been ignorant of its own cost behavior and used pounds of output as the measure of its manufacturing activity, it would have believed that there should have been a reduction of such expenses from February (1,000,000 lb) to March (900,000 lb). Actually, however, an increase in manufacturing expenses from February (3,000 man-hours) to March (3,200 man-hours) should have been expected.

In contrast to the experience of Menlo Chemical Company, this issue of selecting a proper measure of level of activity was clearly seen by the management of Lafayette Brass Company, Otterbein Corporation, and other companies where variable budgeting had been successfully used. These companies do not use physical units of output as the basis for setting up variable budgets of manufacturing expenses, because they know that, owing to the wide variety of products which they manufacture, measurements in terms of tons, pounds, feet, and pieces of output are not common denominators of their manufacturing activity for budgetary purposes. They have decided that for the purpose of establishing budget allowances of manufacturing expenses, productive time, such as that shown in the preceding illustration of Delta Manufacturing Company, should be used as the measure of manufacturing activity. Thus, through the use of productive time, a satisfactory common index of manufacturing activity can be obtained as the basis for setting up budget allowances of manufacturing expenses regardless of the variety of products handled or manufactured by a multiproduct department.

INPUT VERSUS OUTPUT: A CRITICAL APPRAISAL OF SEVERAL DIFFERENT ALTERNATIVES

Although the use of productive time in place of units of output as the measure of level of activity alleviates the problem of product mix at a multiproduct plant, there is still a wide variety of measures of level of activity from which management can make its choice. The selection of a proper measure as the basis for setting up budget allowances of manufacturing expenses has far-reaching implications in the successful application of variable budgeting. The reception of any particular budgetary system by operating management depends primarily upon whether or not it can rely upon the budget report under such a system as a guide for judging actual performance and for planning future courses of action. By using two different measures of level of activity for setting up budget allowances of manufacturing expenses, the analyses of responsibilities for and causes of variation of actual expenditures from that which should have been spent can be entirely different. Discussions in this section will, therefore, center around the several basic measures of input and output most commonly used as the basis for setting up departmental expense budgets. Included among these are: physical units of actual output (Ia), production time necessary to turn out the actual output (Ib), physical units of raw material processed (IIa), production time planned or scheduled to be put in (IIb), and production time actually put in (III). The three measures in terms of production time will be analyzed first to provide a basic framework for understanding the implications involved in the use of these different measures. The other two measures in terms of physical units of actual output and physical units of raw material processed will be discussed in conjunction with the examination of the effect resulting from the use of these different measures upon the successful or unsuccessful application of variable budgeting at the various companies studied.

To illustrate the implications that may arise from the use of these different measures,[2] assume that a manufacturing order of 10,000 lb of product A was received by Anderson Manufacturing Company and put through its manufacturing department during March, 1956. According to the specifications of this order, the manufacture of 100 lb of product A requires the use of 105 lb of material B, the extra 5 lb being allowance for normal waste and spoilage. Accordingly, 10,500 lb of material B (IIa) was requisitioned and put into production. When the production of this order was completed, actual waste and spoilage were less than expected and a total of 10,300 lb of product A (Ia) was produced.

Assume also that, according to studies made by the engineering department, 210 man-hours is required to process 105 lb of material B into product A. For processing 10,500 lb of material B into 10,000 lb of product A, a total of 21,000 man-hours (IIb) of work is planned and scheduled. When the order was completed, the production time actually spent on this order amounted to 23,000 hr (III).

Assume further that, according to studies made by management, manufacturing overhead expenses during this period should consist of $50,000 fixed expenses plus those expenses which will vary with the level of production at the rate of $2 per productive hour. Actual manufacturing overhead incurred during this period amounted to $95,000. There was no other production by this department during March, 1956, except for this order.

Management of Anderson Manufacturing Company wanted to know whether actual manufacturing overhead expenses of $95,000 were more or less than what should have been spent. If actual expenses differed from what should have been spent, it wanted to know what had caused such variation so that necessary corrective steps could be taken in the future.

Depending upon the measure of level of activity selected for setting up budget allowances, three different and contradictory answers could be given to each of the preceding questions. If the production time necessary to turn out the actual output (Ib) were used as the measure of manufacturing activity, at the rate of 210 man-hours for every 100 lb of product A, the manufacture of 10,300 lb of product A actually produced (Ia) would normally require a total productive time of 21,630 hr (Ib). At this level, total budgeted manufacturing overhead expenses should be $93,260 ($50,000 + 21,630 hr × $2 per hour = $93,260). Actual spending of $95,000 would, therefore, be $1,740 more than what should have been spent.

A different answer could be obtained if the production time planned or scheduled to be put in (IIb) were used as the basis for measuring manufac-

---

[2] A more extensive discussion on the implications of the use of different measures of level of activity can be found in Professor C. B. Nickerson's "Cost Accounting: Text, Problems and Cases," Chap. 5, McGraw-Hill Book Co., Inc., New York, 1954.

turing activity. With 21,000 man-hours planned or scheduled to be put in (IIb), the budget allowance of manufacturing overhead expenses for this period should amount to \$92,000 (\$50,000 + 21,000 hr × \$2 per hour = \$92,000). Actual spending of \$95,000 would, therefore, be \$3,000 more than what should have been spent.

Another completely different answer could be obtained if the production time actually put in (III) were used as the measure of manufacturing activity. With 23,000 man-hours actually put in (III) during this period, the budget allowance of manufacturing overhead expenses should amount to \$96,000 (\$50,000 + 23,000 × \$2 per hour = \$96,000). Actual spending of \$95,000 would now be \$1,000 less than what should have been spent for the time actually put in (III).

Advocates for the use of productive time necessary to turn out the actual output (Ib) as the measure of manufacturing activity argue that, if production time actually put in (III) were used as the measure of manufacturing activity for setting up budget allowances, a foreman or department manager could inflate his budget allowances by spending more productive time than that which needs to be spent. In the preceding illustration, they would claim that, using production time actually put in (III) as the measure of manufacturing activity, the budget allowance of manufacturing overhead of this department could be raised to \$96,000 by spending more time (23,000 hr) than that which should have been spent (21,630 hr) so that actual spending of \$95,000 could be looked upon as favorable. Whereas, if the manufacturing activity were measured in terms of production time necessary to turn out the actual output (Ib) (21,630 hr), actual spending of \$95,000 would clearly be \$1,740 more than that which should have been spent (\$93,260) (Ib). Thus, to avoid any padding of budget allowances through inefficiency of operation, this argument claims that measurement of manufacturing activity must be in terms of production time necessary to turn out the actual output (Ib) rather than the production time actually put in (III).

Although the preceding may appear convincing, it has not presented a complete picture. The use of (standard) production time necessary to turn out the actual output (Ib) as the measure of level of activity for setting up budget allowances of manufacturing overhead provides only an analysis which shows the total variance and not an analysis by its causes, such as yield and efficiency. For instance, assume that in the preceding illustration the entire output of 10,300 lb was later found defective and had to be completely scrapped. Using production time necessary to turn out the actual output (Ib) as the measure of manufacturing activity, there would be no activity for this department during March, 1956, because all its output had to be scrapped. Under such circumstances, its budget allowance of variable manufacturing overhead expenses for this period would likewise be nil. However, the fact that the entire output had to be scrapped does not necessarily mean that the manufacturing department is at fault and, therefore, it may not have to incur any variable manufacturing overhead expenses. The material purchased and issued to the production department could have been defective, and such defect might be difficult for the manufacturing department to discover when it did the processing. In such case, the manufacturing department obviously should not be held responsible for the defective product and the manufacturing overhead incident to the processing of this order.

Going back to the preceding illustration, if the manufacturing activity were measured in terms of production time planned to be put in (IIb), with 21,000 man-hours actually scheduled, the budget allowance would become $92,000. Actual spending of $95,000 would thus be $3,000 more than had been planned (IIb). However, because actual output of 10,300 lb (Ia) was 300 lb more than had been expected, a saving of $1,260 in manufacturing overhead resulted (300 lb $\times$ 2.10 hr per pound = 630 hr at $2 per hour = $1,260). While the aggregate of these two effects upon manufacturing overhead ($3,000 − $1,260 = $1,740) is the same as the total variation of actual expenditures from budgeted expenditures, using production time necessary to turn out the actual output (Ib) as the measure, the two analyses of the actual performance of this department present entirely different pictures.

Obviously, the second method (IIb) presents a more complete and detailed picture of what has happened than does the first one (Ib). By using production time planned to be put into production (IIb) as the measure of level of activity, management can now trace the variation of actual expenditures from what should have been spent to two completely different causes. Hence, it can make a more accurate judgment of the extent to which manufacturing overhead expenses are affected by each of these two causes and can better ascertain who should be held responsible for such variations. For these reasons, production time planned or scheduled to be put in (IIb) is a better measure than the productive time necessary to turn out the actual output (Ib) as the basis for setting up budget allowances of manufacturing overhead expenses.

While the production time planned or scheduled to be put in (IIb) is far superior to the production time necessary to turn out the actual output (Ib) as the measure of manufacturing activity in setting up budget allowances of manufacturing overhead expenses, there is still a significant difference between using production time actually put in (III) and production time planned to be put in (IIb). In addition to being influenced by an actual quantity of output more or less than expected, manufacturing overhead expenses can likewise be affected when the production time actually put in (III) differs from the production time planned or scheduled to be put in (IIb). To get a complete picture of what has happened in order to make an accurate appraisal of actual performance and to allow more intelligent planning for the future, the effect upon manufacturing overhead expenses arising from these two different causes should not be confused with one another.

Thus in the preceding illustration, by using production time actually put in (III) as the measure of manufacturing activity, actual spending of $95,000 would be found to be $1,000 less than should have been spent for 23,000 man-hours actually worked (III). However, because 23,000 hr of production time actually put in (III) exceeded 21,000 hr of production time planned to be put in (II*b*) by 2,000 hr, additional manufacturing overhead expenses of $4,000 (2,000 hr at $2 per hour) were incurred. Nevertheless, because of the actual output of 10,300 lb (equivalent to 21,630 man-hours) being better than the original expectation of 10,000 lb (equivalent to 21,000 man-hours), there was a saving in manufacturing overhead expenses amounting to $1,260. The aggregate effect upon manufacturing overhead arising from these three different causes would amount to $1,740 ($4,000 − $1,260 − $1,000 = $1,740). Although this would be the same as the aggregate effect upon manufacturing overhead computed under the two preceding methods, this analysis of what happened with respect to manufacturing overhead expenses during March nevertheless differs completely from the other two analyses.

By its ability to present the most complete and detailed picture of what has happened, the third method, using production time actually put in (III) as the basis for setting up budget allowances of manufacturing overhead, is even better than the method using production time planned or scheduled to be put in (II*b*) as the measure of level of activity. Under this method, not only the effect upon manufacturing overhead due to actual output being more or less than expected is segregated from the effect upon manufacturing overhead due to more or less careful spending, but a distinction is also made on the effect of manufacturing overhead due to actual production time being more or less than planned production time. By helping management make a clear differentiation of the various causes contributing to the variation of actual expenditures from what needed to be spent, and ascertaining to what extent manufacturing overhead has been affected by each of these different causes as well as who should be responsible for such variations, better judgment of actual performance can thus be made and proper courses of action be taken for the future. Only by using actual production time as the measure of level of activity for setting up departmental budget allowances is operating management able to get such a complete picture.

Of the two other measures (I*a* and II*a*) in terms of physical units mentioned earlier, the use of physical units of actual output (I*a*) as the basis for setting up budget allowances of manufacturing overhead expenses at a single product department is as undesirable as the use of production time necessary to turn out the actual output (I*b*). In a previous section of this chapter the use of production time in preference to physical units of output was merely considered as a means of alleviating the problem of product mix at those producing centers where a multitude of products are manufactured or handled. A common fallacy is that, if only one product were manufactured by a department, then the physical units of actual output (I*a*) could be used as an appropriate measure for setting up the budget allowance of manufacturing overhead expenses. Actually, this is not so. The use of physical units of actual output (I*a*) as the measure of manufacturing activity in a single-product department is exactly the same as, and therefore not any better than, the use of production time necessary to turn out the actual output (I*b*) as the measure of manufacturing activity at a multiproduct department.

For example, going back to the previous illustration of Anderson Manufacturing Company, using physical units of actual output (I*a*) as the measure of manufacturing activity, the budget allowance of variable manufacturing expenses would become $4.20 per pound of product A produced (2.10 man-hours per pound of finished product at $2 per hour = $4.20 per pound of finished product). With an actual output of 10,300 lb of product A (I*a*), total budget allowance of manufacturing overhead expenses would be $93,260 ($50,000 + 10,300 lb × $4.20 per pound = $93,260), which is the same as the budget allowance using the production time necessary to turn out the actual output (I*b*) as the measure of level of activity. Therefore, the limitations imposed upon the use of production time necessary to turn out the actual output (I*b*) apply equally to the use of physical units of actual output (I*a*) as the measure of manufacturing activity.[3]

At the companies studied where variable budgeting either had been alleged as inapplicable to the business or had not achieved the result originally expected, physical units of output (I*a*) or its equivalent in standard production time (I*b*) had usually been used as the measure of level of activity in setting up budget allowances of manufacturing expenses. The use of the two improper measures of level of activity at these companies is a major factor contributing to the unreliability of their budget reports as guides to operating management for checking actual performance and for determining future courses of action.

Menlo Chemical Company, which uses tons of chemical produced (I*a*) as the measure of level of activity for setting up budget allowances of manufacturing expenses,[4] is a typical example of such a situation. Through the use of physical units of actual output as the measure of level of activity for

---

[3] The use of physical units of raw material processed (II*a*) as the basis for setting up budget allowances of manufacturing expenses will be discussed later in this section.

[4] See Menlo Chemical Company case in Appendix C.

setting up budget allowances of manufacturing expenses, the management consultant of Menlo Chemical Company had confused the issue of controlling the actual yield of finished products with the problems of controlling the actual expenditure on manufacturing expenses. In the illustration of Anderson Manufacturing Company, it had been shown that, if the entire output of a manufacturing department has to be scrapped, this does not necessarily mean that the manufacturing department is at fault and, therefore, may not incur any manufacturing expenses. The poor yield of finished products may sometimes be beyond the control of the department which does the processing. At Menlo Chemical Company, not only is the control of actual yield of finished products one of its major production problems, but the responsibility for getting a poorer or better yield may also at times lie beyond the realm of the department which does the processing. Under such circumstances, with improperly selected physical units of actual output as the basis for setting up departmental budget allowances, there is little wonder that the operating management at a processing department of Menlo Chemical Company finds that it cannot rely upon the budget report to judge what it should have spent on various manufacturing expenses.

This lack of appreciation of operating conditions and of the implications involved in the use of different measures of level of activity at Menlo Chemical Company could be contrasted with the experience of Milbrae Mining Company.[5] The manufacturing operation at a number of processing centers at Milbrae Mining Company is similar to that at Menlo Chemical Company. In presenting the problem of high cost of operation of Milbrae Mining Company, Mr. Krieg, controller of its parent company, San Rafael Sulphur Company, laid special emphasis on differentiating the variable cost of processing the raw material (IIa) from the variable processing cost of finished products (Ia). Mr. Krieg knew that the control of actual expenditure of manufacturing expenses at Milbrae and the control of the yield of its finished product were two entirely different management problems. During 1955, by keeping operating costs under better control, Milbrae was able to reduce its variable processing cost from $4.17 to $3.40 per ton of raw clays processed, a reduction of 18.5 per cent. By mining better-quality clays, the company was able to step up the yield of its finished product from 44 per cent of raw clays processed in 1954 to 54.4 per cent in 1955. The combination of lower processing cost and improved yield enabled the company to reduce the variable processing cost of finished clay (Ia) from $9.48 in 1954 to $6.24 per ton of finished clay in 1955, a reduction of 34.2 per cent. If actual yield during 1955 could be brought up to 60 per cent instead of 54.4 per cent, the variable processing cost of finished products (Ia) could be further reduced to $5.65 per ton even when the variable cost of processing the raw material (IIa) remained at $3.40 per

[5] See Milbrae Mining Company case in Chap. 4.

ton. The case also shows that the poor quality of raw material put into production at Milbrae Mining Company was entirely out of the control of the superintendent in charge of the processing mill, although he should properly be responsible for the cost of processing the raw material put through the mill.

Whereas the implications involved in the use of different measures of level of activity were clearly seen by the controller of San Rafael Sulphur Company, these same implications had been completely neglected at Menlo Chemical Company. Therefore, the failure of its management consultant to understand clearly the operating conditions of Menlo Chemical Company and his ignorance of the implications involved in the use of different measures of level of activity had resulted in the adoption of an improper measure of level of activity as the basis for setting up budget allowances of manufacturing expenses. This, in turn, led to the unreliability of budget reports and consequent abandonment of the company's old flexible budgeting system.

The experience of Burlingame Manufacturing Company is an example where the use of productive time necessary to turn out the actual output (Ib) has been a major cause leading to the "not so successful" experience of its variable budgeting system. This company uses standard minutes necessary to turn out the actual output (Ib) as the measure of level of activity for setting up its budget allowances of manufacturing overhead expenses. Although the company had used a variable budgeting system for a number of years, until the recent change in top management, the attitude of its operating executives toward the company's budgetary system was far different from the attitude of operating management at those companies where variable budgeting has been successfully used. Up to that time, according to the budget director of Burlingame Manufacturing Company, the reaction within the company toward its budgetary system could be divided into two types. The first consisted of those conscientious people who tried constantly to live within their budgets. The other group did not care what its actual expenditures were in relation to its budget allowance. The predominance of this latter group could be seen by an examination of the company's budget reports (Tables 9–1 and 9–2) for the first six months of 1953. During this period, actual "controllable" manufacturing expenses[6] of $1,338,937 at its "superintendent" division were $379,029 or 39.5 per cent more than the corresponding budget allowance of $959,908.

A major portion of this excessive spending of $379,029 over the budget allowance at the superintendent division could be traced to the machine-

---

[6] "Controllable" overhead expenses at Burlingame Manufacturing Company comprise overhead expenses such as supervision, indirect labor, supplies, and the like. Expenses such as depreciation, rent, insurance, etc., are considered as "noncontrollable" expenses and are, hence, excluded from budget reports.

shop department which was the largest spending unit within the division. During this 6-month period, the machine-shop department spent $286,166 on its controllable manufacturing expenses against a budget allowance of $88,408, almost 225 per cent more than what should have been spent (i.e., according to the budget).

If the budget allowance at Burlingame Manufacturing Company had been a reliable guide to operating management, it certainly would not have taken an indifferent attitude toward such a seemingly alarming variation of actual expenditures from budget allowances. At the machine-shop department of Burlingame Manufacturing Company, control of spoilage and

TABLE 9–1

Burlingame Manufacturing Company

Controllable Expense
Entire Plant

Mr.
Vice-president of Manufacturing   Month ended June 30, 1953

	MONTH		YEAR TO DATE	
	Budget	*Actual*	*Budget*	*Actual*
Divisional:				
Superintendent	$146,468	($195,108)	$ 959,908	($1,338,937)
Industrial relations	7,444	(7,588)	45,463	(47,219)
Plant engineer	23,338	22,603	161,694	(186,569)
Development engineering	44,804	44,415	260,243	(269,527)
Departmental:				
Main office	40,988	(43,341)	265,807	(303,259)
Purchasing	9,435	(9,901)	55,344	(57,680)
Priorities	1,153	1,028	8,284	8,242
Printing	881	(1,186)	5,047	(7,035)
Plant security	8,767	(9,503)	52,296	51,618
Precision equipment engineering	4,836	4,809	33,264	32,549
Total	$288,114	($339,482)	$1,847,350	($2,302,635)
Expenses over budget (red)	. . .	($51,368)	. . .	($455,285)
Expenses under budget—black				
Standard minutes produced	. . .	4,653,300 (22 working days)	. . .	30,344,200 (127 working days)
Cost per 1,000 standard minutes	61.92	(72.96)	60.88	(75.88)

Parentheses denote red figures.

TABLE 9–2

Burlingame Manufacturing Company

Departmental Expenses—Budget & Actual

Mr.
Dept. Plant Superintendent   Month ended June 30, 1953

	Period	MONTH			YEAR TO DATE	
STANDARD MINUTES	Forecast	6,108,100			39,229,800	
	Produced	4,653,300			39,344,200	

		Budget				
ACCOUNT		Cost per M	Dollars	Actual	Budget	Actual
DEPARTMENTS						
3	Farm Machine		$ 8,837	$ 10,149	$ 66,248	$ 66,626
9	Factory and Industrial		12,605	13,255	75,114	83,746
11	Precision Equipment Assembly		1,489	4,177	13,978	26,124
14	Machine Shop		11,154	38,874	88,408	286,166
18	Cast Iron and Paint		4,334	5,407	28,167	47,098
3	Frame and Customer Repair		3,751	3,820	24,367	28,453
42	Gear		2,805	5,913	20,408	53,305
44	Press Steel		10,495	11,522	55,818	80,697
45	Tinning		1,619	1,455	10,418	14,333
	Planning		17,848	19,058	120,375	123,085
	Foundries and Rubber		25,680	28,742	148,385	166,510
	Tool Service and Machine Maintenance		11,972	14,691	76,917	97,305
	Inspection and Salvage		16,636	19,260	114,999	135,595
	Product Engineering		17,243	18,785	116,306	129,894
TOTAL			$146,468	$195,108	$959,908	$1,338,937
A—Actual for Budget						
Expense under Budget—Black						
Expense over Budget—Red (in bracket)				(48,640)		(379,029)
Cost per 1,000 Standard Minutes			31.48	(40.11)	31.63	(44.13)

control of production time are two of the major problems in production management. By the use of standard production time necessary to turn out the actual output (I*b*) as the basis for setting up budget allowances, the budget reports of this machine-shop department, in the form such as those used by the company, present a confused picture as to how much a foreman should spend on various manufacturing expenses during any given period and as to who should be responsible for the variation of actual expenditures from budgeted expenditures. Whenever a foreman found that he had been charged by the accounting department for something for which he should not be held responsible, he would naturally lose his confidence in this type of budget report and would thereafter take an indifferent, if not hostile, attitude toward such a system.

The successful use of variable budgeting at Otterbein Corporation may serve as a good contrast to the experience of Burlingame Manufacturing Company. Both companies are manufacturers of heavy machinery and have many similarities in their manufacturing operations. Instead of the indifferent attitude of operating management as at Burlingame Manufacturing Company, the variable budgeting system at Otterbein Corporation was so well received that it was considered by its operating management as an indispensable tool for helping it to do a better job. One of the important reasons for the enthusiastic attitude at Otterbein Corporation toward its budgetary system was that its budget estimate had been representative of what should have been spent. This, in good part, was due to proper measures of level of activity being selected. By his thorough familiarity with the nature of operations and through his awareness of the implications of different measures of manufacturing activity, the controller of Otterbein Corporation decided that the actual production time (III) was the most appropriate measure of manufacturing activity for setting up budget allowances of manufacturing overhead expenses.[7] Consequently, operating management at Otterbein Corporation found that it could rely upon the budget reports prepared by the controller's department for helping it to judge actual performance and plan future operations. By selecting a proper measure of level of activity and making the budget reports reliable, the controller of Otterbein Corporation laid one of the cornerstones which is fundamental in the successful application of a variable budgeting system.

Between the actual production time (III) used by Otterbein Corporation, which represents the most satisfactory measure of level of activity, and the physical units of actual output (Ia) used by Menlo Chemical Company or the standard production time necessary to turn out the actual output (Ib) used by Burlingame Manufacturing Company, which are the least desirable measures of level of activity, lie two other measures of manufacturing activity. Of these two, production time planned or scheduled to be put in (IIb) has been discussed in the illustration of Anderson Manufacturing Company. The other measure, physical units of raw material processed (IIa) is yet to be covered. Basically, these two measures of input (IIa and IIb) would give identical results if the manufacturing process involved only one raw material and one finished product.

[7] See Otterbein Corporation case in Appendix B.

For instance, in the illustration of Anderson Manufacturing Company discussed earlier, using physical units of raw material processed as the measure of level of activity, the budget allowance of variable manufacturing overhead expenses would become $4 per pound of raw material put into production (2 man-hours per pound of raw material B processed at $2 per hour = $4 per pound). With 10,500 lb of raw material put into production (IIa), the budget allowance of manufacturing overhead expenses for March, 1955, would be $92,000 ($50,000 + 10,500 lb $\times$ $4 per pound = $92,-000), which is the same as the budget allowance using the production time planned or scheduled to be put in (IIb) as the measure of manufacturing activity. Like the production time planned to be put in (IIb), the physical units of raw material processed (IIa) is a far superior measure to the physical units of actual output (Ia) or its equivalent in standard production time (Ib) for setting up budget allowances of manufacturing overhead expenses, because it enables management to differentiate the problem of controlling the yield of a product from the problem of controlling the actual spending of manufacturing overhead expenses. However, like the production time planned to be put into production (IIb), the use of physical units of raw material processed (IIa) is subject to the same limitation arising from mixing the effect upon manufacturing overhead expenses due to variation of actual production time (III) from planned production time (IIb) and the effect upon manufacturing overhead expenses due to more or less careful outlay of such expenditures.

Despite the limitation on the use of physical units of raw material processed (IIa) or production time planned to be put in (IIb) discussed here, sometimes it may be practical to use one of these measures as the basis for setting up budget allowances of manufacturing overhead expenses without endangering the successful application of a variable budgeting system. The experience of Lafayette Brass Company is an example of such a situation. The measure of level of activity used by Lafayette Brass Company for setting up its budget allowances is the production time planned or scheduled to be put in (IIb) translated into standard direct labor dollars at standard labor rates.[8] Prior to the installation of its variable budgeting system, adequate control over the use of its production time had already been achieved by Lafayette Brass Company. Under such circumstances, the limitation imposed upon the use of production time planned to be put in (IIb) was minimized.

For example, returning to the illustration of Anderson Manufacturing Company, assume that 21,000 actual hours (III) was spent to process the 10,500 lb of raw material B into 10,300 lb of product A. The budget allowance using the actual production time (III) as the measure of level of manufacturing activity would then become the same as that using produc-

[8] See Lafayette Brass Company case in Appendix A.

tion time scheduled for production (II*b*) because the latter was also 21,000 hr. Since there was no variation of actual production time (III) from planned or scheduled production time (II*b*), the effect upon manufacturing overhead expenses due to actual production time (III) being different from planned production time (II*b*) would be nil. Therefore, if actual production time (III) could be kept close to the production time planned to be put in (II*b*), the latter could be used as a measure of manufacturing activity as effectively as would the actual production time (III).

However, the successful experience at Lafayette Brass Company does not mean that the limitations upon physical units of raw material processed (II*a*) or production time planned to be in (II*b*) no longer need to be considered. Rather, this experience shows that only through a thorough understanding of the operating conditions of the particular business and by giving full consideration to the implications involved in the use of different measures of level of activity under the particular situation can the normally most desirable measure for the operating conditions of the particular business be identified and adopted.

MACHINE-HOURS VERSUS LABOR-HOURS

When production time is used as the measure of manufacturing activity for setting up budget allowances, further consideration is required of a choice between productive machine time and productive labor time. In certain situations, one of these measures is more representative of the level of activity for manufacturing expenses, whereas under another set of conditions, either one of them may be appropriately used. The extent to which manufacturing operations are mechanized and "automated," the layout and organization of a plant, the flow of manufacturing process, variations in the cost of operating different machines within a department, and management's policy toward labor are some of the factors which need to be considered in the process of selection. Lastly, ease in compiling necessary information has likewise to be weighed in the final decision.

In a fully automated manufacturing department,[9] where manual work has been completely replaced by machine operation and where technical know-how rather than muscular strength or finger dexterity must be used to run a push-button, switch-turning, and dial-flashing operation, machine production time is often a better measure of level of activity for manufacturing expenses. This is especially true when a plant is not continuously operated at its capacity, and when because of their technical training, the operators are kept on the payroll of a department regardless of minor fluc-

[9] Although the word "automation" is a new one developed by the metal-working industries, actual automation has long been achieved and practiced by chemical, petroleum refining, paper, cement, and a number of other processing industries.

tuations in volume. Thus, at Menlo Chemical Company, instead of units of output or productive labor time, productive machine time would be a more appropriate measure of level of activity for setting up budget allowances of manufacturing expenses in a number of its producing departments such as rock grinding, pelletizing, etc.

On the other hand, manual work may still be the predominant operation at another department or company. Under such circumstances, although a variety of mechanical tools may be used by an operator in performing his job, productive labor time is often the only practical and logical measure of its manufacturing activity. A typical example of such an operation is the assembly of small motors at Otterbein Corporation.

In between these two extremes, there are a number of situations where, for the purpose of setting up proper budget allowances, productive labor time may be as equally representative of the manufacturing activity as the productive machine time. For instance, assume the most simple situation of a milling-machine department where there is only one milling machine operated by an hourly rated employee who may be released any day if there is no work scheduled for him the following day.[10] For practical purposes, there will be little difference between measuring the manufacturing activity of this milling-machine department for any month in terms of the time operated by the machine or of the time spent by its operator.

The situation may seem to be complicated in a larger milling-machine department where there are several milling machines and the work load on each machine during any period may be different. For instance, assume that there are five machines in this department and that during March, 1956, two of them were operated at 8 hr a day for 22 working days. Another two were operated at 8 hr a day for 18 working days. The fifth one was operated at 8 hr a day for 15 working days. However, if the cost of operating any of these five machines is identical or close to that of others, for the purpose of determining how much expense should be spent during any month, the manufacturing activity of this department may properly be expressed in terms of the aggregate operating time of these five machines, i.e., 760 machine-hours $(8 \times 22 \times 2 + 8 \times 18 \times 2 + 8 \times 15 \times 1 = 760$ hr). If each of these machines had to be tended by one operator, and if the operator were kept on the payroll of this department only for the time spent at this department, the total productive labor time of 760 man-hours during March, 1956, would, therefore, be the same as the productive machine time.

In most companies, operating statistics of the total productive labor time at any department are usually available at the accounting department,

---

[10] To be released from a department does not necessarily mean that the worker is laid off by the company. It means here that his time at the company will no longer be charged to the department for which he has worked.

which has to compile such statistics for payroll purposes. Under such circumstances, the accounting department usually finds it more convenient to report to the operating management the departmental manufacturing expenses in comparison with the budget allowances on the basis of productive labor time rather than productive machine time.[11] The danger is that they may do so simply because of convenient availability of productive labor time.

A more complicated situation may arise when a manufacturing department has different types of machines with different operating costs. However, if the manufacturing plant is laid out on a product-line basis, and the flow of manufacturing process is such that every production order has to go through each machine in sequence within the department with little or no interruption, it will then be possible to consider all the machines within the department as a single machine unit. The situation will then be similar to the milling-machine department with only one milling machine if the operators could be released from the departmental payroll whenever there is no work scheduled for the following day. The rolling mills at Lafayette Brass Company are an example of such a situation. If, however, the operators are kept on the departmental payroll regardless of temporary fluctuations in the level of activity, then productive machine time will be a more appropriate measure of manufacturing activity for setting up budget allowances. This situation is very much similar to the fully mechanized productive department at Menlo Chemical Company.

The most difficult problem occurs in a manufacturing department where there are a group of heterogeneous machines with varying operating costs and where the flow of the manufacturing process does not require every production order to go through all the machines within the department. For instance, assume that the press (printing) department of Sherwood Press is equipped with five old presses (printing machines) of the same type and size and a new giant rotary press capable of doing the job of five other presses in a given period. Assume also that four operators are required for the operation of each of these presses, large or small, despite the faster speed and greater productivity of the giant press. However, other operating expenses of the giant press and the small presses differ considerably, and the work loads on these presses differ from one another and from period to period depending upon the number and size of production orders scheduled by the production-control department. Since the operating time of the giant press could not be logically added to the operating time of the small presses, a common denominator for the manufacturing activity of different presses is needed for setting up budget allowances of manufacturing ex-

[11] Statistics on the machine production time for any given period are usually available at the production-control department which does the scheduling of production orders.

penses of this department. Frequently, productive labor time is selected as the common denominator for expressing the manufacturing activity of such a department. The use of direct labor-hours at Sherwood Press and the use of standard direct labor-minutes at Burlingame Manufacturing Company are examples of such a practice.

While it may appear "arithmetically" reasonable to add man-hours to man-hours, the use of such logic can make budget allowances "way out of line" from what should have been spent under actual operating conditions if there are wide variations in the cost of operating different machines in this department. For instance, assume that the following estimates had been made by Sherwood Press in setting up manufacturing expense budgets for its press department in 1956:

| 1956 | Total | Press No. | | | | | |
		11	1	2	3	4	5
Estimated machine operating hours	*	2,000	2,000	2,000	2,000	2,000	2,000
Estimated direct labor-hours	48,000	8,000	8,000	8,000	8,000	8,000	8,000
Estimated variable manufacturing expenses	$60,000	$20,000	$8,000	$8,000	$8,000	$8,000	$8,000
Budget allowance per direct labor-hour	$1.25						

* Operating time of Press 11 cannot be added to the operating time of Presses 1 to 5. (Press 11 is the new giant rotary press; Presses 1 to 5 are the small presses.)

Assume also that during March, 1956, the press department operated at a level of 2,560 labor-hours and spent $4,000 on its variable manufacturing (overhead) expenses. At the rate of $1.25 per direct labor-hour, the total budget allowance for 2,560 hr would be $3,200. Actual spending of $4,000 would, therefore, appear to have exceeded the budget allowance of $3,200 by $800 or 25 per cent.

The fact that actual spending of $4,000 had exceeded the budget allowance by $800 according to the above analysis does not mean that the press department had spent more money than should have been spent during this period. To ascertain whether the press department did spend more money than it should have, one should also study the work load of the different presses during this period because the operating cost of Press 11 differs considerably from the operating costs of Presses 1 to 5. Assume that the actual operating time of these machines was 960 direct labor-hours for Press 11, 640 direct labor-hours for Presses 1 and 2, and 320 direct labor-hours for Press 3. In addition, instead of using an average department rate per direct labor-hour, separate rates of variable manufacturing expenses are established for each group of machines with similar operating costs. The budget allowance of variable manufacturing expenses of the press department for March, 1956, would now be as follows:

1956	Total	11	1–5	1	2	3	4	5
					Press No.			
Estimated direct labor-hours	48,000	8,000	40,000	8,000	8,000	8,000	8,000	8,000
Estimated variable manufacturing expenses	$60,000	$20,000	$40,000	$8,000	$8,000	$8,000	$8,000	$8,000
Budget allowance per direct labor-hour	*	$2.50	$1.00	$1.00	$1.00	$1.00	$1.00	$1.00
March, 1956								
Actual direct labor-hours	2,560	960	1,600	640	640	320		
Budget allowance	$4,000†	$2,400	$1,600					

* Average rate for press department: $1.25 per hour.
† Budget allowance would become $3,200 if total productive labor time of 2,560 hr were multiplied by the average rate of $1.25 per hour.

With a budget allowance of $4,000, the actual spending of $4,000 was exactly what it should have been for this period. By taking into consideration the difference in the cost of operating different machines and the work load upon each machine, the second analysis is obviously more representative of the actual operating condition than the first one.

The above illustration is an example that when there is a wide difference between the operating cost of one group of machines and that of other groups, and if the production order does not have to go through every machine in a department, for the purpose of setting up budget allowances of manufacturing expenses, productive labor time does not provide a common denominator for measuring the manufacturing activity of the entire department. It can be a common denominator for measuring the level of activity only when the department consists of a group of machines similar in operating costs. Therefore, in the preceding illustration, in order to know what the variable manufacturing expense of the press department should have been for March, 1956, it is necessary to divide this department into two subdepartments or cost centers, each with a group of homogeneous machines (Press 11 and Presses 1 to 5). Without this subdivision, the use of aggregate productive labor time and an average departmental rate gives a budget allowance which can hardly be representative of what should have been spent under actual operating conditions.

The operating conditions at the press department of Sherwood Press discussed here can be extended to the machine-shop department of Burlingame Manufacturing Company, where there are a wide variety of machines with different operating costs. It had been anticipated by Burlingame Manufacturing Company that, with the use of standard direct labor-minutes, a common denominator of level of activity would be obtained for setting up the budget allowance of manufacturing expenses. It failed to recognize that the productive labor time can be a common denominator of manufacturing activity only for a department consisting of machines similar in operating costs. The wide variation of actual expenditures from budget allowances at Burlingame's machine-shop department and the resultant indifferent attitude of some of the operating management toward the company's budgetary system could be attributed in part to the failure to recognize such implications and to break down the machine-shop department into cost centers, each with a group of machines similar in operating costs.

When a manufacturing department with a variety of machines is subdivided into several cost centers each with a group of machines similar in operating costs, productive machine time again becomes as appropriate a measure of manufacturing activity for setting up budget allowances as productive labor time. For instance, in the preceding illustration of Sherwood Press, the budget allowance for variable manufacturing expenses using productive machine time as the measure of manufacturing activity will be as follows:

1956	Total	Press No. 11	1–5	1	2	3	4	5
Estimated machine operating hours	. . .	2,000	10,000	2,000	2,000	2,000	2,000	2,000
Estimated variable manufacturing expenses	$60,000	$20,000	$40,000	$8,000	$8,000	$8,000	$8,000	$8,000
Budgeted variable manufacturing expenses per machine-hour	. . .	$ 10.00	$ 4.00	$ 4.00	$ 4.00	$ 4.00	$ 4.00	$ 4.00
March, 1956								
Actual machine-hours	. . .	240	400	160	160	80		
Budget allowance	$4,000 = $ 2,400 + $ 1,600							

The budget allowance of $4,000 using productive machine-hours as the measure of manufacturing activity is, therefore, the same as the budget allowance using productive labor-hours as the measure of manufacturing activity.

It has sometimes been argued that it is not practical or economically justified to subdivide a manufacturing department into several cost centers and collect operating statistics on that basis. In the preceding illustration of Sherwood Press, the argument of economic justification should certainly be seriously considered on any proposal to subdivide the press department into six cost centers, each with one press. However, there is a definite need for subdividing this department into two cost centers, each with a group of machines similar in operating costs, if the budgetary tool is to be of value to operating management. This would certainly be more economical than subdividing this department into six cost centers. Furthermore, not only does the foreman of the press department need reliable guidance as to how much money his department should spend, but the plant and cost managers of Sherwood Press need to know the difference in the operating cost of each machine for intelligent pricing. The same cost information is also needed by the production-control department of Sherwood Press for scheduling production orders through the press department to provide the most efficient utilization of its productive facilities. Although the operating statistics of each machine may not have been easily acquired at the accounting department, such information is often readily available at the production department in any efficiently managed manufacturing plant. Therefore, in most cases, very little, if any, additional cost will be incurred by the accounting department in order to collect a summary of operating statistics from the production department and to make the budgetary system really meaningful and helpful to operating management.

MEASUREMENT OF LEVEL OF ACTIVITY
FOR PROFIT-PLANNING PURPOSES

Although productive time is generally preferred as the measure of level of activity for setting up budget allowances of manufacturing expenses at lower supervisory levels, different measures of level of activity should be used for various profit-planning purposes at higher management levels, including forecasts of the financial results of operation for different volumes of business and problems in make or buy, product selection, pricing, planning capital expenditures, and the like. The use of a different measure of level of activity for profit-planning purposes has sometimes led to the belief that variable budgeting is only a tool for helping management control manufacturing overhead expenses and must, therefore, be distinguished from studies of volume-cost relationships for various profit-planning purposes. To be sure, it is true that, in a number of companies, studies of volume-cost relationships are designed solely for helping to solve just one of the many management problems discussed in this book. The possible end uses of the knowledge of volume-cost relationships for a variety of situations may not be recognized all at once. However, in its advanced stage of development at a company where variable budgeting has been successfully used, the same knowledge of volume-cost relationships obtained for purposes of establishing departmental expense budgets can be adapted for various profit-planning purposes. Conversely, realization of the need for knowing the volume-cost relationships of a business to solve various profit-planning problems can lead to the development of variable expense budgets at lower management levels. The reason for using a different measure of level of activity for profit-planning purposes, its relationship with the measure of level of activity for setting up departmental expense budgets, and some of the implications involved in its practical applications will be the main topics of discussion in this section.

The choice of measure of level of activity in studies of volume-cost relationships for various profit-planning purposes is largely dictated by the nature of the problems confronted by management. In forecasting the financial results of operation and in problems such as make or buy, dropping a seemingly unprofitable line of product, price determination, planning of capital expenditures, and the like, management's primary concern is centered around the product or service rendered by a business to its customers. Both the revenues that may be received from and the expenditures that will be incurred for such products have to be taken into consideration in its decisions. Under such circumstances, it is most natural and logical to use units of products produced and sold as the measure of volume of business in studies of volume-cost-profit relationships. Hence, pounds of copper wire, tons of pigment, number of books, and number of vacuum cleaners are used, respectively, at Lafayette Brass Company, Hobson Pigment Company, Sherwood Press, and Olympia Manufacturing Company as the measure of level of activity for various profit-planning purposes.

The use of a different measure of level of activity for various profit-planning purposes from that used for establishing a departmental expense budget does not necessarily mean that the knowledge of volume-cost relationships obtained for the latter purpose cannot be applied to profit-planning purposes. In fact, despite the use of different measures of level of activity, the departmental expense budgets can be made an integral part of profit planning, and if such budgets are properly established, they give management the best assurance of its own costs and expenses. This is analogous to the construction of a house, in which its foundation must be laid first before frames can be erected. The expense budget at lower supervisory levels is the foundation upon which management can build its cost figures for profit-planning purposes.

The practice at Lafayette Brass Company is a typical example of the integration of departmental expense budgets into the forecast of financial results of operations for different volumes of business.[12] In the construction of forecast profit and loss statements and volume-cost-profit diagrams for any of its operating divisions, the necessary direct material and direct labor costs for the contemplated business are built up from the data contained in the standard cost sheets of various products. The variable overhead expenses for the contemplated production and sales are obtained by reference to the variable expense budgets of various departments and the necessary production time at each department in terms of standard direct labor dollars. The fixed overhead expenses of a division comprise the fixed expenses of all departments within the division. With this information on hand, projected profit and loss statements and volume-cost-profit diagrams of any division can be constructed.

A similar approach is used by Sherwood Press in ascertaining the additional cost it will incur on accepting a certain order, even though the volume of the contemplated order is expressed in terms of number of books, whereas the level of activity for manufacturing expenses is measured in terms of productive labor time. On the basis of the specifications of any order, the necessary material and direct labor costs are compiled from standards established by the company's engineering department. Having determined the productive time at various operating centers, the additional manufacturing overhead expenses in relation to that order are obtained from the departmental expense budgets of the respective cost centers. Thus, simply by converting units of output into necessary productive time, the departmental expense budgets are made an integral part of profit planning at these companies, even when a different measure of level of activity is used for establishing the departmental expense budget than that for various profit-planning purposes.

In place of physical units of products produced and sold, dollar volume of sales may also be used as the measure of level of activity in the construction of volume-cost-profit diagrams as a means of studying the possible profit and loss at different volumes of business under any proposed operating plan. At companies where a variety of heterogeneous products are manufactured, the use of this measure provides a common index through which the volumes of business of different products can be combined with one another. For instance, in the machinery and other similar industries, it is not customary to add the number of units of one type of machine to the number of units of another type of machine for measuring the total sales volume of an operating unit which makes different types of machines. Under such circumstances, dollar volume of sales becomes the only logical basis for measuring the aggregate volume of business of such an operating unit.

[12] See Lafayette Brass Company case in Appendix A.

When the dollar volume of sales is used as the measure of level of activity in the construction of volume-cost-profit diagrams, minimum sales volumes necessary to keep a company out of loss and to enable it to reach its profit objective can also be computed mathematically. Instead of using the two formulas

$$V_m = \frac{F}{s_a - v_a} \qquad (9\text{--}1)$$

$$V'_m = \frac{F + P}{s_a - v_a} \qquad (9\text{--}2)$$

in which volumes are expressed in terms of physical units of products, the following formulas can be used:

$$S_m = \frac{F}{1 - V/S} \qquad (9\text{--}3)$$

$$S'_m = \frac{F + P}{1 - V/S} \qquad (9\text{--}4)$$

where V_m = minimum volume in units of products necessary to keep out of loss
S_m = minimum volume in sales dollars necessary to keep out of loss
V'_m = minimum volume in units of products necessary to reach a profit objective of P
S'_m = minimum volume in sales dollars necessary to reach a profit objective of P
S = net sales in dollars
s_a = average selling price per unit of product
V = total variable cost
v_a = average variable cost per unit of product
F = total fixed cost in dollars
P = pretax profit objective in dollars

In a single-product plant or in a plant where the products are more or less of homogeneous character, the use of physical units of output as the measure of level of activity in the constructiton of volume-cost-profit diagrams is usually more desirable than the use of dollar volume of sales, because this method permits the measure of volume of business independent of any influence of selling prices. This is especially true when the volume-cost-profit diagram is used as a means of studying the effects of different price propositions upon the profit position of a company.[13] A volume-cost-price-profit diagram with physical units of products produced and sold as the measure of level of activity usually presents a clearer picture and is easier to understand than one with dollar volume of sales as the measure of volume of business.

At a multiproduct plant, no matter whether physical units of products

[13] See discussions and illustrations on the need and value of volume-cost-profit studies in pricing decisions in Chap. 5.

produced and sold or dollar volume of sales is used as the measure of level of activity in the construction of volume-cost-diagrams, different volume-cost-profit relationships can be obtained with different product mixes if the contributions of different products toward profit are not the same. Therefore, when the actual sales mix realized by a business differs from its anticipated mix, the actual profit would not be the same as the profit forecast for the same volume of business shown in the volume-cost-profit diagram constructed on the basis of anticipated product mixes.

TABLE 9–3

Lafayette Brass Company

Plant 1—Mill Division
Comparison of Sales, Cost, and Profit

	March Actual *	Adjusted Budget †	Volume-Cost ‡ Diagram
	(000 omitted)	(000 omitted)	(000 omitted)
Production, lb	4,616	4,616	
Net pounds sold	4,723	4,723	4,723
Net sales	$2,474	$2,459	$2,456
Net cost of sales at standard	2,188	2,158	2,158
Gross profit at standard	$ 286	$ 301	$ 298
Variations from standard:			
Volume	($ 35)	($ 32)	($ 32)
Other	14		
Total variations	($ 21)	($ 32)	($ 32)
Gross profit, actual	$ 265	$ 269	$ 266
Total commercial costs	83	85	85
Net profit before income taxes and miscellaneous adjustments	$ 182	$ 184	$ 181

* See Appendix A, Table A–6.
† See Appendix A, Table A–7.
‡ See Appendix A, Table A–8 and Fig. A–1.

For instance, Table 9–3 shows that, during March, 1952, actual sales of $2,474,000 for 4,723,000 lb of finished products sold by the mill division of Layafette Brass Company's Plant A differ from corresponding sales of $2,459,000 under the adjusted budget and $2,456,000 from the volume-cost-profit diagram. Similarly, the standard cost of $2,188,000 for the actual finished products sold differs from the corresponding standard (manufacturing) cost of $2,158,000 under the adjusted budget and from the volume-cost-profit diagram. Consequently, the standard gross margin of $286,000 shown under March Actual differs from the corresponding standard gross margin of $301,000 shown under Adjusted Budget and $298,000 in the volume-cost-profit diagram. Figures in Table 9–3 are extracted from Table A–6, Table A–7, Table A–8, and Fig. A–1 of the Lafayette Brass Company case in Appendix A. The main reason for these differences is that the actual product mix in March, 1952, is not the same product mix on the basis of which the original profit budget and volume-cost-profit diagrams were constructed. In addition, variation of actual selling price of a product from that used in the construction of the original profit budget contributes another source of difference in the sales figures. The discrepancy between the sales of $2,459,000 under the adjusted budget and the corresponding sales of $2,456,000 from the volume-cost-profit diagram is due to changes in the mix of outside sales and intercompany sales, for which the volume-cost-profit diagram has not been adjusted.

To those not familiar with how and why studies of volume-cost-profit relationships are used by management, variations of actual profit from predicted profit due to changes in sales mix of products from what has been anticipated may cause suspicion of the accuracy, and hence the value, of the forecast of financial results of operation. Nevertheless, at companies such as Lafayette Brass Company, where variable budgeting has been properly used, the value of volume-cost-profit studies is not destroyed by such variations. Although this will be discussed in detail in Chap. 11, it should be pointed out here that the variation is no criterion for claiming the inadequacy of variable budgeting for profit-planning purposes. This variation in itself is vital as a symbol to management to study the causes of the deviation and to select the course of future action, based on these studies, which will be most desirable. Moreover, the fact that the profit of a company can be changed by having a different product mix makes it more necessary for management to study its volume-cost-profit relationships in planning its sales programs. The reason why this seeming inaccuracy of profit forecasting does not impose any serious limitations on the use of volume-cost-profit studies will be covered in a later chapter (Chap. 11), in which the variation of actual profit from forecast profit will be discussed in more detail.

SUMMARY AND CONCLUSIONS

For the purpose of setting up reliable budget allowances of manufacturing expenses at lower supervisory levels, productive time actually put in (III) is deemed the most desirable measure of the various ones studied in this chapter. The use of this measure makes possible the presentation of a complete picture of what has happened, so that budget reports can be relied upon by operating management as a guide for judging actual performance and for determining the following course of action. Next, but secondary, in desirability as measures are the productive time planned or scheduled to be put in (II*b*) and the physical units of raw material processed (II*a*). The least satisfactory measures are the physical units of actual output (*Ia*) and the productive time necessary to turn out the actual output (*Ib*), because the use of these measures results in the production of budget reports in which the different causes of, as well as responsibilities for, the variation of actual expenditures from budget allowances are confused with one another. Whether or not the less desirable measures can be satisfactorily used depends to a large extent upon the special operating conditions of a particular business. These also dictate the choice of whether machine production time should be preferred over productive labor time.

Failure to make budget allowances representative of what should have been spent under actual operating conditions and bringing a department manager or foreman to account for the expenditures over which he cannot exercise control are major causes leading to the antipathetic attitude of operating management toward unsatisfactory variable budgeting systems. The use of an improper measure of level of activity for setting up departmental budget allowances of manufacturing expenses is one of the major factors contributing to the unreliability of budget allowances as a useful guide to operating management. This can be attributed to the lack of proper understanding of the operating conditions of a particular business and to the failure to realize the implications involved in the use of different measures of level of activity by the person responsible for the design, installation, and administration of variable budgeting itself at these companies.

In studies of volume-cost relationships for profit-planning purposes, a different measure of volume of business has to be used, mainly because the managerial problem is moved up from that of controlling manufacturing expenses at lower supervisory levels to that of calling for a decision by management at top or upper levels. Both the revenue to be received and the expenditures to be incurred have to be taken into consideration in such decisions. It is, therefore, often necessary to use units of products to be produced and sold as the measure of volume of business in such studies.

The use of a different measure of level of activity for profit-planning purposes from that for setting up departmental expense budgets does not mean that the knowledge of volume-cost relationships obtained for setting up manufacturing expense budgets cannot be applied to volume-cost studies for profit-plannig purposes. At a number of companies equipped with variable budgeting systems, the departmental expense budgets are made an integral part of volume-cost studies for various profit-planning purposes simply by converting the contemplated sales and production into necessary production time.

For purposes of cost control, it is possible to make fairly accurate estimates of manufacturing expenses under actual operating conditions through proper selection of the measure of level of activity, regardless of changes in the product mix. However, changes in the product mix may make actual profit differ from that predicted for the same volume of business as shown in the volume-cost-profit diagram if such a diagram is constructed on the basis of a different product mix. To a person not familiar with how and why volume-cost-profit studies are used by management, this seeming inaccuracy of profit forecasting may seem to impose serious limitations. Whether this variation of actual profit from forecast profit really destroys the value of volume-cost-profit studies because of changes in product mix as well as a number of other factors will be discussed in a later chapter.

CHAPTER 10

Importance of
the Time Element

The successful application of variable budgeting depends to a large extent upon the reliability of the budget estimate or allowance at a particular company. In preceding chapters the importance of setting up proper budget estimates and of selecting a proper measure of level of activity in attaining a reliable budget has been analyzed in detail. Discussions in this chapter will be devoted mainly to the role of the time element in bringing out the volume-cost relationships of different manufacturing expenses, its role in the forecast of financial results of operations through volume-cost-profit studies, and the implications arising from the use of budget periods of different lengths upon the reliability of budget estimates.

THE ROLE OF TIME ELEMENT IN VOLUME-COST RELATIONSHIPS

One of the factors which should not be overlooked in the practical application of variable budgeting is the existence of a third factor (dimension), i.e., the time element, in establishing the volume-cost relationships of a manufacturing expense. Depending upon the nature of the particular expense in a particular business, the use of a shorter time period may sometimes completely destroy the volume-cost relationship which would otherwise exist when a longer time period is used. Successful application of variable budgeting requires a proper knowledge of the role of the time element in the volume-cost relationships of each of the different manufacturing expenses. When the budget period selected by management is shorter than the time interval necessary to establish the volume-cost relationships of some of the manufacturing expenses, a clear understanding of the implications involved under such a situation is needed if the budget system is to be successful.

To illustrate the role of the time element in volume-cost relationships, assume that a person X has set up a variable budget for the repairs and maintenance expense of his personal automobile at the rate of 1 cent a mile on the basis that he would spend $15 on repairs and maintenance for every 1,500 miles traveled. Assume also that he travels only 500 miles a month and tries to apply his variable budget strictly on a monthly basis without giving any consideration to the time element involved in the volume-cost relationships of his automobile maintenance expense. He will find that in

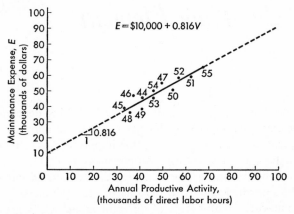

Fig. 10–1. Waltham Chemical Company. Scatter diagram and regression line of maintenance expense in relation to production volume on an annual basis.

one month he spends $15 on repairs and maintenance although his budget allows him only $5. For the other two months, he will find that he spends nothing although his budget tells him he should have spent $5 for each of these months. Does this mean that his variable budget of 1 cent a mile is wrong and hence that the system is inapplicable to his situation? The answer, obviously, is no. If, instead of applying his budget on a rigid monthly basis, he extends the length of his budget period to 3 months, 6 months, or 12 months, he would find that his variable budget system could work out well for him. The reason is that the maintenance expense of his automobile occurs at the rate of $15 for every 1,500 miles traveled. If he travels only 500 miles a month, the use of a short budget period, such as a month, a week, or a day, would make the relationship between his actual maintenance expense and mileage traveled completely erratic. When a longer budget period such as 3 months, 6 months, or 1 year is used, he would have traveled a long enough distance to necessitate repairs and maintenance jobs on his car. Consequently, the volume-cost relationship of his maintenance expense at the rate of 1 cent a mile would be true.

Situations similar to X's maintenance expense on his personal automobile can be found in many companies in different industries. If an intelligent statistical study of past experience is made, the role of the time element in the volume-cost relationships of any expense can be easily discerned. For instance, Fig. 10–1 shows a scatter diagram of the annual maintenance expense of Waltham Chemical Company in relation to its productive activity. Figure 10–2 shows the scatter diagram of its maintenance expense and productive activity on a monthly basis. Because of the nature of the manufacturing operation at this company, its maintenance

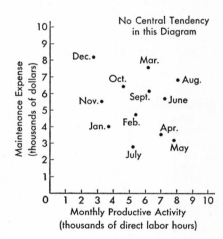

Fig. 10–2. Waltham Chemical Company. Scatter diagram showing lack of correlation between maintenance expense and production volume on a monthly basis.

expense is closely related to the productive activity on an annual basis, and a regression line indicating the volume-cost relationship of this expense at the rate of $E = \$10,000 + 0.816V$ can be drawn.[1] However, owing to the particular nature of this expense at Waltham Chemical Company, the use of a shorter time interval, in this case a month, destroys completely its volume-cost relationships obtained on an annual basis. Therefore, its monthly maintenance expenditures are dispersed throughout the scatter diagram in Fig. 10–2 showing a complete lack of correlation between this expense and productive activity on a monthly basis. Thus, no regression line can be drawn.

Repairs and maintenance of machinery and equipment are not the only expense that requires a relatively long period to bring out its volume-cost relationships. Even for expenses such as operating supplies which are consumed daily in production, a time period longer than a day or a week may be needed to establish its volume-cost relationships. For instance, a

[1] E = expense; V = productive activity.

TABLE 10–1

Waltham Chemical Company

Productive Activity and Maintenance Expense
1944 to 1955

	Productivity Activity	Maintenance Expense
Monthly basis:		
1955, January	3,650 hr	$ 4,000
February	5,380	4,750
March	6,150	7,580
April	6,990	3,560
May	8,040	6,840
June	7,200	5,700
July	5,180	2,800
August	7,740	3,200
September	6,220	6,120
October	4,560	6,460
November	3,220	5,500
December	2,730	8,210
Annual basis:		
1955	67,060 hr	$64,720
1954	46,000	50,000
1953	45,600	46,000
1952	57,000	58,300
1951	62,300	59,400
1950	54,250	50,600
1949	41,000	38,400
1948	35,700	36,000
1947	49,600	55,000
1946	37,400	47,000
1945	33,500	38,500
1944	41,500	45,300

foreman may requisition a certain amount of grease and rags sufficient to last for 4 or 5 weeks' operation. Whether his requisition is filled from stocks on hand or by new purchases, such expense is usually charged to his department at the time when the stock is issued or when an invoice is received. If the variable expense budget of this foreman is set up on a daily or weekly basis, he would find himself overspent on one day or during one week, but underspent for the rest of the month, even though a proper amount of grease and rags is used by him every day. It may be argued that, besides grease and rags, operating supplies consist of a number of other items, and their expenditures may be expected to balance out with one another during any given period. However, whether or not the expenditures of these different items can be balanced out depends upon the length of the period used. The shorter the budget period, the less likely it is that these expenditures will balance out. Depending upon the operating conditions at the particular business, not only a week but sometimes even a month may be found too short a period to bring out the volume-cost relationships of this expense.

Not only different manufacturing expenses behave differently within a business, but the same expense at one company will have a different nature at another company. Consequently, the time interval necessary to bring out the volume-cost relationships of one manufacturing expense may not be the same as that for a similar expense at another business. For example, assume that Y is the owner of a trucking company which operates a fleet of 50 trucks. A variable budget system has also been established for the repairs and maintenance expense of this fleet. While a month is found to be too short a period to establish the volume-cost relationships of maintenance expense of X's personal automobile, Y finds that it works out well for his trucking firm. There are two basic reasons why a month can bring out the volume-cost relationship of the maintenance expense at Y's trucking firm, whereas the same period fails to do so for X's personal automobile. First, being a commercial vehicle, each truck travels many more miles in a month than does X's personal automobile, which travels only 500 miles a month. Because of this higher rate of productive activity, i.e., mileage traveled, it is most likely that each truck would require some maintenance and repair work in a month's period. Under such circumstances, a month may be found to be a long enough period to bring out the volume-cost relationships of maintenance expense on each of these 50 trucks. Secondly, even if a few trucks do not need any repairs and maintenance work during a particular month, other trucks would need such work during this period. By considering 50 trucks as a unit, a month may be found long enough to bring out the volume-cost relationships between the aggregate maintenance expense and their combined mileage. Therefore, although a month is too short a period for establishing the volume-cost relationship of X's automobile maintenance expense, it is found appropriate for Y's fleet of 50 trucks.

The length of budget period selected by management is usually controlled by the length of reporting period of actual expenditures. In the management of any industrial enterprise it is necesary to keep operating executives informed of the actual expenditures of various manufacturing expenses at predetermined time intervals. Since expense budgets are designed to help management keep costs under better control, the length of budget period invariably conforms to the reporting period of actual expenditures.

Owing to the fact that manufacturing expenses are made up of a conglomeration of expenses, each of which has its own peculiar behavior in the particular business, the budget or reporting period selected by management may be longer or shorter than the time interval necessary to bring out the volume-cost relationships of a number of manufacturing expenses.

There is little or no problem for those expenses which need a shorter time interval than the budget period to establish their volume-cost relationships. If such relationships can be established on a daily or weekly basis, they will remain intact on a longer-term basis, such as at monthly, quarterly, or annual intervals. However, the reverse is not true as shown by the earlier illustrations of X's automobile-maintenance expense and Waltham Chemical Company. Under such circumstances, it will be necessary not only for the person responsible for the variable budgeting but also for the operating executives to understand fully the role of time element in the volume-cost relationships of these expenses. In their comparison of actual expenditures against budget allowances of such expenses, judgment has to be exercised as to whether a long enough period has elapsed to make such comparison meaningful. Unless this is done, an otherwise satisfactory budget system could be found unsatisfactory in the same manner as X's trying to apply the variable budget of his automobile maintenance expense on a rigid monthly basis.

The experience of Menlo Chemical Company is a good example of how ignorance of the time factor in volume-cost relationships had led to trouble in the variable budgeting system. One of the reasons given by the company for the unsatisfactory experience with its old flexible budget system was that it found its maintenance budget under this system hardly representative of what the company should have spent under actual operating conditions.[2] According to the budget established by its management consultant, the maintenance expense should vary in direct proportion with changes in volume of production. However, after the system had been put in, the company found that its maintenance expense occurred during the period when the plant was at its lowest level of activity. Conversely, it found that the higher the plant's level of operation, the lower would be its maintenance cost. This was due to the manufacturing operation wherein much of its maintenance work could be done only when the plant was shut down. At such time there would, of course, be no production in the plant.

Actually it was not variable budgeting per se that was inapplicable to the maintenance expense of Menlo Chemical Company. Under its old flexible budget system, weekly budgets had been introduced by its management consultant for every manufacturing expense of this company. On the same weekly basis, actual expenditures were compared against their corresponding budget allowances without giving any consideration to the role of time element in the volume-cost relationships of these expenses. Because of the nature of its fully mechanized operation, the maintenance expenses of Menlo Chemical Company behave much like the maintenance expense of

[2] Maintenance expense at Menlo Chemical Company constitutes approximately 25 per cent of its total (standard) processing cost and is, therefore, a significant item to the company (see Appendix C).

X's personal automobile or the maintenance expense of Waltham Chemical Company. The reason advanced by this company for its dissatisfaction with the flexible budget system is nothing more than X saying that his variable budget of 1 cent a mile for his automobile maintenance expense was wrong because he had spent nothing on the day he drove 210 miles from Boston to New York but had to spend $15 on repairs and maintenance on the day when his car was not driven, having been left with his mechanic for a checkup.

Among the real causes of trouble in the old flexible budget system at Menlo Chemical Company was the use of too short a budget period and disregard of this time factor in the volume-cost relationships of different manufacturing expenses. These, in turn, were the result of the complete lack of understanding by this management consultant of the peculiar nature of operation at this company and his unimaginative imitation of some practice that might have worked at some other companies. This management consultant had established the wrong budget estimates,[3] had selected the improper measure of level of activity,[4] and had introduced a budget and reporting period which were utterly meaningless under the operating conditions of Menlo Chemical Company. A week is too short a period to bring out the volume-cost relationships of a number of manufacturing expenses at Menlo Chemical Company, of which maintenance expense is only a predominant one. Therefore, even if he had established the correct budget estimate and selected the proper measure of level of activity, his introduction of weekly budgets and his ignorance of the time factor in the volume-cost relationships of different manufacturing expenses would have brought the flexible budget system at Menlo Chemical Company into trouble.

In addition to the incompetence of its management consultant, Menlo Chemical Company itself had contributed to this unsuccessful experiment with its old flexible budgeting system. All the blunders made by this management consultant could have been discovered and corrected by the company before the system was actually put in. It was not until a year after the old flexible budgeting system had been discarded that management of Menlo Chemical Company realized that its weekly budgets were meaningless and started to budget all its expenses on monthly and annual bases only.[5]

In contrast to the indiscriminate use of weekly budgets at Menlo Chemical Company, at companies where variable budgeting has been successful, monthly budgets are generally used for most manufacturing expenses and the role of the time element in the volume-cost relationships of these

[3] See Chap. 8 and Appendix C.
[4] See Chap. 9 and Appendix C.
[5] See Appendix C.

different expenses is usually taken into consideration by management. For instance, the controller of Otterbein Corporation stated:

"A month is the shortest practical budget period at our company. For a number of manufacturing expenses, 3 months would be a better budget period, although their actual expenditures would have to be reported to management at least once a month. Under such circumstances, management would have to exercise its judgment to determine whether or not a long enough period has elapsed to permit any intelligent comparison of actual expenditures against budget estimates of such expenses." [6]

Through this thorough knowledge of the operating conditions and complete understanding of the role of time element in the volume-cost relationships of different manufacturing expenses, an important cornerstone in the successful application of variable budgeting was laid at these companies, of which Otterbein Corporation is an example.

The fact that most companies use monthly budgets for their manufacturing expenses and that Menlo Chemical Company had an unsatisfactory experience with its weekly budgets does not mean that for certain special items weekly budgets should not be used. A typical example of such an exception is indirect labor, especially if the incurrence of this expense is dependent upon daily volume of production. Since labor statistics at most companies are collected and compiled on daily and weekly bases, there is little practical difficulty in reporting this item on a weekly basis. However, whether or not management wants indirect labor reported and compared with its budget allowance on a weekly basis depends to a large extent upon the importance and size of this expense at the particular company. For instance, at Otterbein Corporation indirect labor constitutes only 10 per cent of its direct productive labor, whereas at Lafayette Brass Company indirect labor constitutes almost 50 per cent of direct productive labor at some departments. Therefore, even though Lafayette Brass Company had used monthly budgets for all its manufacturing expenses, at the time when the field study was made, it was contemplating the use of weekly budgets for its indirect labor expense so that more prompt information could be provided to operating management and more timely action taken. On the other hand, because this expense is only of minor significance at Otterbein Corporation, they do not feel it necessary to report such expense on a weekly basis.

In summary, the role of time element in establishing the volume-cost relationships of a manufacturing expense is one of the important factors which should not be overlooked in the practical application of variable budgeting. Different manufacturing expenses require different minimum time periods to bring out their volume-cost relationships. Since the length

[6] See Appendix B.

of budget period usually conforms to the length of reporting period selected by management, some manufacturing expenses will need time intervals longer than the budget period to bring out their volume-cost relationships. Under such circumstances, judgment must be exercised in the comparison of actual expenditures against budget allowances as to whether a long enough period has elapsed to make such comparison meaningful. Failure to understand the operating conditions at the particular business and to appreciate the role of time element in the volume-cost relationships of different manufacturing expenses together with the use of an improperly selected budget period are among the reasons leading to some alleged failures of variable budgeting, which might otherwise have been satisfactorily used.

THE ROLE OF TIME ELEMENT IN VOLUME-COST-PROFIT STUDIES

In studies of volume-cost relationships for forecasting financial results of operations at different volumes of business, an implicit assumption frequently used is that the production of a given period will be completed and sold during the same period. Naturally, no business would like to produce for commercial purposes anything that it does not expect to be able to sell. And, given a long enough period, all production will be sold. However, both for the purpose of planning its operations and for keeping itself informed of operating progress, the budget period used by management is often shorter than the one that can allow for a complete synchronization of sales and production. Under such circumstances, even when everything is under proper control by management, actual reported profits are often found to be different from the ones predicted by volume-cost-profit studies for the actual volume of business experienced. In order to avoid any misconception about the reliability of volume-cost-profit studies as a tool of management, it is important for the person responsible for the preparation of such studies, as well as for the operating management making use of such studies, to understand fully the role of time element in volume-cost-profit studies and to be familiar with the relationships between the predicted profit and the reported profit as well as the reasons contributing to their difference.

The following illustration, the Owen Manufacturing Company, shows a situation where reported profit differs from predicted profit and yet everything is under management's control. The reasons for such variation, including the role played by the time element or length of budget period, are readily brought out from the facts therein.

Assume that management of Owen Manufacturing Company had forecasted that its sales and production for 1955 would be 1,000,000 units. The selling price of its product and the company's cost structure were expected to be as follows:

	Per Unit of Product	Total per Year
Selling price	$1.00	
Variable cost of sales:		
Material	$0.10	
Direct labor	0.20	
Variable manufacturing expenses	0.10	
Total variable cost of sales	0.40	
Gross contribution	$0.60	
Fixed manufacturing expenses		$200,000
Selling and administrative expenses		200,000

On the basis of preceding estimates, a volume-cost-profit diagram, as shown in Fig. 10–3, was constructed and a pre-tax profit of $200,000 was expected for the predicted volume.

Since the forecast profit and loss in Fig. 10–3 is on an annual basis, the length of budget period would appear to be too long to enable management to make a timely comparison of the result of current operation against its predetermined objective. In order to facilitate this comparison on a more current basis, a volume-cost-profit diagram on a quarterly basis, shown in Fig. 10–4, was prepared. The fixed expenses in this diagram are one-fourth of the same expenses on an annual basis, on the assumption that they are evenly spread throughout the year. With these estimated sales at an average

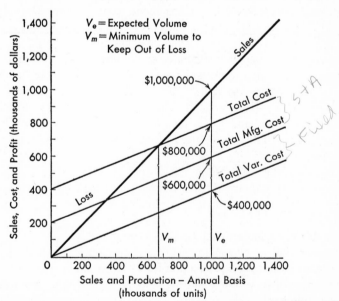

Fig. 10–3. Owen Manufacturing Company. Volume-cost-profit diagram: forecast for 1955, annual basis.

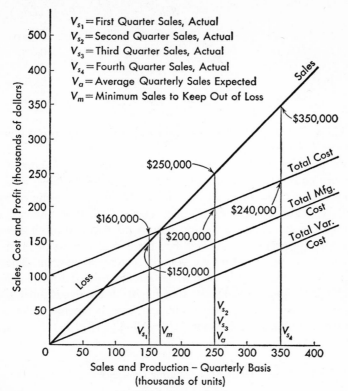

Fig. 10-4. Owen Manufacturing Company. Volume-cost-profit diagram: quarterly basis for 1955.

quarterly rate of 250,000 units, an average quarterly profit of $50,000 was set as the objective.

Actual 1955 sales and production in physical units experienced by Owen Manufacturing Company are as follows:

	Production	Sales
First quarter	200,000	150,000
Second quarter	250,000	250,000
Third quarter	300,000	250,000
Fourth quarter	250,000	350,000
1955—total	1,000,000	1,000,000

There was no inventory at the beginning and at the end of the year.

Assume further that everything during 1955, including selling price, product mix, material cost, wage rate, production efficiency, etc., turned out as management had expected. According to the volume-cost-profit studies previously made by the company, its quarterly profit for the volume of business actually realized would be as follows:

	Sales	Profit (Loss)
First quarter	$ 150,000	($ 10,000)
Second quarter	250,000	50,000
Third quarter	250,000	50,000
Fourth quarter	350,000	110,000
1955—total	$1,000,000	$200,000

A detailed profit and loss statement from which the above profit figures are extracted is shown in Table 10–2.

Since everything was under management's control, would actual reported *quarterly* profit of Owen Manufacturing Company be the same as that predicted by the volume-cost-profit diagram for the actual volume of business realized? The answer is generally no. Depending upon the accounting method used by the company for inventory valuation and profit determination, a variety of profit figures could be obtained, and most of them would differ from those predicted by the volume-cost-profit diagram. The multitude of such variations can be seen by an examination of Table 10–3 which tabulates the various profit figures that might be obtained under different methods of accounting. Detailed profit and loss statements under each of these selected methods are shown in Tables 10–4 to 10–10.

TABLE 10–2

Owen Manufacturing Company

Profit and Loss Statement
Forecasted by Volume-Cost-Profit Diagram—1955

	Per Unit	First Quarter	Second Quarter	Third Quarter	Fourth Quarter	1955
Sales	$1.00	$150,000	$250,000	$250,000	$350,000	$1,000,000
Variable cost:						
Materials	$0.10	15,000	25,000	25,000	35,000	100,000
Labor	0.20	30,000	50,000	50,000	70,000	200,000
Variable manufacturing expense	0.10	15,000	25,000	25,000	35,000	100,000
Total variable cost	$0.40	$ 60,000	$100,000	$100,000	$140,000	$ 400,000
Gross contribution	$0.60	$ 90,000	$150,000	$150,000	$210,000	$ 600,000
Fixed manufacturing expense	...	$ 50,000	$ 50,000	$ 50,000	$ 50,000	$ 200,000
Selling and administrative expense	...	50,000	50,000	50,000	50,000	200,000
Total fixed cost	...	$100,000	$100,000	$100,000	$100,000	$ 400,000
Net profit before income taxes	...	($ 10,000)	$ 50,000	$ 50,000	$110,000	$ 200,000

TABLE 10–3

Owen Manufacturing Company

Comparison of Reported Profit Under Different Conventional Accounting Methods
with Profit Predicted by Volume-Cost-Profit Diagram for Identical Operations

	First Quarter	Second Quarter	Third Quarter	Fourth Quarter	1955
Profit (loss) per					
1 Volume-cost-profit diagram	($10,000)	$50,000	$50,000	$110,000	$200,000
2 Standard cost methods					
2a Normal production volume of 200,000 units	2,500	50,000	62,500	85,000	200,000
2b Normal production volume of 250,000 units	–0–	50,000	60,000	90,000	200,000
2c Standard production volume = expected sales * and lifo for finished goods inventory	6,667	50,000	60,000	83,333	200,000
2d Standard production volume = expected sales * and fifo for finished goods inventory	6,667	43,333	60,000	90,000	200,000
3 Actual cost methods:					
3a Last-in first-out	2,500	50,000	58,333	89,167	200,000
3b Average	2,500	47,917	56,845	92,738	200,000
3c First-in first-out	2,500	47,500	56,667	93,333	200,000
Operating statistics in physical units:					
Production	200,000	250,000	300,000	250,000	1,000,000
Sales	150,000	250,000	250,000	350,000	1,000,000
Beginning inventory	–0–	50,000	50,000	100,000	–0–
Ending inventory	50,000	50,000	100,000	–0–	–0–
Increase (decrease) in inventory	50,000	–0–	50,000	(100,000)	–0–

* Expected sales are same as actual sales in this illustration.

TABLE 10-4

Owen Manufacturing Company

Profit and Loss Statement Reported under Standard Cost Method
with a Normal Production Volume of 200,000 Units per Quarter—1955

	Per Unit	First Quarter	Second Quarter	Third Quarter	Fourth Quarter	1955
Sales	$1.00	$150,000	$250,000	$250,000	$350,000	$1,000,000
Standard cost of sales						
Material	$0.10	15,000	25,000	25,000	35,000	100,000
Labor	0.20	30,000	50,000	50,000	70,000	200,000
Variable manufacturing expenses	0.10	15,000	25,000	25,000	35,000	100,000
	$0.40	$ 60,000	$100,000	$100,000	$140,000	$ 400,000
Fixed manufacturing expenses	0.25	37,500	62,500	62,500	87,500	250,000
Standard cost of sales	$0.65	$ 97,500	$162,500	$162,500	$227,500	$ 650,000
Standard gross margin	$0.35	$ 52,500	$ 87,500	$ 87,500	$122,500	$ 350,000
Volume variance		–0–	12,500cr.	25,000cr.	12,500cr.	50,000cr.
		$ 52,000	$100,000	$112,500	$135,000	$ 400,000
Selling and administrative expenses		50,000	50,000	50,000	50,000	200,000
Net profit		$ 2,500	$ 50,000	$ 62,500	$ 85,000	$ 200,000
Net profit per volume-cost-profit diagram		($ 10,000)	$ 50,000	$ 50,000	$110,000	$ 200,000
Difference in net profit		+$ 12,500	–0–	+$ 12,500	–$ 25,000	–0–

166

Beginning inventory:					
Units	-0-	50M	50M	100M	-0-
Fixed manufacturing expenses at standard *	-0-	$ 12,500	$ 12,500	$ 25,000	-0-
Cost of goods manufactured:					
Units	200M	250M	300M	250M	1,000M
Fixed manufacturing expenses at standard *	$ 50,000	$ 62,500	$ 75,000	$ 62,500	$ 250,000
Volume variance †					
Units	-0-	50M	100M	50M	200M
Fixed manufacturing expenses at standard *	-0-	$ 12,500cr.	$ 25,000cr.	$ 12,500cr.	$ 50,000cr.
Ending inventory:					
Units	50M	50M	100M	-0-	-0-
Fixed manufacturing expenses at standard *	$ 12,500	$ 12,500	$ 25,000	-0-	-0-
Cost of sales:					
Units	150M	250M	250M	350M	1,000M
Fixed manufacturing expenses at standard *	$ 37,500	$ 62,500	$ 62,500	$ 87,500	$ 250,000
Increase (decrease) inventory:					
Units	50M	-0-	50M	(100M)	-0-
Fixed manufacturing expenses at standard *	$ 12,500	-0-	$ 12,500	($ 25,000)	-0-

* Standard fixed manufacturing expenses per unit of product = $50,000 ÷ 200M = $0.25 per unit.
† Based upon production volume.

167

TABLE 10–5

Owen Manufacturing Company

Profit and Loss Statement Reported under Standard Cost Method
with a Normal Production Volume of 250,000 Units per Quarter—1955

	Per Unit	First Quarter	Second Quarter	Third Quarter	Fourth Quarter	1955
Sales	$1.00	$150,000	$250,000	$250,000	$350,000	$1,000,000
Standard cost of sales:						
Material	$0.10	15,000	25,000	25,000	35,000	100,000
Labor	0.20	30,000	50,000	50,000	70,000	200,000
Variable manufacturing expenses	0.10	15,000	25,000	25,000	35,000	100,000
	$0.40	$ 60,000	$100,000	$100,000	$140,000	$ 400,000
Fixed manufacturing expenses	0.20	30,000	50,000	50,000	70,000	200,000
Standard cost of sales	$0.60	$ 90,000	$150,000	$150,000	$210,000	$ 600,000
Standard gross margin	$0.40	$ 60,000	$100,000	$100,000	$140,000	$ 400,000
Volume variance—F (U)		(10,000) dr.	–0–	10,000 cr.	–0–	–0–
		$ 50,000	$100,000	$110,000	$140,000	$ 400,000
Selling and administrative expenses		50,000	50,000	50,000	50,000	200,000
Net profit (loss)		–0–	$ 50,000	$ 60,000	$ 90,000	$ 200,000
Net profit per volume-cost-profit diagram		($ 10,000)	$ 50,000	$ 50,000	$110,000	$ 200,000
Difference in net profit		+$ 10,000	–0–	+$ 10,000	–$ 20,000	–0–

Beginning inventory:					
Units	-0-	50M	50M	100M	-0-
Fixed manufacturing expenses at standard *	-0-	$ 10,000	$ 10,000	$ 20,000	-0-
Cost of goods manufactured:					
Units	200M	250M	300M	250M	1,000M
Fixed manufacturing expenses at standard *	$ 40,000	$ 50,000	$ 60,000	$ 50,000	$ 200,000
Volume variance †					
Units	(50M)	-0-	50M	-0-	-0-
Fixed manufacturing expenses at standard *	$ 10,000dr.	-0-	$ 10,000cr.	-0-	-0-
Ending inventory:					
Units	50M	50M	100M	-0-	-0-
Fixed manufacturing expenses at standard *	$ 10,000	$ 10,000	$ 20,000	-0-	-0-
Cost of sales:					
Units	150M	250M	250M	350M	1,000M
Fixed manufacturing expenses at standard *	$ 30,000	$ 50,000	$ 50,000	$ 70,000	$ 200,000
Increase (decrease) in inventory:					
Units	50M	-0-	50M	(100M)	-0-
Fixed manufacturing expenses at standard *	$ 10,000	-0-	$ 10,000	($ 20,000)	-0-

* Standard fixed manufacturing expenses per unit of product = $50,000 ÷ 250M = $0.20 per unit.
† Based upon production volume.

TABLE 10–6

Owen Manufacturing Company

Profit and Loss Statement Reported under Standard Cost Method
with Expected (Quarterly) Sales Volume as Standard Volume of Production
and Lifo Treatment of Finished Goods Inventory—1955

	Per Unit	First Quarter	Second Quarter	Third Quarter	Fourth Quarter	1955
Sales	$1.00	$150,000	$250,000	$250,000	$350,000	$1,000,000
Standard cost of sales:						
Material	$0.10	15,000	25,000	25,000	35,000	100,000
Labor	0.20	30,000	50,000	50,000	70,000	200,000
Variable manufacturing expenses	0.10	15,000	25,000	25,000	35,000	100,000
	$0.40	$ 60,000	$100,000	$100,000	$140,000	$ 400,000
Fixed manufacturing expenses		50,000	50,000	50,000	62,381	212,381
Standard cost of sales		$110,000	$150,000	$150,000	$202,381	$ 612,381
Standard gross margin		$ 40,000	$100,000	$100,000	$147,619	$ 387,619
Volume variance—F (U)		16,667cr.	–0–	10,000cr.	(14,286)dr.	12,381cr.
		$ 56,667	$100,000	$110,000	$133,333	$ 400,000
Selling and administrative expenses		50,000	50,000	50,000	50,000	200,000
Net profit		$ 6,667	$ 50,000	$ 60,000	$ 83,333	$ 200,000
Net profit per volume-cost-profit diagram		($ 10,000)	$ 50,000	$ 50,000	$110,000	$ 200,000
Difference in net profit		+$ 16,667	–0–	+$ 10,000	–$ 26,667	–0–

Beginning inventory:					
Units	-0-	50M	50M	100M	-0-
Fixed manufacturing expenses at standard	-0-	$ 16,667*	$ 16,667*	50M—$ 16,667* 50M— 10,000‡	-0-
Cost of goods manufactured:					
Units	200M	250M	300M	250M	1,000M
Fixed manufacturing expenses at standard	$ 66,667*	$ 50,000†	$ 60,000‡	$ 35,714§	$ 212,381
Volume variance:					
Units	50M	-0-	50M	100M	-0-
Fixed manufacturing expenses at standard	$ 16,667cr.*	-0-	$ 10,000cr.‡	($ 14,286)dr.§	$ 12,381cr.
Ending inventory:					
Units	50M	50M	100M	-0-	-0-
Fixed manufacturing expenses at standard	$ 16,667*	$ 16,667*	50M—$ 16,667* 50M— 10,000‡	-0-	-0-
Cost of sales:					
Units	150M	250M	250M	350M	1,000M
Fixed manufacturing expenses at standard	$ 50,000*	$ 50,000†	$ 50,000‡	50M—$ 16,667* 50M— 10,000‡ 250M— 35,714§	$ 212,381
Increase (decrease) in inventory:					
Units	50M	-0-	50M	(100M)	
Fixed manufacturing expenses at standard	$ 16,667*	-0-	$ 10,000‡	($ 26,667)	

* Standard fixed manufacturing expense per unit of product = $50,000 ÷ 150M = 33⅓¢ per unit.
† Standard fixed manufacturing expense per unit of product = $50,000 ÷ 250M = 20¢ per unit.
‡ Standard fixed manufacturing expense per unit of product = $50,000 ÷ 250M = 20¢ per unit.
§ Standard fixed manufacturing expense per unit of product = $50,000 ÷ 350M = 14.286¢ per unit.

TABLE 10–7

Owen Manufacturing Company

Profit and Loss Statement Reported under Standard Cost Method with Expected (Quarterly) Sales Volume as Standard Volume of Production and Fifo Treatment of Finished Goods Inventory—1955

	Per Unit	First Quarter	Second Quarter	Third Quarter	Fourth Quarter	1955
Sales	$1.00	$150,000	$250,000	$250,000	$350,000	$1,000,000
Standard cost of sales:						
Material	$0.10	15,000	25,000	25,000	35,000	100,000
Labor	0.20	30,000	50,000	50,000	70,000	200,000
Variable manufacturing expenses	0.10	15,000	25,000	25,000	35,000	100,000
	$0.40	$ 60,000	$100,000	$100,000	$140,000	$ 400,000
Fixed manufacturing expenses		50,000	56,667	50,000	55,714	212,381
Standard cost of sales		$110,000	$156,667	$150,000	$195,714	$ 612,381
Standard gross margin		$ 40,000	$ 93,333	$100,000	$154,286	$ 387,619
Volume variance		16,667cr.	-0-	10,000cr.	14,286dr.	12,381cr.
		$ 56,667	$ 93,333	$110,000	$140,000	$ 400,000
Selling and administrative expenses		50,000	50,000	50,000	50,000	200,000
Net profit		$ 6,667	$ 43,333	$ 60,000	$ 90,000	$ 200,000
Net profit per volume-cost-profit diagram		($ 10,000)	$ 50,000	$ 50,000	$110,000	$ 200,000
Difference in net profit		+$ 16,667	–$ 6,667	+$ 10,000	– $ 20,000	–0–

Beginning inventory:					
Units	-0-	50M	50M	100M	-0-
Fixed manufacturing expenses at standard	-0-	$ 16,667*	$ 10,000†	$ 20,000‡	-0-
Cost of goods manufactured:					
Units	200M	250M	300M	250M	1,000M
Fixed manufacturing expenses at standard	$ 66,667*	$ 50,000†	$ 60,000‡	$ 35,714§	$ 212,381
Volume variance:					
Units	50M	-0-	50M	(100M)	-0-
Fixed manufacturing expenses at standard	$ 16,667cr.*	-0-	$ 10,000cr.‡	$ 14,286dr.§	$ 12,381cr.
Ending inventory:					
Units	50M	50M	100M	-0-	-0-
Fixed manufacturing expenses at standard	$ 16,667*	$ 10,000†	$ 20,000‡	-0-	-0-
Cost of sales:					
Units	150M	250M	250M	350M	1,000M
Fixed manufacturing expenses at standard	$ 50,000*	50M—$ 16,667* 200M—$ 40,000†	50M—$ 10,000† 200M—$ 40,000‡	100M—$ 20,000‡ 150M—35,714§	$ 212,381
Increase (decrease) in inventory:					
Units	50M	-0-	50M	(100M)	-0-
Fixed manufacturing expenses at standard	$ 16,667*	($ 6,667)	$ 10,000	($ 20,000)	-0-

* Standard fixed manufacturing expense per unit of product = $50,000 ÷ 150M = 33⅓¢ per unit.
† Standard fixed manufacturing expense per unit of product = $50,000 ÷ 250M = 20¢ per unit.
‡ Standard fixed manufacturing expense per unit of product = $50,000 ÷ 250M = 20¢ per unit.
§ Standard fixed manufacturing expense per unit of product = $50,000 ÷ 350M = 14.286¢ per unit.

TABLE 10–8

Owen Manufacturing Company

Profit and Loss Statement Reported under Actual Cost Method
with Inventory Valuation Based on Last-In First-Out Method—1955

	Per Unit	First Quarter	Second Quarter	Third Quarter	Fourth Quarter	1955
Sales	$1.00	$150,000	$250,000	$250,000	$350,000	$1,000,000
Cost of sales:						
Material	$0.10	15,000	25,000	25,000	35,000	100,000
Labor	0.20	30,000	50,000	50,000	70,000	200,000
Variable manufacturing expenses	0.10	15,000	25,000	25,000	35,000	100,000
	$0.40	$ 60,000	$100,000	$100,000	$140,000	$ 400,000
Fixed manufacturing expenses		37,500	50,000	41,667	70,833	200,000
Total cost of sales		$ 97,500	$150,000	$141,667	$210,833	$ 600,000
Gross profit		$ 52,500	$100,000	$108,333	$139,167	$ 400,000
Selling and administrative expenses		50,000	50,000	50,000	50,000	200,000
Net profit		$ 2,500	$ 50,000	$ 58,333	$ 89,167	$ 200,000
Net profit per volume-cost-profit diagram		($ 10,000)	$ 50,000	$ 50,000	$110,000	$ 200,000
Difference in net profit		+$ 12,500	–0–	+$ 8,333	–$ 20,833	–0–

Beginning inventory:					
Units	-0-	50M	50M	100M	-0-
Fixed manufacturing expenses	-0-	$ 12,500*	$ 12,500*	50M—$ 12,500* 50M— 8,333‡	-0-
Cost of goods manufactured:					
Units	200M	250M	300M	250M	1,000M
Fixed manufacturing expenses—total	$ 50,000*	$ 50,000†	$ 50,000‡	$ 50,000§	$ 200,000
Ending inventory:					
Units	50M	50M	100M	-0-	-0-
Fixed manufacturing expenses	$ 12,500*	$ 12,500*	50M—$ 12,500* 50M— 8,333‡	-0-	-0-
Cost of sales:					
Units	150M	250M	250M	350M	1,000M
Fixed manufacturing expenses	$ 37,500*	$ 50,000†	$ 41,667‡	50M—$ 12,500* 50M— 8,333‡ 250M— 50,000§	$ 200,000
Increase (decrease) in inventory:					
Units	50M	-0-	50M	(100M)	-0-
Fixed manufacturing expenses	$ 12,500*	-0-	$ 8,333‡	($ 20,833)	-0-

* Fixed manufacturing expense per unit of product = $50,000 ÷ 200M = 25¢ per unit.
† Fixed manufacturing expense per unit of product = $50,000 ÷ 250M = 20¢ per unit.
‡ Fixed manufacturing expense per unit of product = $50,000 ÷ 300M = 16.667¢ per unit.
§ Fixed manufacturing expense per unit of product = $50,000 ÷ 250M = 20¢ per unit.

TABLE 10–9

Owen Manufacturing Company

Profit and Loss Statement Reported under Actual Cost Method
with Inventory Valuation Based on Average Method—1955

	Per Unit	First Quarter	Second Quarter	Third Quarter	Fourth Quarter	1955
Sales	$1.00	$150,000	$250,000	$250,000	$350,000	$1,000,000
Cost of sales:						
Material	$0.10	15,000	25,000	25,000	35,000	100,000
Labor	0.20	30,000	50,000	50,000	70,000	200,000
Variable manufacturing expenses	0.10	15,000	25,000	25,000	35,000	100,000
	$0.40	$ 60,000	$100,000	$100,000	$100,000	$ 400,000
Fixed manufacturing expenses		37,500	52,083	43,155	67,262	200,000
Total cost of sales		$ 97,500	$152,083	$143,155	$207,262	$ 600,000
Gross profit		$ 52,500	$ 97,917	$106,845	$142,738	$ 400,000
Selling and administrative expenses		50,000	50,000	50,000	50,000	200,000
Net profit		$ 2,500	$ 47,917	$ 56,845	$ 92,738	$ 200,000
Net profit per volume-cost-profit diagram		($ 10,000)	$ 50,000	$ 50,000	$110,000	$ 200,000
Difference in net profit		+$ 12,500	–$ 2,083	+$ 6,845	–$ 17,262	–0–

Beginning inventory:					
Units	-0-	50M	50M	100M	-0-
Fixed manufacturing expenses	-0-	$ 12,500ᵃ	$ 10,417ᵉ	$ 17,262ᶠ	-0-
Cost of goods manufactured:					
Units	200M	250M	300M	250M	1,000M
Fixed manufacturing expenses	$ 50,000ᵃ	$ 50,000ᵇ	$ 50,000ᶜ	$ 50,000ᵈ	$ 200,000
Ending inventory:					
Units	50M	50M	100M	-0-	-0-
Fixed manufacturing expenses	$ 12,500ᵃ	$ 10,417ᵉ	$ 17,262ᶠ	-0-	-0-
Cost of sales:					
Units	150M	250M	250M	350M	1,000M
Fixed manufacturing expenses	$ 37,500	$ 52,083ᵉ	$ 43,155ᶠ	$ 67,262	$ 200,000
Increase (decrease) in inventory:					
Units	50M	-0-	50M	(100M)	-0-
Fixed manufacturing expenses	$ 12,500ᵃ	($ 2,083)	$ 6,845	($ 17,262)	-0-

ᵃ Fixed manufacturing expense per unit of product = $50,000 ÷ 200M = 25¢ per unit.
ᵇ Fixed manufacturing expense per unit of product = $50,000 ÷ 250M = 20¢ per unit.
ᶜ Fixed manufacturing expense per unit of product = $50,000 ÷ 300M = 16.667¢ per unit.
ᵈ Fixed manufacturing expense per unit of product = $50,000 ÷ 250M = 20¢ per unit.
ᵉ Fixed manufacturing expense per unit of product = $62,500 ÷ 300M = 20.833¢ per unit.
ᶠ Fixed manufacturing expense per unit of product = $60,417 ÷ 350M = 17.262¢ per unit.

TABLE 10-10

Owen Manufacturing Company

Profit and Loss Statement Reported under Actual Cost Method
with Inventory Valuation Based on First-In First-Out Method—1955

	Per Unit	First Quarter	Second Quarter	Third Quarter	Fourth Quarter	1955
Sales	$1.00	$150,000	$250,000	$250,000	$350,000	$1,000,000
Cost of sales:						
Material	$0.10	$ 15,000	$ 25,000	$ 25,000	$ 35,000	$ 100,000
Labor	0.20	30,000	50,000	50,000	70,000	200,000
Variable manufacturing expenses	0.10	15,000	25,000	25,000	35,000	100,000
	$0.40	$ 60,000	$100,000	$100,000	$140,000	$ 400,000
Fixed manufacturing expenses		37,500	52,500	43,333	66,667	200,000
Total cost of sales		$ 97,500	$152,500	$143,333	$206,667	$ 600,000
Gross profit		$ 52,500	$ 97,500	$106,667	$143,333	$ 400,000
Selling and administrative expenses		50,000	50,000	50,000	50,000	200,000
Net profit		$ 2,500	$ 47,500	$ 56,667	$ 93,333	$ 200,000
Net profit per volume-cost-profit diagram		($ 10,000)	$ 50,000	$ 50,000	$110,000	$ 200,000
Difference in profit		+$ 12,500	-$ 2,500	+$ 6,667	-$ 16,667	-0-

178

Beginning inventory:					
Units	–0–	50M	50M	100M	–0–
Fixed manufacturing expenses	–0–	$ 12,500*	$ 10,000†	$ 16,667‡	–0–
Cost of goods manufactured:					
Units	200M	250M	300M	250M	1,000M
Fixed manufacturing expenses	$ 50,000*	$ 50,000†	$ 50,000‡	$ 50,000§	$ 200,000
Ending inventory:					
Units	50M	50M	100M	–0–	–0–
Fixed manufacturing expenses	$ 12,500*	$ 10,000†	$ 16,667‡	–0–	–0–
Cost of sales:					
Units	150M	250M	250M	350M	1,000M
Fixed manufacturing expenses	$ 37,500*	50M—$ 12,500* 200M— 40,000†	50M—$ 10,000† 200M— 33,333‡	100M—$ 16,667‡ 250M— 50,000§	$ 200,000
Increase (decrease) in inventory:					
Units	50M	–0–	50M	(100M)	–0–
Fixed manufacturing expenses	$ 12,500*	($ 2,500)	$ 6,667	($ 16,667)	–0–

* Fixed manufacturing expense per unit of product = $50,000 ÷ 200M = 25¢ per unit.
† Fixed manufacturing expense per unit of product = $50,000 ÷ 250M = 20¢ per unit.
‡ Fixed manufacturing expense per unit of product = $50,000 ÷ 300M = 16.667¢ per unit.
§ Fixed manufacturing expense per unit of product = $50,000 ÷ 250M = 20¢ per unit.

Table 10–3 shows that, although on an annual basis the reported profit under any conventional accounting method in this illustration would agree with the profit predicted by the volume-cost-profit diagram, the quarterly profits obtained under these conventional methods provide an array of figures, most of which differ from the ones predicted by the volume-cost-profit diagram (Fig. 10–4 or Table 10–2). Out of 28 quarterly profit figures provided by the seven selected "acceptable" accounting methods, only four agree with the profit shown by the volume-cost-profit diagram in this illustration.

Over and above this multitude of profit figures per se which Owen Manufacturing Company might obtain by using different accounting methods, the degree of variation of some of these reported quarterly profits from their counterparts predicted by the volume-cost-profit diagram could be astoundingly alarming to a person unfamiliar with the intricacies of accounting. For instance, during the first quarter of 1955, when sales were at their low volume of 150,000 units, a loss of $10,000 is indicated by the volume-cost-profit diagram. In place of this loss, the conventional methods of accounting could produce profit figures ranging from nothing (2b) to as high as $6,667 (2c and 2d) in this illustration. During the fourth quarter of 1955, when actual (sales) volume of business reached its highest peak of 350,000 units, a profit of $110,000 is shown by the volume-cost-profit diagram. However, for the same volume of business, the reported profits which range from $83,333 (2d) to $93,333 (3c) are much less than the predicted profit of $110,000.

One of the main reasons for the variation of reported profits from the profit predicted by the volume-cost-profit diagram for the same volume of business realized is the unavoidable difference between production volume and sales volume in a short period of time. In the preceding illustration of Owen Manufacturing Company, although its total production and total sales are identical on an annual basis, they differ on a quarterly basis during the first, third, and fourth quarters of 1955. Under any conventional method of accounting, when current production exceeds current sales (in physical units), part of the fixed manufacturing expense of the current period is carried over through increased inventory into the next period. By deferring to the future the fixed manufacturing expenses incurred during the current period, the reported cost charged against the revenues of the current period is reduced below what has been actually incurred during this period. Conversely, when the sales volume exceeds production volume (in physical units), some of the fixed manufacturing expenses carried over from the preceding period are added to the fixed manufacturing expenses of the current period through reduction of inventory in determining the proper accounting charges against the revenues of the current period.

However, in the construction of the volume-cost-profit diagram, by assuming a complete synchronization of sales and production, the fixed manufacturing expenses charged against the revenues of the current period comprise only the fixed manufacturing expenses incurred during the current period. Hence, if sales volume does not equal the production volume, through the intricacies of carry-over of fixed manufacturing expenses from a preceding period into the next period, the reported profit would be found to differ from the profit predicted by the volume-cost-profit diagram for the same (sales) volume of business. The difference between the predicted profit and the profit reported under the conventional method of accounting is made up of the difference between the "fixed manufacturing expenses carried over from the preceding period" and "the fixed manufacturing expenses carried into the next period." [7] Generally, the reported profit would be higher than the profit predicted by the volume-cost-profit diagram when there is an increase in inventory, and the reported profit would be less

---

[7] When standard cost with standard overhead rate established on the basis of *normal volume* of production (2a or 2b) is used as the basis of inventory valuation, such as at Lafayette Brass Company, the difference between the profit forecast by the volume-cost-profit diagram for the actual (sales) volume of business realized and the profit reported under the standard cost method can be easily determined by the difference between the volume variance computed on the basis of actual production volume and the volume variance computed on the basis of actual sales volume. The reason is that the difference between these two volume variances is equivalent to the difference between the fixed manufacturing expenses carried over from the preceding period and the fixed manufacturing expenses carried over to the next period as shown by the following computation:

$$Var_p = (Vol_p - Vol_n) \times R$$
$$Var_s = (Vol_s - Vol_n) \times R$$
$$Var_p - Var_s = (Vol_p - Vol_s) \times R$$

Substitute
$$Vol_p - Vol_s = Inv_e - Inv_b$$

Then
$$Var_p - Var_s = (Inv_e - Inv_b) \times R$$
$$= Inv_e \times R - Inv_b \times R$$
$$= FME_{ei} - FME_{bi}$$

where Var_p = volume variance based upon production volume
  Var_s = volume variance based upon sales volume
  Vol_p = actual production volume
  Vol_s = actual sales volume
  Vol_n = normal production volume
  R = standard fixed manufacturing cost per unit of product at normal production volume
  Inv_e = ending inventory
  Inv_b = beginning inventory
  FME_{bi} = fixed manufacturing expenses carried over from preceding period through beginning inventory
  FME_{ei} = fixed manufacturing expenses carried into next period through ending inventory

In the profit and loss statement of the Mill Division of Lafayette Brass Company's Plant A for March, 1952, the volume variance of $35,000 under March Actual was computed on the basis of March production volume. The corresponding volume variance of $32,000 under Adjusted Budget was computed on the basis of March sales. The variation of reported profit from profit forecast due to this variation of production volume from sales volume alone is represented by the difference of $3,000 between these two volume variances (see Appendix A, Table A–6).

than the predicted profit when there is a reduction in inventory. Therefore, as inventories of Owen Manufacturing Company were built up during the first and third quarter of 1955, its reported profits are found to be larger than the ones predicted by the volume-cost-profit diagram. And, as its inventories were used up during the fourth quarter of 1955, the reported profits are found to be less than the one predicted by the volume-cost-profit diagram (see Table 10–3).

In addition to the variation of production volume from sales volume, the difference between reported profit and the profit predicted by the volume-cost-profit diagram is also dependent upon the method of inventory valuation used by a company in its profit determination. Since the fixed manufacturing expenses per unit of product carried over from the preceding period into the next period would differ with different methods of inventory valuation, different profit figures for the same operation could result from the use of different accounting methods. Consequently, an array of profit figures is found in Table 10–3 even for the identical operation of the business, simply because of the use of different methods of accounting.

Because of this involvement of accounting methods in determining the periodic profit of a business, exceptions can be found to the general belief that, when production volume equals sales volume, reported profit would be the same as that predicted by the volume-cost-profit diagram. For instance, during the second quarter of 1955, the production volume of Owen Manufacturing Company was the same as its sales volume. However, Table 10–3 shows that the reported profits for this quarter under three of the seven selected conventional methods (2d, 3b, and 3c) differ from those predicted by the volume-cost-profit diagram. This is due to the fact that the company had stocks on hand at the beginning of the second quarter and the fixed manufacturing expenses per unit of product carried over from the preceding quarter were not the same as the fixed manufacturing expenses allocated to each unit of product produced during the second quarter. Thus, by the use of various first-in first-out (2d and 3c) and average (3b) methods of inventory valuation, part of the fixed manufacturing expenses incurred during the current period is substituted for the fixed manufacturing expenses carried over from the preceding period (at a different dollar figure but for the same physical quantity) in the preparation of profit and loss statements.

The result is that the reported profits under these three methods differ from the profit predicted by the volume-cost-profit diagram even though the sales volume of this period equals its production volume (in physical quantity).

Therefore, only under certain qualified conditions would the general statement be true that the reported profit would be the same as the profit predicted by the volume-cost-profit diagram when production volume equals sales volume. One of these qualifications is that the statement would hold if there is no stock on hand at the beginning of a period. Under such circumstances, any accounting method would provide the same profit figure as that predicted by a volume-cost-profit diagram. The agreement of reported profits of Owen Manufacturing Company with predicted profit on an annual basis in Table 10–3 is an example of such a situation. A second qualification is that, if there is a beginning inventory, the general statement would still hold, provided that the fixed manufacturing expenses per unit of product carried over from the preceding period equals the fixed manufacturing expenses charged to each unit of product produced during the current period. Under such circumstances, the fixed manufacturing expenses charged against the revenue of the current period would be the same as the fixed manufacturing expenses incurred during this period. Such a situation can usually be found when standard cost with standard overhead rate established on the basis of normal volume of production is used as the basis of inventory valuation (see 2*a* and 2*b* for the second quarter of 1955 in Table 10–3). A third qualification is that if there is a beginning inventory, and if the fixed manufacturing expenses per unit of product carried over from the preceding period do not equal the fixed manufacturing expenses charged to each unit of product produced during the current period, the general statement could still hold, provided that the last-in first-out method is used as the basis of inventory valuation and profit determination (see 2*c* and 3*a* for the second quarter of 1955 in Table 10–3). Under such circumstances, the fixed manufacturing expenses charged against the revenues of the current period are the same fixed manufacturing expenses incurred during the current period.

Owing to the intricacies of accounting methods, exceptions could also be found to a general statement previously made that the reported profit would be higher than the profit predicted by the volume-cost-profit diagram when there is an increase in inventory and that the reported profit would be less than that predicted by the volume-cost-profit diagram when there is a reduction in inventory. Table 10–11 shows that, with severe seasonal fluctuations of production volume and wide variations between sales volume and production volume from one season to another, the use of the first-in first-out method of inventory valuation as a means of profit determination produced a reported profit less than the one predicted by the volume-cost-profit diagram during the second quarter, in spite of a build-up of inventory (in physical units). It also shows that the reported profit during the third quarter became more than the one predicted by the volume-cost-profit diagram, although there is a reduction in inventory during this period.

What is important in the preceding illustrations of Owen Manufacturing Company is their revelation of the need to appreciate the role of the time

TABLE 10–11

Owen Manufacturing Company

Profit and Loss Statement Reported under Actual Cost Method
with Inventory Valuation Based upon First-In First-Out Method—1955

	Per Unit	First Quarter	Second Quarter	Third Quarter	Fourth Quarter	Total
Sales	$1.00	$100,000	$350,000	$200,000	$350,000	$1,000,000
Cost of sales:						
Material	$0.10	10,000	35,000	20,000	35,000	100,000
Labor	0.20	20,000	70,000	40,000	70,000	200,000
Variable manufacturing expenses	0.10	10,000	35,000	20,000	35,000	100,000
	$0.40	$ 40,000	$140,000	$ 80,000	$140,000	$ 400,000
Fixed manufacturing expenses		25,000	56,250	43,750	75,000	200,000
Cost of sales		$ 65,000	$196,250	$123,750	$215,000	$ 600,000
Gross margin		$ 35,000	$153,750	$ 76,250	$135,000	$ 400,000
Selling and administrative expenses		50,000	50,000	50,000	50,000	200,000
Net profit (loss)		($ 15,000)	$103,750	$ 26,250	$ 85,000	$ 200,000
Net profit per volume-cost-profit diagram		($ 40,000)	$110,000	$ 20,000	$110,000	$ 200,000
Difference in profit		+$ 25,000	–$ 6,250	+$ 6,250	–$ 25,000	–0–

Beginning inventory:					
Units	-0-	100M	150M	50M	-0-
Fixed manufacturing expenses	-0-	$ 25,000*	$ 18,750†	$ 25,000‡	-0-
Cost of goods manufactured:					
Units	200M	400M	100M	300M	1,000M
Fixed manufacturing expenses	$ 50,000*	$ 50,000†	$ 50,000‡	$ 50,000§	$ 200,000
Ending inventory:					
Units	100M	150M	50M	-0-	-0-
Fixed manufacturing expenses	$ 25,000*	$ 18,750†	$ 25,000‡	-0-	-0-
Cost of goods sold:					
Units	100M	350M	200M	350M	1,000M
Fixed manufacturing expenses	100M—$ 25,000*	100M—$ 25,000* 250M— 31,250†	150M—$ 18,750† 50M— 25,000‡	50M—$25,000‡ 300M— 50,000§	$ 200,000
Increase (decrease) in inventory:					
Units	100M	50M	(100M)	(50M)	-0-
Fixed manufacturing expenses	$ 25,000*	($ 6,250)	$ 6,250	($ 25,000)	-0-

* Fixed manufacturing expense per unit of product = $50,000 ÷ 200M = 25¢ per unit.
† Fixed manufacturing expense per unit of product = $50,000 ÷ 400M = 12.5¢ per unit.
‡ Fixed manufacturing expense per unit of product = $50,000 ÷ 100M = 50¢ per unit.
§ Fixed manufacturing expense per unit of product = $50,000 ÷ 300M = 16.667¢ per unit.

element in comparing actual results of operation against the forecast results of operation by volume-cost-profit studies. These illustrations show that, even when everything is under management's control, reported profit could differ from predicted profit purely because of the lack of synchronization of sales volume and production volume and/or because of the accounting method used by a company. Generally, the longer the budget period, the closer reported profit would be to forecast profit, and vice versa. Although the production volume of most businesses would usually differ from their sales volume even on an annual basis, the reported profit under any conventional method of accounting on an annual basis is usually closer to the profit predicted by volume-cost-profit studies than reported profits on quarterly or monthly bases. Since it is usually necessary for management to keep itself informed of current operations on monthly and quarterly bases, it becomes imperative for the person responsible for the preparation of volume-cost-profit studies and the operating management making use of such studies to be aware of the possible difference due to time element and accounting practice of reported profit from predicted profit, to understand the relationships between these different profit figures, and to familiarize themselves with the reasons contributing to such differences. Whether or not the value of volume-cost-profit studies as a tool of management is hampered by this variation of reported profit from predicted profit because of the role played by the time and other elements will be further discussed in the following chapter.[8]

[8] The time element and accounting practices are among the causes that make the actual cost of a business differ from its anticipated cost. Examples of the effect of cost changes due to this and other factors are found in Chap. 11.

CHAPTER 11

Variation of Actual Profit
from Forecast Profit

In earlier chapters it has been shown that with an intelligently designed and properly administered variable budgeting system it is possible
to make reasonably accurate estimates of what the various costs and expenses should be at different levels of operation. It has also been shown
that these budget estimates can be used not only as management's guides
for keeping costs and expenses under better control but also as a basis for
forecasting financial results of operation at different volumes of business,
thereby helping management evaluate its operating plans. However, the job
of predicting what the profit of a business will be next year is much more
complex and difficult than that of estimating what its costs and expenses
should be during any period. Variations of actual profit from that which
has been expected, i.e., budgeted, by management may frequently be found.
To those not familiar with how and why volume-cost-profit studies are used
by management, this variation of actual profit from forecast profit can be
a source of misunderstanding and confusion about the real value of volume-
cost-profit studies. It is, therefore, necessary to examine in this chapter
(1) the nature of forecast profit, (2) some of the factors that can contribute
to the variation of actual profit from forecast profit, and (3) the true effect
of this variation upon the usefulness of volume-cost-profit studies as a
managerial tool.

What is forecast profit? In a simple definition, a forecast profit is, and
represents nothing more than, management's expectation of the result of
operations in financial terms if a specific set of operating plans are carried
out under certain operating conditions over a given period or periods of

187

time. It should be noted that, in order to arrive at any forecast profit, there must be a set of operating plans. Since it is usually possible to have alternative plans of conducting a business, the forecast profit under one set of plans may often differ from that under another set. It should also be noted that, in order to arrive at the forecast profit for any set of operating plans, consideration must be given to the conditions or atmosphere under which such operating plans are to be carried out. With different operating conditions, varying results can be expected from the same set of operating plans. By properly appraising the circumstances which it meets and will meet, and by intelligently assessing the different operating plans, management can decide upon and undertake the program which, in its judgment, is the most desirable. The "official" forecast profit of a business for any given period is, therefore, merely a statement of what management expects to accomplish with this selected program under certain conditions which, in its opinion, will most likely prevail during this period.

One of the difficulties in profit forecasting, as pointed out earlier, is to predict with exactitude the volume of business in the period ahead. Because of the nonuniform response of various costs and expenses of a business to changes in volume of business, profit seldom fluctuates in direct proportion to changes in volume of business. In order to plan their operation intelligently, many managements have found it desirable to study what their profit will be at varying volumes of business under each set of operating plans, what minimum volumes of business they must achieve in order to keep themselves out of loss and reach their profit objective, whether it will be possible for the company to attain such volumes, and so forth. This naturally leads to the use of variable budgeting and volume-cost-profit studies.

Volume, of course, is not the sole determinant of the revenue, cost, and profit of a business. The final profit of a business is also dependent upon such other factors as selling price, product mix, cost structure, operating efficiency, and the like. Consequently, if the actual selling price, product mix, cost structure, or operating efficiency realized by a business were not the same as those anticipated by management, and on the basis of which the original forecast profit had been established, the actual profit of a business would naturally differ from the forecast profit even when this forecast profit had been adjusted to the volume of business actually realized.

For instance, Dayton Manufacturing Company had estimated that it could sell 4,000,000 lb of product X at a price of $1.20 per pound during 1956. Its variable cost was estimated to be $0.60 per pound of product X, and its total fixed cost for the entire year was estimated to be $1,600,000. A pre-tax profit of $800,000 was estimated and is shown in the following summarized profit forecast:

	Thousands of Dollars	Dollars per Pound
Sales	$4,800	$1.20
Total variable cost	2,400	0.60
Gross contribution	$2,400	$0.60
Total fixed cost	1,600	
Pre-tax profit	$ 800	

A volume-cost-profit diagram, as shown in Fig. 11–1, was constructed in order to study the probable profit or loss at different volumes of business.

Assume that during 1956 Dayton Manufacturing Company sold a total of 3,600,000 lb of product X. Its actual variable cost per pound of product X and its actual total fixed cost were the same as expected. However, the selling price actually realized by the company was $1.10 per pound instead of the original expectation of $1.20 per pound.

TABLE 11–1

Dayton Manufacturing Company

Comparison of Actual Profit with Forecast Profits:
Actual Selling Price Being 10% Less Than Original Expectation—1956

	Actual		Adjusted Budget *		Original Budget	
	(000 omitted)	$ per lb	(000 omitted)	$ per lb	(000 omitted)	$ per lb
Sales	$3,960	$1.10	$4,320	$1.20	$4,800	$1.20
Total variable cost	2,160	0.60	2,160	0.60	2,400	0.60
Gross contribution	$1,800	$0.50	$2,160	$0.60	$2,400	$0.60
Total fixed cost	1,600	...	1,600	...	1,600	
Pre-tax profit	$ 200	...	$ 560	...	$ 800	
Pounds forecast					4,000,000	
Pounds actually produced and sold	3,600,000		3,600,000			
Net selling price, forecast	...		$1.20 per lb		$1.20 per lb	
Net selling price, actually realized	$1.10 per lb.					

* Adjusted to actual volume of 3,600,000 lb.

The actual result of operation of Dayton Manufacturing Company is shown in Table 11–1, in which it is compared against both the original objective and the expected result of operation adjusted to the actual volume of business. The pre-tax profit actually realized by the company was $200,000. However, according to the adjusted budget in Table 11–1 and

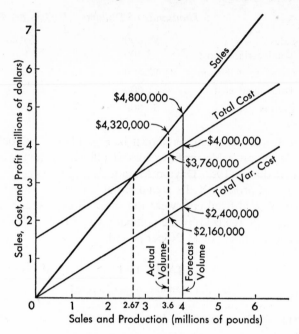

Fig. 11–1. Dayton Manufacturing Company. Volume-cost-profit diagram based upon original budget for 1956.

the volume-cost-profit diagram in Fig. 11–1, a pre-tax profit of $560,000 had been predicted for the volume of business actually realized. The reason for this variation of actual profit from forecast profit is that the selling price of $1.10 per pound actually realized by the company was $0.10 less than the anticipated selling price of $1.20 per pound. With total sales of 3,600,000 lb, this reduction in selling price is reflected in the difference of $360,000 between the actual and forecast profit.

Changes in product mix, like changes in selling price, can also cause the actual profit to differ from the forecast profit. For example, assume that Dayton Manufacturing Company produces two products A and B instead of a single product X. The original plan for 1956 was to sell 2,000,000 lb of product A at $1.00 per pound and 2,000,000 lb of product B at $1.40 per pound. The variable costs of these products were estimated to be $0.45 per pound for product A and $0.75 per pound for product B. The total fixed cost of the company was estimated to be $1,600,000. A pre-tax profit of $800,000 was expected, as shown by the original budget in Table 11–2. The probable profit and loss at various other volumes of operation is shown by the volume-cost-profit diagram in Fig. 11–1.

Assume further that during 1956 the company produced and sold 1,200,000 lb of product A and 2,400,000 lb of product B, a total of

TABLE 11-2

Dayton Manufacturing Company

Comparison of Actual Profit with Forecast Profits:
Actual Product Mix Being Different from Forecast Product Mix—1956

| | Adjusted Budget* | | Total | | Actual | | | |
| | | | | | Product A | | Product B | |
	(000 omitted)	$ per lb	(000 omitted)	$ per lb	(000 omitted)	$ per lb	(000 omitted)	$ per lb
Sales	$4,320	$1.20	$4,560	$1.267	$1,200	$1.00	$3,360	$1.40
Total variable cost	2,160	0.60	2,340	0.650	540	0.45	1,800	0.75
Gross contribution	$2,160	$0.60	$2,220	$0.617	$ 660	$0.55	$1,560	$0.65
Total fixed cost	1,600	...	1,600					
Pre-tax profit	$ 560	...	$ 620					
Pounds actually produced and sold	3,600,000		3,600,000		1,200,000		2,400,000	

| | Total | | Original Budget | | | |
| | | | Product A | | Product B | |
	(000 omitted)	$ per lb	(000 omitted)	$ per lb	(000 omitted)	$ per lb
Sales	$4,800	$1.20	$2,000	$1.00	$2,800	$1.40
Total variable cost	2,400	0.60	900	0.45	1,500	0.75
Gross contribution	$2,400	$0.60	$1,100	$0.55	$1,300	$0.65
Total fixed cost	1,600					
Pre-tax profit	$ 800					
Pounds forecast	4,000,000		2,000,000		2,000,000	

* Adjusted to actual volume of 3,600,000 lb at original product mix.

3,600,000 lb. The actual selling price and the variable cost of each of its two products were the same as anticipated. The actual fixed cost during this period was likewise the same as the original expectation.

The actual result of operation of Dayton Manufacturing Company is shown in Table 11–2, in which it is compared against the original objective and the expected result of operation adjusted to the actual volume of business at the original product mix. According to the adjusted budget in this exhibit or the volume-cost-profit diagram in Fig. 11–1, the company should earn a pre-tax profit of $560,000 with a total sales volume of 3,600,000 lb. However, the pre-tax profit actually realized by the company amounted to $620,000, exceeding the forecast profit by $60,000.

The variation of actual profit from forecast profit in this case is due to two reasons: First, the actual product mix of the company differed from the product mix originally anticipated. *And,* secondly, the gross contribution toward fixed cost and profit (i.e., excess of selling price over variable cost) of product A was not the same as that of product B. Instead of an expected product mix of 1 lb of product A to 1 lb of product B, the product mix actually realized by Dayton Manufacturing Company in 1956 was 1 lb of product A to 2 lb of product B. Since product A contributed $0.55 per pound toward fixed cost and profit and product B contributed $0.65 per pound, this variation of actual product mix from expected product mix resulted in an increase in the average gross contribution of all products (i.e., product A plus product B) from $0.60 per pound (original expectation) to $0.617 per pound (actually realized). Consequently, an additional profit of $60,000 over what had been originally predicted for the same (total) volume of business was realized (3,600,000 lb at $0.016667 = $60,000).

It should be noted that a change in product mix alone may not necessarily affect the profit of a business. In the preceding illustration, the actual profit differs from the forecast profit, because the variation in product mix is accompanied at the same time by a difference in the gross contribution of product A and product B toward the company's fixed cost and profit. If, however, the gross contribution of these two products had been the same, then despite the variation of actual product mix from forecast product mix, the actual profit could still have been the same as that predicted for the actual volume of business.

For example, assume that the selling price and the variable cost of product A of Dayton Manufacturing Company were $1.00 and $0.40 per pound, respectively, yielding a gross contribution of $0.60 per pound. The selling price and variable cost of product B were $1.40 and $0.80 per pound, respectively, yielding also a gross contribution of $0.60 per pound. The total fixed cost of the year was $1,600,000. As in the preceding illustration, the actual selling price and variable cost of each product and the actual fixed cost of the company were the same as expected. Assume also that the company had expected to sell 2,000,000 lb of product A and 2,000,000 lb of product B. Actual sales realized by the company were 1,200,000 lb of product A and 2,400,000 lb of product B.

The actual result of operation in this example, the original budget, and the expected result of operation adjusted to the actual (total) volume of business at original product mix are shown in Table 11–3. From this exhibit, it can be seen that despite a variation of actual product mix (1 lb of product A to 2 lb of product B) from the anticipated product mix (1 lb of product A to 1 lb of product B), the actual pre-tax profit of $560,000 realized by Dayton Manufacturing Company agrees with the forecast profit for its actual volume of business. As mentioned above, the reason is that, in this particular case, the gross contribution toward fixed cost and profit of both product A and product B was identical ($0.60 per pound), a condition making the average gross contribution of all products remain the same at $0.60 per pound regardless of changes in product mix. Consequently, the actual profit in this example agrees with the forecast profit for the actual volume of business, although the actual product mix differs from the anticipated product mix.

Besides changes in selling price and product mix, changes in the variable and/or fixed cost of a business from original expectations can also cause the actual profit to differ from the forecast profit. For instance, assume, as in the first illustration of Dayton Manufacturing Company, that its management had planned to produce and sell 4,000,000 lb of product X in 1956 at a price of $1.20 per pound. The variable cost was estimated to be $0.60 per pound of product X; the total fixed cost for the company, $1,600,000. The selling price actually realized in this case was the same as that expected. The company produced and sold a total of 3,600,000 lb during this period.

Assume that, instead of the original expectation of $0.60 per pound, the actual variable cost of Dayton Manufacturing Company was $0.70 per pound. The actual fixed cost in this case was the same as that expected. Comparisons of the actual result of operation with the original objective and with the expected result of operation adjusted to the actual volume of business are shown in Table 11–4. From this exhibit, it can be easily seen that, because of the increase of $0.10 per pound in variable cost from the original expectation of $0.60 per pound, the actual profit of $200,000 fell short of the forecast profit (budgeted profit adjusted to the actual volume) of $560,000 by $360,000 (3,600,000 lb at $0.10 = $360,000).

In the preceding example, the actual profit can differ from the forecast profit if, instead of the variable cost (per unit of product), the actual fixed cost has differed from the original expectation. Assume that the actual fixed cost of Dayton Manufacturing Company amounted to $1,800,000, exceed-

TABLE 11-3

Dayton Manufacturing Company

Comparison of Actual Profit with Forecast Profits:
Actual Product Mix Being Different from Forecast Product Mix—Example 2

| | Adjusted Budget * | | Actual | | | | | |
| | | | Total | | Product A | | Product B | |
	(000 omitted)	$ per lb	(000 omitted)	$ per lb	(000 omitted)	$ per lb	(000 omitted)	$ per lb
Sales	$4,320	$1.20	$4,560	$1.267	$1,200	$1.00	$3,360	$1.40
Total variable cost	2,160	0.60	2,400	0.667	480	0.40	1,920	0.80
Gross contribution	$2,160	$0.60	$2,160	$0.600	$ 720	$0.60	$1,440	$0.60
Total fixed cost	1,600	...	1,600					
Pre-tax profit	$ 560	...	$ 560					
Pounds actually produced and sold	3,600,000		3,600,000		1,200,000		2,400,000	

| | Original Budget | | | | | |
| | Total | | Product A | | Product B | |
	(000 omitted)	$ per lb	(000 omitted)	$ per lb	(000 omitted)	$ per lb
Sales	$4,800	$1.20	$2,000	$1.00	$2,800	$1.40
Total variable cost	2,400	0.60	800	0.40	1,600	0.80
Gross contribution	$2,400	$0.60	$1,200	$0.60	$1,200	$0.60
Total fixed cost	1,600					
Pre-tax profit	$ 800					
Pounds forecast	4,000,000		2,000,000		2,000,000	

* Adjusted to actual volume of 3,600,000 lb at original product mix.

194

TABLE 11–4

Dayton Manufacturing Company

Comparison of Actual Profit with Forecast Profits:
Actual Variable Cost Being Different from Original Expectation—1956

	Actual		Adjusted Budget *		Original Budget	
	(000 omitted)	*$ per lb*	*(000 omitted)*	*$ per lb*	*(000 omitted)*	*$ per lb*
Sales	$4,320	$1.20	$4,320	$1.20	$4,800	$1.20
Total variable cost	2,520	0.70	2,160	0.60	2,400	0.60
Gross contribution	$1,800	$0.50	$2,160	$0.60	$2,400	$0.60
Total fixed cost	1,600	...	1,600	...	1,600	
Pre-tax profit	$ 200	...	$ 560	...	$ 800	
Pounds forecast					4,000,000	
Pounds actually produced and sold	3,600,000		3,600,000			

* Adjusted to actual volume of 3,600,000 lb.

ing the original expectation of $1,600,000 by $200,000. The incurrence of an additional amount in fixed cost over what had been originally expected would naturally be reflected in the actual profit of the company which, as shown by Table 11–5, was reduced to $360,000—$200,000 less than the forecast profit of $560,000 for the actual volume of business realized.

TABLE 11–5

Dayton Manufacturing Company

Comparison of Actual Profit with Forecast Profits:
Actual Fixed Cost Being Different from Original Expectation—1956

	Actual		Adjusted Budget *		Original Budget	
	(000 omitted)	*$ per lb*	*(000 omitted)*	*$ per lb*	*(000 omitted)*	*$ per lb*
Sales	$4,320	$1.20	$4,320	$1.20	$4,800	$1.20
Total variable cost	2,160	0.60	2,160	0.60	2,400	0.60
Gross contribution	$2,160	$0.60	$2,160	$0.60	$2,400	$0.60
Total fixed cost	1,800	...	1,600	...	1,600	
Pre-tax profit	$ 360	...	$ 560	...	$ 800	
Pounds forecast					4,000,000	
Pounds actually produced and sold	3,600,000		3,600,000			

* Adjusted to actual volume of 3,600,000 lb.

Variations of actual profit from anticipated profit such as those illustrated in the preceding examples of Dayton Manufacturing Company may easily be interpreted as prima-facie evidence of the unreliability of volume-cost-profit studies and volume-cost-profit diagrams as a means of helping management forecast its future profit and evaluate its operating plans. One may conclude that, although analyses of this nature appear to be highly useful, their real value is seriously impaired by their failure to take into consideration many inevitable changes, such as selling prices, product mixes, cost structure, operating efficiency, and the like, which can readily cause the actual profit to differ from the forecast profit.

In order to prevent possible misunderstanding and/or misapplication of volume-cost-profit studies as a managerial tool, it is necessary to discuss here briefly the decision-making function of management and the role of profit forecasting in this decision-making process. The primary functions and responsibilities of management are to size up the situation which faces it and will face it, to decide upon a course or program of action in view of the situation it sees, and to carry out the decision which it has made. The final decision is usually made after a study of several alternative programs and an examination of the various conditions which are most likely to occur.

One of the criteria used by management in selecting its final operating plan is, of course, its profit opportunity.[1] Because profit usually does not fluctuate in direct proportion to changes in volume of business and because it is difficult to predict exactly the future volume of business, managements of a number of companies have come to realize that they can make better evaluations of the profit opportunities or the lack of profit opportunities of various operating plans under consideration by studying the relationship between volume, cost, and profit under each plan.

After management has made its final selection, the official profit forecast of a business, including both the fixed profit budget and the related volume-cost-profit diagram, as pointed out earlier in this chapter, represents nothing more than what management hopes to accomplish with its selected operating program—a program which, in its judgment, will most likely give the desired results under certain operating conditions that will probably occur over a particular period of time.

With the passage of time, new situations will develop of such significance that new decisions will have to be made and new operating plans will have to be set up. The development of new operating conditions and/or new operating plans will, of course, make the original profit forecast, which is established on the basis of an older set of operating conditions and operating plans, no longer representative of what the profit should be and will be under the new conditions. In the discussion of setting up proper budget estimates it has been pointed out that, if there is any significant change in operating conditions that will make the budget estimates no longer representative of what the cost should be under the new conditions, the budget

---

[1] Other criteria which may be used by management are to maintain steady employment, to fulfill its social responsibilities, and so forth.

estimates should be and are revised at the companies studied.[2] Similarly, with the revision of cost estimates, profit forecast should likewise be revised to reflect the new operating conditions. If the old profit forecast had not been revised, the actual profit under the new operating conditions would, of course, differ from the old forecast profit.

The question now is whether the value of these volume-cost-profit studies is impaired or destroyed by the variation of actual profit from forecast profit because of changes in selling prices, product mixes, and cost structures.[3] One of the purposes of volume-cost-profit studies is to enable management to choose the most desirable and most reasonable operating plans toward achieving the profit objective of a business under the circumstances foreseeable at the present (i.e., at the moment when a decision has to be made by management). Admittedly, the operating conditions which will actually occur in the future may differ from those foreseeable at the present, and the present operating plans may be revised to meet the new operating conditions, resulting in a variation of actual profits from those which are predicted *today*. But this does not mean that the value of properly established volume-cost-profit studies is thus impaired. Their value has to be judged from their purposes. As mentioned previously, one of the objectives of volume-cost-profit studies is to help management make better evaluation of its operating plans in terms of profit opportunities or the lack thereof. If volume-cost-profit studies failed to provide management with reliable cost and profit information for the specific operating plan under the specific operating conditions which it has in mind, they would certainly be useless. On the other hand, if volume-cost-profit studies do provide management with reliable cost and profit information for the operating plan and operating conditions which it has in mind, such studies will be found of immeasurable value whenever cost and profit are used as the criteria for weighing future operating plans even though conditions may change.

In formulating and evaluating its operating plans, management must, of course, take into consideration not only possible changes in volume of business but also such other factors as selling price, product mix, cost structure, and so forth. By studying the volume-cost-profit relationships under different sets of operating plans with different selling prices, product mixes, and cost structure, management is provided with a means of selecting and deciding upon the most desirable set of operating plans. Its sales and production efforts can then be channeled into the course which, in its judgment, will be the most rewarding. As brought out by the cases studied here, at companies such as Lafayette Brass Company, where volume-cost-

[2] See Chap. 8 and Appendices A and B.
[3] See Dayton Manufacturing Company.

profit studies have been properly and successfully used, due consideration is given to these other factors in formulating and selecting their operating plans.

The experience of Sherwood Press,[4] Messina Plastics Company,[5] Milbrae Mining Company,[6] Olympia Manufacturing Company,[7] and Hobson Pigment Company [8] indicates that in order to make better decisions in what to produce and what to sell, in setting up selling prices of their products, volume-cost or volume-cost-profit studies themselves are definitely needed by management.

A second purpose of volume-cost-profit studies is to help management appraise its performance in the period just ended so that better action can be taken for the future. Under a properly designed and administered variable budgeting system, the variations of actual profit from forecast profit are often segregated into different elements, such as operating efficiency, volume of business, selling price, product mix, and so forth. Information like this is a valuable guide to management for ascertaining the real causes of the variation of actual profit from planned profit, in judging how well a job has been done in the period just ended, and for seeking better and improved plans for the period ahead.[9] Without variable budgeting and volume-cost studies, managements in a number of companies experienced difficulty in determining whether good or poor profit showing was caused by operating efficiency, changes in volume of business, or other discernible factors.[10]

Thus conceived, it can be readily seen that at companies such as Lafayette Brass Company, where variable budgeting has been properly and successfully used, the variation of actual profit from forecast profit, as shown in Table 9–3 and discussed in Chap. 9, does not impair or destroy the value of volume-cost-profit studies for helping management make better operating plans. The segregation of this variation into different elements, such as done by Lafayette Brass Company, provides management with fundamental information for helping judge its past performance, thereby leading toward better plans for the future.

[4] See Chaps. 3 and 5.
[5] See Chap. 4.
[6] See Chap. 4.
[7] See Chap. 5.
[8] See Chap. 2.
[9] See Dayton Manufacturing Company.
[10] See Chap. 6 and Appendices A, B, and C.

APPENDICES

Appendix A

LAFAYETTE BRASS COMPANY

Lafayette Brass Company is the largest independent brass-products manufacturer in the United States. It produces and sells brass and copper sheets, wires, rods, and tubes of various shapes and sizes. Besides these basic brass products, the company also manufactures a complete line of brass plumbing goods, automobile tire valves, and aerosol dispensers. The company operates two brass mills, one fabricating mill, and one foundry in this country as well as a mill in Canada. In 1952 the company employed over 5,000 people, and its sales amounted to more than $125,000,000.

Prior to 1942 the company had used an actual process cost system. Following the entrance of the United States into World War II, the company's business increased from $31,000,000 in 1940 to $61,000,000 in 1942. As the company's activities expanded, the top management of the company began to feel that its cost accounting system, which was based upon past actual costs, did not provide them with sufficient and timely information for proper pricing, product costing, and inventory valuation. The management also felt that past actual costs did not indicate whether the company had used the most efficient method of operation in the past and, therefore, it was improper to use past averages as future objectives for planning and control purposes. In order to find a more efficient system of coping with management's needs, the company called in one of the most reputable accounting firms to study its problems. As a result of this study and following the recommendations made by the accounting firm, a standard cost system was installed in the company in 1944.

Under the standard cost system, standard unit product cost is established for each product. Standard material cost per unit of product is based upon standard specifications established by the engineering department, with due allowances for reasonable waste and spoilage. Standard labor cost is established on the basis of standard methods of operation and standard efficiency of performance which is determined by time and motion studies and by attainment in the past. Standard material prices and standard wage rates are based upon those current at the beginning of the year. Standard overhead rate is obtained by dividing the standard overhead expenses by the standard direct labor dollars contained in the company's normal volume of operation. Standard overhead expenses at the company's normal volume of operation is determined on the basis of past experience and the management's judgment as to what should be the reasonable expenses at that volume. The normal volume of operation is the average volume of production which is necessary to meet average sales requirements over a long period of time. It is not the full-capacity volume but an attainable volume when the effects of good years and bad years are averaged out. It permits all overhead expenses to be absorbed by the company's products over the long period.

In introducing the standard cost system, the company revamped its accounting classification and procedures so that standards could be tied to the books and variances could be recorded during the regular process of monthly closing. All variations of actual costs from standards are treated as deductions from the gross profit of the current period and are, therefore, not capitalized into inventories. For illustration, in March, 1946, the company manufactured 1,000,000 lb of F-12 ¼-in. rod and the actual cost of production for this item averaged 40 cents per pound. The standard cost for this item was 38 cents per pound. The variation of the actual cost from standard cost was 2 cents per pound, or $20,000 for 1,000,000 lb. The finished goods added to the inventory were valued at 38 cents per pound, and the total variance of $20,000 was treated as a deduction from gross profit for the month.

Through the use of this standard cost system, the company arrived at a satisfactory basis of establishing unit product costs to assist management in setting prices or in determining which product could bring the most profit to the company. The system also provided the company with a consistent basis of spreading overhead and avoided the distortion under the previous actual past cost system that inventory valuation per unit of product would be low when the company was operating at high levels of activity and inventory valuation per unit of product would be high when the company was operating at low levels of activity. The system also assisted the company in standardizing its production methods and processes for more efficient operation. By segregating the different types of variances of actual costs from standards, the company could locate the causes of such variation and was thus able to take rapid managerial action on any excessive variation. The system also allowed the company to plan on a systematic basis and to achieve greater cooperation and coordination of effort within the company.

The standard cost system worked well during World War II, but when the war came to an end the company experienced a decline in sales. In 1945, the company's sales dropped to $52,900,000 from its wartime peak of $67,500,000 established in 1943. While the decline in sales during this 2-year period amounted to 22 per cent only, the drop in net profits before taxes was more severe. The company earned only $3,100,000 before taxes in 1945 in comparison to $7,600,000 earned in 1943, a drop of 59 per cent. Conditions in 1946 improved somewhat because of the lifting of ceiling prices by the U.S. Office of Price Administration, but the profit situation in 1947 was more disappointing than in 1945. The company's net profit in that year declined to $2,700,000 while sales rose to $60,700,000. Confronted with this problem of decline in profits, the company decided that a tighter control over costs must be exercised.

Of the company's basic brass products, manufacturing costs constituted the major portion of their selling prices. Through the use of the standard cost system, the company had achieved good control over direct material and direct labor costs. However, the company discovered that, as the company's volume of production and sales declined, its actual overhead costs greatly exceeded their standards. In its effort to control the unabsorbed overhead expenses, the company found it difficult to pinpoint responsibility of such variation because standard overhead expenses were not set up according to functions of responsibility. The comany also realized that many of the overhead expenses were fixed and would not drop proportionately with any decline in the level of activity as the standard cost would do. Therefore, the standard cost system was found to be unsatisfactory as a means of controlling overhead expenses. Besides manufacturing overhead, the company also found that its commercial costs, i.e., selling and administrative expenses, had been saddled with high-cost wartime practices. In order to keep the company's manufacturing overhead and commercial costs under effective control, the company decided in 1947 that, in addition to the standard cost system then in use, budgetary control should be used as a means of keeping these expenses within bounds and that flexible (or variable) budgets be used to control manufacturing overhead.

Under the budgetary control system, responsibility for cost control is assigned to the foreman or department head of each cost center. While the standard cost sheets do indicate standards for direct material and direct labor for each unit of product passing through any cost center, the standard overhead rate used for costing and inventory valuation purposes does not indicate how much overhead expense each cost center should spend for the actual volume of production when different from normal production. In order that costs could be controlled at points where they are actually expended and responsibilities for keeping these costs under control be affixed, budgets of manufacturing expenses are established for each cost center at all levels of production. A cost center is a department which is placed under the complete authority and responsibility of one man and, therefore, there would be no overlapping of responsibility. The foreman of each department is then charged with the responsibility of keeping his actual expenses in line with his budget allowances. The company's Atwood Plant is divided into four major divisions, viz., casting shop, rolling mill, rod and wire mill, tube and pipe mill. Each of these major divisions is, in turn, divided into several departments by functions. For instance, the wire and rod mill is divided into extrusion department, draw block department, and packing and shipping department. Each department has a foreman, and a budget is set up for each of these departments.

To accommodate the advance in philosophy from cost control by products to cost control by functions, the company had to modify its accounting procedure to fit into management's new requirements. One of these modifications was the change from "pure" accounts to "mixed" accounts. Under the old system, overhead expenses of any cost center were not charged to the cost of that department but were accumulated with overhead expenses of other departments "purely" according to account classification. The total overhead expenses thus accumulated were absorbed into costs of finished products by applying the standard burden rate. Under the new system, overhead expenses of each cost center are charged to the cost of operating that department. The total departmental budget allowance for that cost center and those for other cost centers would be added together. The aggregate of various departmental allowances thus obtained would then be absorbed into costs of finished products by applying standard overhead rates.

For budgetary purposes, the same accounting classification is used as that for accounting purposes. Since the underabsorbed or overabsorbed overhead expenses under the old system would now be segregated into different types of variances by their causes, it became necessary to reclassify some of the accounts and to modify the accounting procedure to conform to the new practices.

In setting up budgets at the lowest supervision level, only those expenses controllable by the foreman are included in his budgets. The company feels that no foreman or department head should be held responsible for costs or expenses over which he cannot exercise full control. Therefore, the budgets for a typical manufacturing department include only such items as supervision and clerical salaries, handling, tool setting, cleaning and sweeping, indirect labor, overtime and night bonus, lost time, tool maintenance labor, machine maintenance labor, and other maintenance labor. Included also in his budgets are items such as supplies, water, fuel and electricity, tool maintenance supplies, machine maintenance supplies, spoiled work, and other indirect charges. In addition, he is held responsible for supplementary wage costs which include payroll taxes, workmen's insurance, vacations, and holidays. For accounting purposes, these items are further broken down into detailed subaccounts. When the budgetary system was first installed, each of these detailed subaccounts was budgeted. However, the company found the practice to be impractical, and budgets are now established on the basis of subaccounts only, each of which may have a group of detailed accounts of similar nature.

Responsibility of establishing and keeping up with the budgets of any department is vested in the foreman of that department. The company feels that the man whose performance is to be judged by the budget must be the man who makes up the budget, because a person cannot be held responsible for performance under a budget that he has not taken part in creating.

At the outset, in installing its expense budget system, resistance from its foremen and department heads was experienced. The company found that the people on the operating line did not like to be told by the "squirrel in the glass tower" what they could do with their jobs. It took a great deal of salesmanship from management to convince the foreman that his budget was not designed as a whip for his boss to hold over his head but was a part of an over-all profit project for his division, in which he played a considerable part and the company needed his help to achieve the common goal.

The budget department now supplies the foreman with all necessary information in making up his budgets, and he is given all the help and advice the budget department can furnish, including the limitations within which the foreman must operate to yield a satisfactory margin of profit. Nevertheless, the budget thus established is primarily the foreman's budget, not that of the budget department.

All budgeted items are expressed in terms of dollars. For certain indirect labor expenses such as supervisory and clerical salaries, handling, and the like, the fixed portion of budget allowance is first figured in terms of the number of men required and then converted into dollars by multiplying their salary and wage rates. For expenses such as gas, oil, electricity, and supplies used in large quantities, budget allowances are based upon physical quantities used and then converted into dollars. In reporting actual performances, should there be any significant variation of actual expenditures from budget allowances due to price changes, the variation would be segregated and reported as such.

The level of activity, which determines budget allowances for manufacturing expenses under the flexible budget, is measured in terms of standard direct labor dollars contained in the work done. The standard direct dollars contained in the work done for any product are the standard direct labor dollars necessary to produce the "required" output in a standard number of operations. For instance, to produce a ½-in.-size rod, it is necessary to extrude the rod in four standard operations. Sometimes after four standard operations it might be found that the rod measured to ⅝ in. and another operation is needed to reduce the rod to ½-in. size. The measurement of the level of production activity under the flexible budget is based upon the standard direct labor dollars necessary for the four standard operations, not upon the standard direct labor dollars for the five actual operations. The company decided upon the use of standard direct labor dollars for the standard number of operations as the measurement of level of activity because of the practicality and ease in getting figures on that basis as well as the degree of significance of that measurement. The company does not use standard direct labor-hours because, through the use of standard wage rates, standard direct labor dollars achieve the same purpose as standard direct labor-hours but save the company from the extra work of accumulating statistics on the basis of standard direct labor-hours. Pounds of output are not used as the measurement of level of activity to determine budget allowances for manufacturing expenses under the flexible budget because each product contains a different value per pound. More expenses are incurred in the manufacture of ¾-in. tubes than ¾-in. rods, but the ¾-in. tube weighs much less than the ¾-in. rod. From the standard cost sheets, physical units of output are converted into standard direct labor dollars so that a more accurate measurement of production activity can be obtained to determine budget allowances for manufacturing expenses.

Budget allowances for each manufacturing expense at different levels of activity in any cost center are established on the basis of experience for the past twelve months and the company's profit objective for the coming year. A scatter diagram is made for each manufacturing expense, and a straight line is drawn through the diagram. This regression line, tempered with management's policy for the next year, is used as a basis to negotiate with the department head involved the fixed budget and flexible budget for the particular manufacturing expense under study.

For each manufacturing expense, the budget estimates are divided into two segments, a "flexible" budget covering only the variable portion of the budget allowances at different volumes of business and a "fixed" budget representing the fixed part of the budget allowance applicable to all levels of operation. As mentioned earlier, this fixed portion of budget allowance is determined on the basis of the regression line obtained from the scatter diagram and checked by the management's judgment as to the minimum requirement at any level of activity. Table A–1 shows the fixed budget of manufacturing expenses for Department A of the Mill Division at the company's main plant for 1952. In that exhibit the average monthly fixed budget for salaries in 1952 was based upon three men on monthly payroll whose salaries were $650, $695, and $700, respectively, or a combined total of $2,045 per month. In addition to these three men on monthly payroll, the combined salaries of men on weekly payroll averaged $15,205 per month. Therefore, the average monthly fixed budget for salaries in 1952 was $17,250 per month. It should be noted that the word "fixed" as used here has three meanings, viz., fixed by month, fixed by salary working day, and fixed by factory working day. One of the columns in Table A–1 indicates on what basis each manufacturing expense is fixed. Since there are different numbers of working days in each calendar month, the fixed budget allowance for each calendar month as shown in Table A–1 differs from month to month.

The flexible budget of manufacturing expenses is expressed in tabular forms as shown in Table A–2. Within the department's practical range of activity, the flexible budget allowance is computed and tabulated at intervals of every 5 per cent change in the level of activity. When the actual level of activity for the month is determined, the flexible budget allowance for the level of activity nearest the actual level of activity is taken to be the variable budget allowance for that month.

The total budget allowance for each manufacturing expense in any month is the sum of its fixed budget allowance for that particular month and its variable budget allowance selected from the variable budget table. Table A–3 shows that Department A of the Mill Division produced 4,516,154 lb during the month of March, 1952. The budget allowance for direct labor (or the standard direct labor) for the work done during that month was $80,380. The standard direct labor at normal level of production was $94,570. Therefore, the department operated at 84.9 per cent activity level during that month. Budget allowances for manufacturing expenses were obtained by adding the fixed budget for the month of March and the variable budget at 85 per cent level of activity, which was the nearest level of activity in the budget allowance table.

In setting up budget standards, the company tries to make the budget as realistic as possible. The company discovered that some people were inclined to do a little padding in establishing their own standards whereas others were overly ambitious in estimating the savings they could make. The budget department tries to avoid both extremes through persuasion. In case of disagreement, appeal is made to the next higher level of supervision of the man setting the budget.

Besides being used as a device to control manufacturing expenses, the company's budget system is also applied to control selling and administrative expenses. While the manufacturing expenses are controlled by both fixed and flexible budgets, selling and administrative expenses are controlled by fixed budgets only. The head of each selling and administrative department is charged with the responsibility of preparing and keeping up with his budget in the same manner as the foreman of a manufacturing department would do.

Monthly expense budget reports such as the one shown in Table A–3 are prepared and presented to the foreman or head of each department on the fifteenth day of the following month. This report compares the actual expenses of the department with its budget allowances and shows the amount of variation of each item from its budget allowance. At the bottom of each report, exceptional variations, both favorable and unfavorable, during the month are explained in the form of remarks. These explanations are based upon an analysis of what was charged to the account and the foremen's version of what happened during the month.

The management of the company feels that good cost control is only one of the means by which the company can maintain itself in a profitable position. In order to achieve desired results in terms of profit, cost control alone is not sufficient, and management must plan and control the company's operation in the most intelligent way. To this end, management uses a profit budget to guide it in planning and controlling the company's future course of business.

In establishing its profit budgets, the company does not follow the usual orthodox approach of starting with sales estimates. Instead, the company starts with the dividends which need to be paid and the profit which should be earned. From its profit requirement, the company figures out what sales it must achieve and at what cost and efficiency level it must operate in order to reach the desired profit goal.

Two types of profit budgets are being used by the company. The first one is a long-term profit budget. The long-term profit budget is a projection of what the company hopes to do in the way of profit for several years ahead and consequently in the way of sales and production during this period. In making up this budget, consideration is given to the company's production capacities, the growth trend of the company and industry as a whole, the company's competitive position within the industry, cost and price level required, etc.

The second type of profit budget is a short-term profit budget. The short-term profit budget covers only the period of one year and is management's plan for the period immediately ahead. This budget provides management with a means of recognizing profit opportunities or lack of profit opportunities during the coming year so that proper action can be taken in advance. In making up plans for the next year, the profit budget also provides management with a tool to coordinate the effort of various departments in sales, production, procurement, and finance.

The short-term profit budget is prepared during the month of December prior to the year covered by the budget and is presented to the board of directors for approval. After it is approved by the board, the profit budget becomes the company's fixed objective for that year. Usually the profit budget will not be changed unless drastic changes in business conditions tell management that it needs to be revised. In such case, the revision also will have to be presented to the board of directors for approval.

A comparison of the actual results of operation with profit budgets is presented monthly to top management in two ways. The actual result of operation of each plant is compared with the fixed profit budget of the plant. This comparison shows management whether the company is meeting its planned profit schedule. Although the actual volume of operation may differ from that set up on the profit budget, no adjustment in the fixed budget is made. Table A–5 shows the comparison of the actual result of operation of the company with profit budgets for March, 1952, by plants.

On another report, each plant is broken down by its major divisions and the comparison on this report is made between the actual result of operation of each division with the adjusted profit budget of that division. The adjusted profit budget of each division is the fixed profit budget of that division adjusted to the actual volume of operation. This report shows management how good a job was done on what each division has actually sold and produced. Table A–6 shows the comparison of actual results of operation by divisions of the company's Plant 1 with its adjusted profit budgets for March, 1952. Table A–7 shows the adjusted profit budgets and the original profit budgets of Plant 1 by divisions.

Two years after the installation of the budgetary system at Lafayette Brass Company, the brass industry went through a recession. Net sales of the company fell to $54,700,000 from $74,900,000 of the previous year, and the company for the first time since the war experienced an operating loss of $2,600,000. As a part of the study in coping with the adverse situation, a break-even analysis was made for each of the eleven divisions of the company.

In preparing a break-even chart for any division, the company had first to assume a certain pattern of product mix for that division. On the basis of this product mix, direct material and direct labor costs could be figured from standard cost sheets. Having converted the physical units of output into standard direct labor dollars, variable and fixed overhead costs at different levels of operation are obtained from the variable and fixed budgets for manufacturing expenses. Selling and administrative expenses are obtained from fixed budgets for these expenses. With the above information on hand, a break-even chart was drawn up for each division.

As a result of this study, the company found that, although it had done a good job in controlling its variable costs, its break-even point was high because of high fixed costs. A detailed analysis of fixed costs was made, and the company found that its fixed costs could be classified into three categories. The first type of fixed costs are those real fixed costs which are incurred with the passing of time and are not related to the volume of production. Included in this category are such costs as depreciation of building and equipment, property taxes, insurance, minimum plant protection, etc. The second type of fixed costs are those determined by current management policies. Into this category fall all organization salaries, research and development, welfare, bonuses, canteens, hospitals, etc. The third type of fixed costs are those semivariable costs which are usually considered fixed while operating within certain volume brackets. The company decided that the first type of fixed costs or its real fixed costs were the basic fixed costs outside the control of management. However, the last two types of fixed costs are subject to cost reduction.

Further analysis was made of each department's fixed cost, and the respective department head was asked by top management to review his fixed budget and to make some contribution to the job that had to be done by eliminating or reducing all costs not consistent with the reduced volume without impairing the efficiency of the organization. Practically every department agreed to reduction,

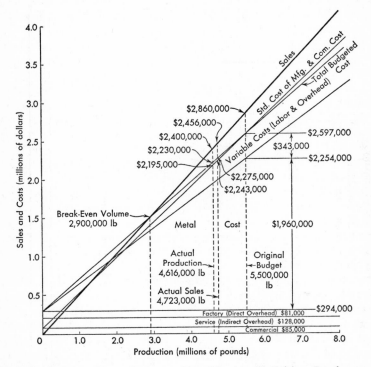

Fig. A–1. Lafayette Brass Company. Plant No. 1, mill division. Break-even chart for 1952.

and budgets were revised accordingly. New break-even charts were constructed, and the break-even point was found to have been pushed way down the line. During the next year, sales rose to $91,900,000 and profits shot up to $8,100,000. The management of the company felt very pleased with the efforts they made in 1949. Figure A–1 shows the break-even chart of Mill Division in 1952.

In 1953, the management of the company felt that they had a very satisfactory budgetary system in use. They were very pleased with the accuracy by which they were able to guide their business. Since 1949 sales and profits had risen steadily and had continued to make a record each year. In 1952, the company's sales reached $126,800,000 and profit before taxes was $12,300,000.

FIXED BUDGET

TABLE A–1

Lafayette Brass Company
Master Budget Sheet
Main Plant

Date Effective—January 1, 1952

Department A
Fixed Budget

Subaccount	Av. Month	Fixed per Month	Fixed per Day	Basis	Jan.	Feb.	Mar.	Apr.	May	June	July	Aug.	Sept.	Oct.	Nov.	Dec.
					Standard Direct Labor Normal $94,570			Lb Production 5,500,000								
10 Salaries	$17,250	$2,045	$ 735.75	1 & 2	$18,100	$17,550	$17,550	$17,550	$17,550	$16,640	$15,760	$17,550	$17,550	$18,830	$14,820	$17,550
12 Handling	7,500		362.90	3	7,920	7,650	7,650	7,650	7,650	7,200	6,750	7,650	7,650	8,280	6,300	7,650
14 Tool setting	100		4.85	3	105	100	100	100	100	95	90	100	100	110	85	100
16 Cleaning	500		24.20	3	530	510	510	510	510	480	450	510	510	550	420	510
18 Other indirect labor	900		43.55	3	950	920	920	920	920	865	810	920	920	995	755	920
20 Overtime and night bonus	...															
22 Lost time	...															
30 Tool maintenance labor	1,000		48.40	3	1,055	1,020	1,020	1,020	1,020	960	900	1,020	1,020	1,105	840	1,020
32 Machine maintenance labor	3,000		145.15	3	3,170	3,060	3,060	3,060	3,060	2,880	2,700	3,060	3,060	3,310	2,520	3,060
34 Other maintenance labor	...															
40 Supplies	2,000		96.75	3	2,110	2,040	2,040	2,040	2,040	1,920	1,800	2,040	2,040	2,210	1,680	2,040
42 Water, fuel, electricity	2,800		135.50	3	2,955	2,855	2,855	2,855	2,855	2,690	2,520	2,855	2,855	3,090	2,350	2,855
44 Tool maintenance supplies	500		34.20	3	530	510	510	510	510	480	450	510	510	550	420	510
46 Machine maintenance supplies	2,000		96.75	3	2,110	2,040	2,040	2,040	2,040	1,920	1,800	2,040	2,040	2,210	1,680	2,040
48 Spoiled work	...															
49 Other indirect supplies	500		24.20	3	530	510	510	510	510	480	450	510	510	550	420	510
50 Supplemental wage cost	11,115		537.80	3	11,735	11,340	11,340	11,340	11,340	10,670	10,005	11,340	11,340	12,270	9,335	11,340
Total	$49,165	$2,045	$2,280.00		$51,800	$50,105	$50,105	$50,105	$50,105	$47,280	$44,485	$50,105	$50,105	$54,060	$41,625	$50,105

Basis of monthly distributon:
Calendar month 1
Salaried working days 2
Factory working days 3

FLEXIBLE BUDGET
5% changes

TABLE A-2

Lafayette Brass Company
Master Budget Sheet
Main Plant

Date Effective—January 1, 1952

Department A
Flexible Budget

		Standard Direct Labor $94,750 Normal							Lb Production 5,500,000					
Subaccount	Var. Rate per D.L. $	60%	65%	70%	75%	80%	85%	90%	95%	100%	105%	110%	115%	120%
10 Salaries	0.0254	$ 1,440	$ 1,560	$ 1,680	$ 1,800	$ 1,920	$ 2,040	$ 2,160	$ 2,280	$ 2,400	$ 2,520	$ 2,640	$ 2,760	$ 2,880
12 Handling	0.1161	6,590	7,135	7,685	8,235	8,785	9,335	9,880	10,430	10,980	11,530	12,080	12,630	13,180
14 Tool setting	0.0058	325	355	380	410	435	465	490	520	545	570	600	625	655
16 Cleaning	0.0141	800	870	935	1,000	1,070	1,135	1,200	1,270	1,335	1,400	1,470	1,535	1,600
18 Other indirect labor	0.0105	595	645	695	745	790	840	890	940	990	1,040	1,090	1,140	1,190
20 Overtime and night bonus	0.0581	3,295	3,570	3,845	4,120	4,390	4,665	4,940	5,215	5,490	5,765	6,040	6,315	6,590
22 Lost time	0.0027	130	140	150	160	170	185	195	205	215	225	235	245	260
30 Tool maintenance labor	0.0523	2,960	3,205	3,450	3,700	3,945	4,190	4,435	4,685	4,930	5,175	5,425	5,670	5,915
32 Machine maintenance labor	0.1618	9,180	9,945	10,710	11,475	12,240	13,005	13,770	14,535	15,300	16,065	16,830	17,595	18,360
34 Other maintenance labor	0.0263	1,490	1,615	1,740	1,865	1,990	2,110	2,235	2,360	2,485	2,610	2,735	2,860	2,980
40 Supplies	0.0785	4,455	4,825	5,200	5,570	5,940	6,310	6,680	7,055	7,425	7,795	8,170	8,540	8,910
42 Water, fuel, electricity	0.1221	7,025	7,610	8,200	8,780	9,365	9,950	10,535	11,120	11,705	12,290	12,875	13,460	14,045
44 Tool maintenance supplies	0.0233	1,320	1,430	1,540	1,650	1,760	1,870	1,980	2,090	2,200	2,310	2,420	2,530	2,640
46 Machine maintenance supplies	0.1488	8,385	9,085	9,785	10,480	11,180	11,880	12,580	13,275	13,975	14,675	15,370	16,070	16,770
48 Spoiled work	0.0403	2,290	2,485	2,645	2,865	3,055	3,245	3,440	3,630	3,820	4,010	4,200	4,395	4,585
49 Other indirect supplies	0.0405	2,300	2,490	2,680	2,870	3,065	3,255	3,445	3,640	3,830	4,020	4,215	4,405	4,595
50 Supplemental wage costs														
Total	0.9266	$52,580	$56,965	$61,320	$65,725	$70,400	$74,480	$78,855	$83,250	$87,625	$92,000	$96,395	$100,775	$105,155

TABLE A–3

Lafayette Brass Company
Department A

Expense Budget Report
Month of March, 1952

Direct Labor in Normal Production—$94,570
Department A Production—4,516,154 lb

Activity Level—84.9%

Actual Expense	Budget Allowance		Description	Variation	Variation Year to Date
$ 80,203	$ 80,380	01	Direct labor	$ 177 S	$ 531 L
$ 19,138	$ 19,590	10	Salaries	$ 452 S	$1,178 S
17,994	16,985	12	Handling	1,009 L	432 L
505	565	14	Tool setting	60 S	192 S
1,755	1,645	16	Cleaning	110 L	208 S
2,112	1,760	18	Other indirect labor	352 L	596 L
5,220	4,665	20	Overtime and night bonus	555 L	1,427 L
150	185	22	Lost time	35 S	82 L
4,407	5,210	30	Total maintenance labor	803 S	305 S
17,186	16,065	32	Machine maintenance labor	1,121 L	2,762 L
2,366	2,110	34	Other maintenance labor	256 L	307 L
$ 70,833	$ 68,780		Total labor charges	$2,053 L	$3,109 L
			Supplies and Services		
9,247	8,350	40	Supplies	897 L	2,136 L
12,300	12,805	42	Water, fuel, electric	505 S	983 S
1,988	2,380	44	Tool maintenance supplies	392 S	105 S
15,352	13,920	46	Machine maintenance supplies	1,432 L	2,491 L
00	00	48	Spoiled work	00	00
3,864	3,755	49	Other indirect supplies	109 L	586 S
14,272	14,595	50	Supplemental wage costs	323 S	951 S
$127,856	$124,585		Total departmental overhead	$3,271 L	$5,111 L

Remarks: Actual costs exceed budget by 2.6 per cent principally because of machine maintenance costs on the Preheating Furnace and Large Breakdown Mill which broke down on March 12. Supply costs also were higher than standard because of large usage of bichromate of soda. Actual expense for grinding rolls included above amounted to $2,852.

S indicates savings.
L indicates losses.

TABLE A–4

Lafayette Brass Company
Mill Division

Summary of Actual Costs vs. Standard
Month of March, 1952

Normal Production—5,500,000 lb—100.0%
March Production—4,616,320 lb— 84.0%

Plant Activity—94.1%

(1) Summary of *Direct Labor* Cost Variations:

	Actual Direct Labor	Budget Direct Labor	Direct Labor Variations		Normal Direct Labor	Activity Level % of Normal
			March	To Date		
Dept. A	$ 80,203	$ 80,380	$ 177	$ (531)	$ 94,570	84.9
Dept. B	27,871	27,961	90	1,146	34,115	82.0
Dept. C	39,435	40,690	1,255	3,315	50,130	81.2
Total	$147,509	$149,031	$1,522	$3,930	$178,815	83.4

(2) Summary of *Direct O.H.* Variations (see Expense Budget Report attached)

	Actual	Budget Allowance	Variance	Variation to Date	Actual as % of Budget Allowances
Dept. A	$127,856	$124,585	$(3,271)	$(5,111)	102.6
Dept. B	36,891	38,989	2,098	4,719	94.6
Dept. C	37,478	36,582	(896)	(1,189)	102.4
Total	$202,225	$200,156	$(2,069)	$(1,581)	101.0

(3) Summary of *All* Actual Cost Variations from Standard Costs of Production:

Variations Subject to Cost Reductions:		
Direct Labor Costs Less Than Standard	$1,522	
Direct Overhead Costs in Excess of Standard	(2,069)	$ (547)
Yield Variations due to Scrap Performance:		
Gain as result of scrap being less than standard MATL YIELD	$1,665	
Gain on Direct Labor D.L. YIELD	3,317	
Gain on Overhead OH YIELD	6,932	11,914
Total Variations Controllable within Mill Division		$11,367
Higher Unit Costs Resulting from Actual Volume Being Less Than Normal		(35,005)
Proportionate Share of Indirect Overhead Variations		2,573
Total Variations from Standard Cost of Production		$(21,065)

actual results vs.
NON-ADJUSTED profit budget -
for company

TABLE A–5

Lafayette Brass Company

Profit and Loss Statement
March, 1952

(000 Omitted)

	Plant 1		Plant 2		Total	
	March Actual	*Profit Budget*	*March Actual*	*Profit Budget*	*March Actual*	*Profit Budget*
1. Production, lb	8,946	9,500	5,320	5,000	14,266	14,500
Gross Pounds Sold:						
To Customer	7,381	7,500	5,143	4,600	12,524	12,100
To Inter Plant	1,664	2,000	321	400	1,985	2,400
Less: Returns	(37)	...	(17)	...	(54)	...
2. Net Pounds Sold	9,008	9,500	5,447	5,000	14,455	14,500
3. Net Sales after Returns:						
Customer	$4,165	$4,216	$2,634	$2,358	$6,799	$6,574
Inter Plant	841	1,005	151	172	992	1,177
Less:						
Freight	(157)	(160)	(116)	(110)	(273)	(270)
Discounts Allowed	(20)	(21)	(16)	(14)	(36)	(35)
4. Net Sales	$4,829	$5,040	$2,653	$2,406	$7,482	$7,446
5. Net Cost of Sales at Standard	4,202	4,390	2,382	2,153	6,584	6,543
6. Gross Profit at						
Standard	$ 627	$ 650	$ 271	$ 253	$ 898	$ 903
% of Sales	13.0	12.9	10.2	10.5	12.0	12.1
7. Variations from Standard:						
Volume	($ 21)	...	($ 10)	($ 20)	($ 31)	($ 20)
Other	18	...	(14)	...	4	...
Total Variations	($ 3)	...	($ 24)	($ 20)	($ 27)	($ 20)
8. Gross Profit Actual	$ 624	$ 650	$ 247	$ 233	$ 871	$ 883
% of Sales	12.9	12.9	9.3	9.7	11.6	11.8
9. Selling Expense	$ 92	$ 90	$ 70	$ 68	$ 162	$ 158
10. Administrative	53	50	28	25	81	75
11. Other (Income) or Deduction, Net	31	30	19	15	50	45
12. Total Commercial Costs	$ 176	$ 170	$ 117	$ 108	$ 293	$ 278
13. Net Profit before Income Taxes and Miscellaneous Adjustment	$ 448	$ 480	$ 130	$ 125	$ 578	$ 605
14. % of Sales	9.3	9.5	4.9	5.2	7.7	8.1

TABLE A–6

Lafayette Brass Company

Plant 1

Profit and Loss Statement
March, 1952

(000 Omitted)

actual results vs. adjusted profit, budget by division

	Mill Division		Rolling Div.		Total Plant 1	
	March Actual	Adj. Budget	March Actual	Adj. Budget	March Actual	Adj. Budget
1. Production, lb	4,616	4,616	4,328	4,328	8,946	8,946
Gross Pounds Sold:						
To Customer	3,571	3,571	3,810	3,810	7,381	7,381
To Inter Plant	1,177	1,177	487	487	1,664	1,664
Less: Returns	(25)	(25)	(12)	(12)	(37)	(37)
2. Net Pounds Sold	4,723	4,723	4,285	4,285	9,008	9,008
3. Net Sales after Returns:						
Customer	$1,971	$1,960	$2,194	$2,175	$4,165	$4,135
Inter Plant	590	589	251	248	841	837
Less:						
Freight	(77)	(80)	(80)	(76)	(157)	(156)
Discounts Allowed	(10)	(10)	(10)	(11)	(20)	(21)
4. Net Sales	$2,474	$2,459	$2,355	$2,366	$4,829	$4,795
5. Net Cost of Sales at Standard	2,188*	2,158*	2,014*	2,011*	4,202*	4,169*
6. Gross Profit at						
Standard	$ 286	$ 301	$ 341	$ 325	$ 627	$ 626
% of Sales	11.6	12.2	14.5	13.9	13.0	13.0
7. Variations from Standard:						
Volume	($ 35)	($ 32)	$ 14	$ 10	($ 21)	($ 22)
Other	14	. . .	4	. . .	18	. . .
Total Variations	($ 21)	($ 32)	$ 18	$ 10	($ 3)	($ 22)
8. Gross Profit Actual	$ 265	$ 269	$ 359	$ 355	624	604
% of Sales	10.7	10.9	15.2	14.3	12.9	12.6
9. Selling Expense	$ 44	$ 45	$ 48	$ 45	$ 92	$ 90
10. Administrative Expense	25	25	28	25	53	50
11. Other (Income) or Deduction, Net	14	15	17	15	31	30
12. Total Commercial Costs	$ 83	$ 85	$ 93	$ 85	$ 176	$ 170
13. Net Profit before Income Taxes and Miscellaneous Adjustment	$ 182	$ 184	$ 266	$ 250	$ 448	$ 434
14. % of Sales	7.4	7.5	11.3	10.7	9.3	9.0

* Net cost of sales at standard for March actual differs from that of adjusted budget because the adjusted budget is based upon a product mix different from that of the actual.

Original budget vs. adjusted profit budget by division

TABLE A-7

Lafayette Brass Company

Plant 1

Original and Adjusted Profit Budgets
March, 1952

(000 Omitted)

	Mill Division		Rolling Division		Total Plant 1	
	Original Budget	Adj. Budget	Original Budget	Adj. Budget	Original Budget	Adj. Budget
1. Production, lb	5,500	4,616	4,000	4,328	9,500	8,946
Gross Pounds Sold:						
To Customer	4,000	3,571	3,500	3,810	7,500	7,381
To Inter Plant	1,500	1,177	500	487	2,000	1,664
Less: Returns	...	(25)	...	(12)	...	(37)
2. Net Pounds Sold	5,500	4,723	4,000	4,285	9,500	9,008
3. Net Sales after Returns:						
Customer	$2,211	$1,960	$2,005	$2,175	$4,216	$4,135
Inter Plant	750	589	255	248	1,005	837
Less:						
Freight	(90)	(80)	(70)	(76)	(160)	(156)
Discounts Allowed	(11)	(10)	(10)	(11)	(21)	(21)
4. Net Sales	$2,860	$2,459	$2,180	$2,336	$5,040	$4,795
5. Net Cost of Sales at Standard	2,512	2,158	2,878	2,011	4,390	4,169
6. Gross Profit at Standard	$ 348	$ 301	$ 302	$ 325	$ 650	$ 626
% of Sales	12.2	12.2	13.9	13.9	12.9	13.0
7. Variations from Standard:						
Volume	...	($ 32)	...	$ 10	...	($ 22)
Other	...	...	...	...	...	...
Total Variations	...	($ 32)	...	$ 10	...	($ 22)
8. Gross Profit Actual	$ 348	$ 269	$ 302	$ 335	$ 650	$ 604
% of Sales	12.2	10.9	13.9	14.3	12.9	12.6
9. Selling Expense	$ 45	$ 45	$ 45	$ 45	$ 90	$ 90
10. Administrative Expense	25	25	25	25	50	50
11. Other (Income) or Deduction, Net	15	15	15	15	30	30
12. Total Commercial Costs	$ 85	$ 85	$ 85	$ 85	$ 170	$ 170
13. Net Profit before Income Taxes and Miscellaneous Adjustment	$ 263	$ 184	$ 217	$ 250	$ 480	$ 434
14. % of Sales	9.2	7.5	9.9	10.7	9.5	9.0

TABLE A–8

Lafayette Brass Company

Plant 1—Mill Division

Sales, Costs, and Profit at Three Selected Volumes
on the Break-even Chart *
1952

(000 Omitted)

	"Normal" Volume	*March Sales Volume*	*March Production Volume*
Sales, lb	5,500	4,723	4,616
Net Sales (52¢/lb av)	$2,860	$2,456	$2,400
Costs:			
Metal (35.7¢/lb)	$1,960	$1,686	$1,646
Direct Labor (3.255¢/lb)	179	154	151
Direct Overhead—Variable (2.58¢/lb)	142	122	119
Direct Overhead—Fixed	81	81	81
Indirect Overhead—Variable (0.4¢/lb)	22	19	18
Indirect Overhead—Fixed	128	128	128
Total Manufacturing Cost	$2,512	$2,190	$2,145
Standard Manufacturing Cost (45.7¢/lb)	$2,512	$2,158	$2,110
Gross Margin at Standard	$ 348	$ 298	$ 290
Volume Variance	. . .	32	35
Gross Profit Actual	$ 348	$ 266	$ 255
Commercial Costs:			
Selling Expense	$ 45	$ 45	$ 45
Administrative Expense	25	25	25
Other Expense	15	15	15
	$ 85	$ 85	$ 85
Net Profit	$ 263	$ 181	$ 170

* See Fig. A–1.

Appendix B

OTTERBEIN CORPORATION

In the summer of 1953, Mr. Charles Vanderlip, the controller of Otterbein Corporation, made the following remarks on budgeting:

"Budgetary control is the road map for management at Otterbein Corporation. It assists us in planning our business and is used as a device to control all phases of our operation. Through this system we establish our goal, coordinate the effort of our management, measure our actual performance against our objective, and focus our attention on those items where actual performance markedly differs from our predetermined objective. Variable budgeting is just an integral part of this successful system at our company."

Otterbein Corporation is a manufacturer of steam and gas turbines, electric motors and generators, heat-transfer apparatus, industrial process equipment, centrifugal blowers, compressors and expanders, superchargers for diesel engines, strainers, tube cleaners, and other industrial equipment. In 1953 the company had five manufacturing divisions in the eastern United States and employed more than 4,000 persons.

The company had its first experience with budgeting when a sizable decline in sales and an operating loss in 1938 prompted Mr. W. S. Otterbein, the former chief executive of the company, to request Mr. Vanderlip to make a forecast of the company's future business. A profit and loss budget was thus prepared for the company under the direction of Mr. Vanderlip on the basis of anticipated sales for the coming year and the company's past experience. This was a fixed budget, and the company expected that it would help management in planning the future course of business and in controlling the company's costs and expenses as well.

However, soon after the introduction of budgetary control, Mr. Otterbein passed away and a new president was brought into the company in 1942. Because of this change in top management and the lack of manpower following the entrance of the United States into World War II, the budgetary system was abandoned by the company in order to concentrate its efforts on war production.

When the war came to an end, the company experienced another change in top management. Mr. T. A. Wakefield was elected in 1943 to be the chairman of the board of directors and the president of the company. In 1946, Mr. O. B. Otterbein was elected president of the company. By that time, the postwar reconversion and a strike in 1946 had resulted in a drop in the company's shipments of more than 50 per cent from its wartime peak. To help Mr. Wakefield and the company in coping with the situation, Mr. Vanderlip suggested to Mr. Wakefield that the company reintroduce the budgetary system. From its experience with the previous budgetary system, the company had learned the strength and weakness of a fixed budget in its practical application. In installing the new budgetary system, necessary improvements and modifications would be made so that the company's management from top to bottom could be assisted by the system in running their business. One of these improvements was in the use of variable budgeting to control manufacturing cost. At first Mr. Wakefield thought that the system would be too complicated to work out. However, he was finally willing to give it a trial.

Under the new system, estimates of new orders by product lines for the succeeding year are first made by the company's district sales managers. These estimates are consolidated at the company's headquarters and checked with the estimates made by the company's divisional sales managers. Each divisional sales manager is a specialist in the line of products for which he is responsible. The divisional sales managers make their estimates on the basis of their knowledge of total availability of business to the industry, the degree of competition within the industry, current trends of prices, wages, and costs, and the company's experience in the past. Mr. Vanderlip, who studies the general economic and business condition for the company, gives assistance to the divisional sales managers in making their estimates.

After the estimates for new orders are completed, the company's sales department estimates the volume of shipments by product lines for the next year. These estimates are made on the basis of a backlog of orders on the books, the estimated new orders to be received, the length of production cycle for each product, the manufacturing facilities of the company at the time, the availability of manpower and materials for the coming period, the status of jobs currently in the process of production, and shipping commitments on orders already received. Extensive consultation and full cooperation with the manufacturing department are indispensable in making such estimates.

On the basis of estimated shipments, preliminary estimates of costs and expenses for the succeeding year are made by the various manufacturing and nonmanufacturing departments. When these estimates are sent to the controller's department, Mr. Vanderlip consolidates them and prepares a forecast of results of operations (profit or loss) by divisions and for the company as a whole. This forecast of profit and loss is presented to the first budget meeting for the succeeding year, in which the executives of the company review and discuss the estimates. If the forecast result of operations are considered to be satisfactory and attainable by the executives at that meeting, the forecast becomes the budget or objective for the result of operations for the ensuing year. At times, it is found necessary to revise the preliminary estimates at the meeting in order to arrive at a desirable profit goal for the budgeted period.

After the objectives of the company have thus been established by the executives, the various divisions and departments now prepare with the assistance of the controller's department detailed budgets for orders, costs, expenses, and profits for their respective departments. These detailed budgets are again combined by the controller to see if the result will meet the objective established by the company. If the goal is attainable, these detailed budgets become the formal budgets for the respective departments. Sometimes when the detailed expense budgets do not agree with the amount provided for in the budget for the result of operations, it will become necessary to revise the detailed budgets through consultation with the respective department heads.

Under the company's earlier budgetary system, budgets were prepared at the divisional level only. The result was found to be unsatisfactory for control purposes because no definite responsibility could be established for cost control. The procedure was therefore changed under the new system, and budgets are now prepared by departments. Departmentalization for budget preparation is carried down to the lowest supervision level according to foremanship responsibility so that cost control can be exercised at points where actual expenditures are made. Therefore, for budgetary purposes, the company's Tecumseh Division is first broken down into departments according to major functions such as manufacturing, engineering, sales, administrative, etc.; each of these departments is, in turn, further divided into smaller departments according to its organizational structure. For instance, the manufacturing department is broken down into receiving and store (C10), shipping (C11), turbocharger (C12), machine (C13), assembly (C14), plate and weld (C15), assembly and test turbines (C16), general factory (C17), foundry (C21), etc. Some of these departments are further divided into subdepartments where different foremen are in charge. Hence, the machine department (C13) is divided into lathe department (C130), horizontal boring mill (C131), milling machine (C132), radial drill (C133), screw machine (C134), vertical boring mill (C136), and forge mill (C137). In 1953 there were approximately 70 departments in the Tecumseh Division where departmental budgets were prepared.

The company's accounting system, which was designed to collect needed information with a minimum of clerical work and to furnish management with timely reports for intelligent interpretation, facilitates the preparation of budgets and comparison of actual performance against budgets. The same accounting classification is used for budgetary purposes as that used for accounting purposes, and every item of expense is budgeted.

The company uses a job order cost system. To budget direct material and direct labor costs, estimated costs on the basis of engineering specification and the company's past experience are used. Cost estimates are made by the cost analyst in the company's cost department, who analyzes the direct material and direct labor costs on every order that goes through the mill. The company is in a unique position in having a cost analyst who is a combination of an accountant and engineer. To do his work efficiently and quickly would take years of experience and background knowledge of the company's products, manufacturing processes, and their costs.

For each job order, identity for direct material and direct labor is maintained throughout the process of production even after the work has been completed as parts. Factory overhead is added to the manufacturing cost through the application of standard burden rates. The company's finished product usually consists of an assembly of numerous parts. By adding factory overhead to the final assembled cost the company eliminates the necessity of adding overhead separately to each of the thousand parts which go into the manufacture of one generator. Through this simplification of accounting procedure, and elimination of all other detailed accounting which serves no useful purpose, the controller's department was able to provide satisfactory service to the company without noticeably increasing their work load even though the company's sales had been doubled in recent years.

In preparing budgets for factory, engineering, and administrative expenses, three types of budgets are used under the new system. These are (1) fixed or period budgets, (2) project budgets, and (3) variable budgets.

Fixed or period budgets are established for those departments, such as accounting, treasury, sales engineering, and the like, where expenses would usually be fixed within the budget period. Changes in the company's volume of business during the budget period usually would have little effect on these expenses. These budgets are prepared by the respective department heads or managers on the basis of the company's past experience and management's expectation and policy for the planned period. Sometimes, when significant changes in any of these department's expenses are expected during the budgeted period, the annual fixed budgets will be broken down into semiannual or quarterly budgets in order to reflect the changes in the planned period and to avoid distortion in comparing actual expenses with average monthly budgets as these monthly allowances are obtained by averaging the annual allowances into equal monthly parts.

Project budgets are used for research and development expenses where specific amounts have been approved by management for certain specific projects. This type of budget is also used for controlling expenditures for plant, equipment, and property. Forms of progress reports showing budget allowances and actual expenditures for these two types of expenses are given in Tables B–1 and B–2.

Variable (or flexible) expense budgets are used for factory expenses. From its experience with the previous fixed budgetary system, the company had learned that certain items of manufacturing expenses, such as supplies and the like, would vary with changes in the level of manufacturing activities. Certain manufacturing expenses, such as indirect labor, had a fixed relation to time as well as a variable relation to the volume of production. Other items of factory expenses, such as depreciation or real estate taxes, would continue even when there was no production in the factory. Therefore, fixed budgets, though indispensable for planning purposes, did not serve as a satisfactory means in controlling factory expenses when the actual volume of production differed from the anticipated volume of production. Under the new system, variable budgeting is used as a means to control manufacturing expenses.

In preparing departmental variable expense budgets at the foremanship level, only controllable expenses are included in the budgets and the foreman is made responsible for all controllable expenses incurred within his department. The company feels that the foreman of any department should not be held responsible for those manufacturing expenses which are incurred as a result of top management decision and over which the foreman could not exercise any control. Therefore, the foreman of a milling-machine department would be held responsible for all the payroll expenses within his department and his other operating costs such as supplies, expendable tools, semidurable tools and equipment, repairs to machinery and equipment, repairs and replacement of jigs and fixtures, spoiled and defective works, instruction and training, and miscellaneous expenses. Included in his payroll expenses are hourly wages paid to helpers, errand boy, sweepers, and cleaners; compensation paid for clerical work in his department; compensation of the foreman and other supervisory personnel; overtime and night-shift bonus; lost productive time and extra work; pro-rata accrual, applicable to the current period, of estimated annual cost of vacations and holidays for hourly employees within his department; pensions; social security taxes; and employee insurance applicable to his department. Included in the supplies are expenses for such items as lubricating oils, greases, cutting compound, cleaning compound, cotton waste, bolts, washers, etc. Included in the expendable tools are such items as drills, cutter blades, ring gauges, and other hand tools and instruments of a portable nature. Costs of repairing such tools and equipment are also included in that account. Included in semidurable tools and equipment are those tools and equipment which do not fall into the category of expendable tools, but because of their size, portability, and relatively small unit cost they are not capitalized for practical purposes. Fixed expenses such as depreciation, property insurance, and taxes are not included in the foreman's departmental budgets because they are out of his personal control and responsibility. They would be included in the summarized budgets for the machine departments and total factory expenses for the Tecumseh Division. Likewise, the milling-machine department foreman would not be held responsible for the portion of general factory expenses and power plant expenses redistributed to his department for planning, costing, and accounting purposes.

For every budgeted expense, the budget allowance is expressed in terms of dollars. In figuring allowances for indirect labor, supervision, and the like, the number of men required at the anticipated level of production activity is established and translated into dollar allowances on the basis of their salary or wage rates. However, for other expenses, such as supplies, the company does not use any physical measuring units to arrive at dollar allowances because there are several hundred items involved in one account and it would not be feasible or economically justified for the company to go into such detail. Mr. Vanderlip said that if the company tried to control these supplies, item by item, it would be like putting a $300 policeman to guard a $100 ring.

The level of activity, which determines the amount of budget allowance for manufacturing expense under variable budget, is measured in terms of productive labor-hours, i.e., actual direct labor-hours. Other measures of level of activity had been considered but were rejected as not feasible. Unit of output is not used because the wide variety of the company's product as well as their big assortment of sizes makes this measurement unrepresentative of the company's manufacturing activity. Measurement in terms of per cent of plant capacity is considered impracticable because the company has known from its past experience that sometimes one machine might be loaded with work while others might be lying idle. Direct machine-hours are not used because the company has not in the past accumulated any statistics on that basis. The cost of compiling another set of statistics merely for budgetary purposes is deemed to be unjustified. The company does not use direct labor dollars to measure its level of activities because this measurement is subject to distortion by changes in wage rates.

Direct labor-hours are considered fairly representative of the company's level of production activity. Since it had already been compiled for payroll purposes and was, therefore, readily available for budgetary purposes, it was selected as the measure of the company's level of manufacturing activities.

The variable expense budget for each factory expense is expressed by three elements, viz., the fixed element, the variable element, and the level of activity. In Table B-3, budget report for the milling-machine department, the first column gives the names of the expense accounts. The second column represents the fixed element of the monthly budget allowance. The third column is the budget standard for the variable element expressed in terms of dollars per productive labor-hour. The last line of the fourth column gives the budgeted productive labor-hours for the month. The last line of the fifth column gives the actual productive hours for the month. The total budget allowance for each expense, shown in the fourth column, is the sum of the fixed monthly allowance (column 2) and the product of the actual productive labor-hours multiplied by the variable allowance per productive labor-hour (column 3).

Budget standards for each department's manufacturing expenses are established on the basis of past experience and expected changes during the budget period. In earlier years a scatter diagram was drawn for each manufacturing expense and the budget line for that expense would be drawn on the diagram. Mr. Vanderlip pointed out that many persons would extrapolate the budget line to a theoretical zero volume to obtain the fixed element. He said that it would be mere chance or luck if the fixed element of any expense at zero volume obtained through extrapolation would be the actual expense at that volume. At Otterbein Corporation, the budget line on the scatter diagram is considered representative of a relationship between volume and expense only within the range of activity experienced by the company in the past, and no extrapolation would be made beyond that range. Mr. Vanderlip also said that most people would look down on past experience and would not take it as the right standard. At Otterbein Corporation, past experience is considered to be the right standard, unless it could be proved otherwise. Many times it did. In such case, the standard would be corrected.

In recent years, because the range of activities at Otterbein Corporation has not been very large, no scatter diagram has been drawn for any manufacturing expense. Instead, the vice-president in charge of manufacturing and the works controller would first determine the probable range of manufacturing activity for the ensuing year. Budget allowances for each expense at the possible high level and low level of activities would be determined. Based on these two budget allowances, the fixed element and the variable element of the budget standard for any level within the anticipated range of activity could then be calculated.

For instance, in October, 1952, the company started preparing its budgets for 1953. During the first six months of 1953 the milling-machine department would be expected to work at levels ranging from 6,500 to 8,500 productive labor-hours per month. Based on the department's most recent experience during the first nine months of 1952 and the company's expectation for 1953, three and a half men would be needed for indirect labor if the department operated at 6,500 productive labor-hours per month. At the operating level of 8,500 productive labor-hours per month, four and a half men would be needed for indirect labor. By applying the wage rates for these workers, budget allowances for indirect labor would be $828 and $1,008 at levels of 6,500 and 8,500 productive labor-hours per month, respectively. The variable element of the budget standard was obtained by dividing the estimated increase of $180 in indirect labor expense from $828 to $1,008 per month by the corresponding increase of 2,000 hr in manufacturing activity from 6,500 hr to 8,500 hr per month. Therefore, the variable element of the budget allowance for indirect labor in the milling-machine department would be $0.090 per productive labor-hour. The fixed element of the budget allowance was obtained by subtracting from the total budget allowance of $828 at 6,500 productive labor-hours the variable allowance of $585 (0.090 per productive labor-hour × 6,500 hr) for the same level. Therefore, the fixed element of the budget allowance for indirect labor expense in the milling-machine department would be $243 per month. The monthly budget allowance for indirect labor in the milling-machine department for the anticipated high level and low level during the first six months of 1953 and for actual April, 1953, production would be as follows:

	Level of Activity		
	6,500 Hr	6,889* Hr	8,500 Hr
Fixed allowance	$243	$243	$ 243
Variable allowance (at $0.090 per hour)	585	620	765
Total budget allowance	$828	$863	$1,008
Cost per productive labor-hour	$0.1275	$0.1250	$0.1186

* Actual productive labor-hours of milling-machine department in April, 1953.

While the level of activity used in figuring budget allowances for any manufacturing department, such as the milling-machine department, is based on the productive labor-hours of that particular department, the level of activity of the maintenance department and other service departments is measured by the productive labor-hours of the plant as a whole, as it is the duty of the maintenance department to keep all the machines in good operating condition. The size of the maintenance crew is decided by the vice-president in charge of manufacturing, who makes sure that there will be enough people to take care of the work. All other expenses of the maintenance department are controlled by means of variable expense budget.

As mentioned earlier, the company's result of operations budget is based on the anticipated level of activity for the budget period. However, factory expenses are added to the cost of production at standard rates which are established on the basis of normal level of activity. The normal level of activity differs from the anticipated level of activity in that it does not represent the company's expectation for the next year but the company's judgment for a reasonable balance between the company's capacity to produce and its ability to sell over a number of years. By the nature of its business, the company knows from past experience that its sales and production will fluctuate from period to period. Mr. Vanderlip said that, if the anticipated level of activity for the current period were used in absorbing manufacturing overhead, the results would be misleading with regard to the company's inventory valuation, costing, and pricing of the products. Since the result of operations budget is intended to show management in advance costs and expenses that will be incurred at the anticipated level of activity and that, if the anticipated level of activity does not happen to be the same as the normal level of activity used in establishing standard rates for overhead absorption, there will be an overabsorption or underabsorption of the company's budgeted manufacturing expenses. These underabsorbed and overabsorbed manufacturing expenses are included in the "result of operations" budget as factory burden variance, as shown in Table B–4.

The decision to use a month as the basic budget period for checking actual performance was made by top management who wanted to be kept informed of the actual result of operations on that basis. Mr. Vanderlip thought a month to be the shortest practical budget period in his company, although he was of the opinion that a 3-month period might be better than a 1-month period in eliminating temporary peaks and valleys in expenditures. In establishing standards of monthly budget allowance for each manufacturing expense, it is usually assumed that the operating set-up of that department will remain the same for the entire budget year. However, should any significant changes, such as installation of new machinery, changes in plant layout, etc., be expected during the budget year and when such changes would materially affect the manufacturing expenses in that department, the budget year would be broken down into several semiannual or quarterly periods and different monthly standards would be set up for each of these periods to reflect such changes. For instance, the monthly budget standard of the milling-machine department as shown in Table B–3 covered only the first six months of 1953.

Budget standards for each foreman's controllable expenses are established jointly by the assistant controller, who is also the works controller, and the factory budget analyst with the cooperation of the respective foreman. The factory budget analyst, who is an assistant to the factory superintendent, does the preliminary statistical work. The budget standard of any factory department has to be reviewed and agreed to by the foreman of that department. If the foreman thinks the budget unreasonable, he can object to the budget, and he is free to call upon the controller for explanation. Since he is the person responsible for the expenses in his department, his agreement as to what his expenses should be during the next year is an indispensable factor if the administration of the budget system is to be successful.

Once the budget standard is established, the company usually will not revise it during the budget year if operating conditions reveal that only a minor revision of standard might be needed. Even when major changes are needed, the company will usually deliberately resist revising the standard until the budget for the following year is prepared. The red flags on budget reports will make the responsible person look into the situation more carefully, even though he knows that the standard is in need of adjustment.

From its past experience, the company learned that actual manufacturing expenses would usually fall within the budget allowance when the level of activity was rising. The company also learned that when the level of activity was declining actual manufacturing expenses would usually be higher than the budget allowances. Mr. Vanderlip explained that both of these two situations were caused by the time lag of indirect expenses in responding to change in volume of production. The company does not establish different standards for any manufacturing expense to fit into the upswing or downswing of business. However, at any time when the volume of activity drops significantly, the company polices its budgets more vigorously to keep its costs and expenses under control.

The company does not relate the compensation of any of its foremen or supervisors to his budget performance. The company is afraid that, if it adopted an incentive plan in which the foreman's earnings would be tied to his budget performance, some foremen would try to make their budget standards as loose as possible so that they could easily meet their budget standards and get the most benefits for themselves out of the incentive plan. Those foremen who did not do so would become dissatisfied when they discovered that other persons had deliberately taken part in such practices. The result would be suspicion, chaos, and fighting among the foremen themselves and between the foremen and top management in trying to loosen the standard on one hand and to tighten the standard on the other. Moreover, on many occasions savings in manufacturing costs and expenses could not be attributed to closer supervision by the foreman or to more effort by the workers. The installation of better machinery and equipment, improved methods and procedures, better plant layout, and many other decisions made by top management could result in savings in manufacturing expenses. If the foreman's earnings were tied to the budget standard, and when any change in budget standard would likely have adverse effects on his earnings, he would resist such changes in standard even if he knew that such high-cost standard was no longer justified under the new operating conditions. Under these circumstances, the company would "be run by the budget" instead of the budget being used as a means to assist the management for more efficient operation and control. Furthermore, Mr. Vanderlip said that the cost of premium under an incentive plan and the cost of administering such a plan might very well offset the possible savings in manufacturing expense derived from such a plan.

Monthly budget reports on controllable factory expenses are prepared by the the accounting department and presented to each foreman, showing a comparison of his actual expenses against his budget allowances for the month immediately preceding and for the period covering the year to date. When there was any significant variation of actual expense from its budget allowance, the accounting department, by digging into its accounting records, would explain on the budget report, as shown in Table B–3, what had been charged to that expense account during the month. With the report supplied by the accounting department, the foreman would be able to find out the causes for such variation. Any necessary action to correct the situation would have to be taken by the foreman himself or by the vice-president in charge of manufacturing. Monthly budget reports for nonmanufacturing departments are prepared in the same manner by the accounting department and presented to the respective departmental foremen or managers. Summarized budget reports of related departments and of total factory expenses are prepared for higher executives.

In the manufacturing expense budget reports, direct material and direct labor are not included. For each job order, comparison of actual direct material and direct labor costs with their estimated costs are shown on the job order sheet. Therefore, upon completion of his work, the foreman of each department would be able to tell whether there had been any variation of actual costs from the estimated costs and to know the causes for such variation. Mr. Vanderlip said that among the causes of direct material cost variation were higher or lower prices paid for the material, use of substitute material, and more or less efficient operation. Among the causes of direct labor cost variation were the use of more or less expensive labor, more or less efficient operation, and the use of new equipment or processes.

For top management, reports on the actual result of operations in comparison with budgets are prepared by the controller's department on a monthly and quarterly basis. These reports are prepared by departments (product lines), by divisions, and for the company as a whole. These reports, together with reports on order booking and shipment, keep top management informed whether the company has been able to meet their objectives. If not, top management will decide on the necessary action to correct the situation.

On the report for the result of operations, as shown in Table B–4, comparisons of actual results with budgeted results are also made in terms of percentage of net sales. These percentage comparisons are the key figures used by top management in checking actual direct material and direct labor costs with their estimated costs. Because the actual shipment would most likely differ from the budgeted shipment, comparison of actual direct material and direct labor costs with their budgeted costs established on the basis of anticipated shipment in terms of absolute figures would be misleading unless these absolute figures are translated into percentage of net sales. If there was any significant variation of the actual percentage costs with the budgeted percentage costs, investigation would be made to ascertain whether such variations were caused by changes in selling price, changes in material or labor costs, or changes in both.

It might also be noted that in Table B–4 on the result of operations report, the actual factory burden variance consisted in fact of two elements, i.e., (1) volume variance and (2) budget variance. The volume variance is the result of actual level of activity being different from the normal level of activity. The budget variance is the result of actual expenditures of manufacturing expenses being different from their budgeted allowance. At Otterbein Corporation, the two variances are not separated on its books because the work involved would be tremendous and by the nature of the company's "custom-tailored" business "you would not know what to do with them after you got them separated." Mr. Vanderlip said that the company already had sufficient means to control its operation by carefully watching its sales and keeping close control of expenses at points where they were incurred.

The company's budgetary committee consists of the president, vice-president in charge of manufacturing, vice-president in charge of sales engineering, divisional vice-presidents, secretary-treasurer, controller, and division controllers. The controller also serves as the budget director of the company. In the factory, the budget analyst is an assistant to the factory superintendent. All routine work in the preparation of budgets and reports for actual results is done by the company's accounting department, and there is no separate budget department in the company. Mr. Vanderlip said that the company did not incur any additional cost in administering its present budgetary system. The budget reports merely substituted reports that would have been made without the budgetary system.

The new budgetary system was well accepted throughout the company, and the company had been very successful in administering this budgetary system. Mr. Vanderlip attributed this success, in part, to the cooperation between the accounting department and the factory department. The accounting department provided all the necessary information to the factory department both in the preparation of budgets and the reporting of actual results. The factory department made its own decisions on the amount of budget allowance and took the responsibility for following up any variance. The company did not reprimand its foreman for spoiled and defective work. Otherwise, the foremen would not report such work. Through the collection of true information and cooperative discussions with its foremen, the company was able to find ways and means of improving its operation.

The budgetary reports are the only documents by which the factory foremen can tell how well they have operated their departments. Through Mr. Vanderlip's salesmanship, they became interested in the system and were very cooperative in the installation and administration of the budget.

Besides selling the system to the factory people, Mr. Vanderlip had to sell the system to top management too. Originally, the company's top management did not believe in control through reports and budgets. Mr. Vanderlip waited patiently until the company was in need of such a system and was then able to convince top management of its usefulness first. It was an evolutionary process. Although appreciation of its value was slow in coming, top management each year became more convinced of its usefulness. At first, the company's top management was only interested in budgets for bookings, shipments, and net profits. All other budgets were left to the rest of the executives. Since 1950, reports on results of operations presented to the board of directors have been related to budgets at the request of the company's chairman of the board.

In conclusion, Mr. Vanderlip said that the budgetary system at Otterbein Corporation was set up to assist its management in more efficient operation. Control could be exercised only through people. An accounting or budget system must be shaped to the persons with whom one deals. The high degree of success in the company's budgetary system was achieved through salesmanship and without dictatorial authority. It was budgeting by cooperation and persuasion rather than by compulsion. Mr. Vanderlip's final advice on setting up a variable budget system was as follows:

"1. The budget covers only a small segment, not a wide range, of the production curve.

2. Do not be highly theoretical about the fixed amount of the budget.

3. The budget should be established according to the organization you have, not what you do not have.

4. Do not cross responsibility in establishing budgets.

5. Budgets should not be limited to controlling expenses but should be used as a means of controlling all phases of operation. It is the road map of management."

TABLE B-1

Otterbein Corporation

PROGRESS REPORT

Page _____ of _____

☐ Product Improvement Expense
☐ Company Sponsored Research Projects

Division _____   As of _____ 19___

Description	Order No.	Current Month Expenditures	Current Year						Total Project	
			Expenditures				Budget	Unexpended Balance	Amount Expended	Amount Estimated
			Eng. & Draft.	Patterns	Tooling	Mfg. & Test	Total			

TABLE B–2
Otterbein Corporation

PROGRESS REPORT
of Capital Expenditures

Division _____ As of _____ 19____ Page ____ of ____

Description	Budget			Authorized		Appropriations			
	Project No.	Project Amount	Expended Prior Years	Current Year Budget	Autho. No.	Amount	Expenditures		Balance Unexpended	Unauthorized Balance of Budget
							Current Month	Year to Date		

230

TABLE B–3
Otterbein Corporation

BUDGET REPORT   Controllable   Expenses

Division B

Department C 13 Machine Group

Subdepartment C 132 Milling Machine Department

	First 6 Months Budget			This Month			Year to Date			
Account	Fixed Amount per Month	Per Productive Labor-hour	Budget		Actual	Difference	Budget Original	App'd. Adj.	Actual	Difference (Month of April / 1953)
2 Indirect labor	$ 243	0.0900	$ 863		$ 924	($ 61)	$ 3,713		$ 4,096	($ 383)
3 Salaries	318		318		360	(42)	1,272		1,242	30
4 Supervision	616	0.1032	1,327		1,388	(61)	5,607		5,670	(63)
5 Lost production time and extra work	...	0.0038	26		6	20	116		87	29
6 Instruction and training	...	0.0065	45		...	45	198		2	196
7a Overtime bonus	...	0.0700	482		6	476	2,132		1,245	887
7b Night-shift bonus	195	0.0283	195		174	21	862		745	117
8 Vacations and holidays	1,052	...	1,052		1,052	...	4,208		4,208	...
9 Social security taxes	498	...	498		498	...	1,992		1,992	...
10 Pensions	1,222	...	1,222		1,204	18	4,888		4,817	71
11 Employee welfare insurance	227	...	227		259	(32)	908		991	(83)
12 Compensation insurance	91	...	91		73	18	364		360	4
Total payroll expense	$4,267	0.3018	$ 6,346		$ 5,944	$402	$26,260		$25,455	$ 805
13 Supplies	...	0.0518	357	(1)	88	269	1,578		568	1,010
14 Expandable tools	...	0.3690	2,542	(2)	3,062	(520)	11,239		10,473	766
15 Semidurable tools and equipment	...	0.0152	104	(3)	5	99	463		552	(89)
16 Repairs to machinery, equipment and furniture	...	0.0624	430	(4)	580	(150)	1,900		1,749	151
17 Repairs and replacement—jigs and fixtures	...	0.0108	75		79	(4)	329		309	20
20 Spoiled and defective work	...	0.0634	437		300	137	1,931		1,138	793
64 Miscellaneous	...	...	...		...	...	...		25	(25)
Total	$4,267	0.8744	$10,291		$10,058	$233	$43,700		$40,269	$3,431

Personnel { Productive (number of persons)					46	
Indirect					5	
Total					51	
Hourly Rate	F	s	Vot			
Productive Labor Hours { Inventory			7,500		6,567	611
Expense and development					322	
Total			30,000		6,889	

Year to Date: Inventory 29,079; Expense and development 1,379; Total 30,458; Difference (458)

Notes to Budget Report (as shown at the back of the report):
(1). 13   Make studs and bolts $22; naphtha $5; oil $22; abrasives $5; miscellaneous $34.
(2). 14   Sander belts $123; side mills $285; cutter blades $51; standard tools $224; Kennametal tools $30; end mills $14; files and handles $40; saw blades $19; taps $14; drills $67; dress grinding wheels $112; repair cutters $56; make broaches $124; repair pyrometer $77; make lathe tools $57; grind tools and cutters $1,759.
(3). 15   Install air line for babbitt pots 5.
(4). 16   Lamps, sockets, etc., $36; repair: water cooler $11; Keyseater $59; shaper $12; grinders $23; milling machines $314; lathes $79; drill press $29; steel $8; belting 9.

231

TABLE B-4

Otterbein Corporation

Comparison of Budgeted and Actual Results of Operations
B   Division   Period Ending   April 30, 1953

	Current Month					Year to Date					
	Budget		Actual		% Budget Attained	Budget		Actual		Variance	% Budget Attained
	Amount	%	Amount	%		Amount	%	Amount	%		
Net shipments	$471,000	101.9	$532,245	102.6	113	$1,884,000	101.9	$1,882,608	102.0	($ 1,392)	100
Less cost of											
Purchased auxiliaries	3,642		7,599		218	14,568		16,738		(2,170)	115
Installation	3,642		3,431		93	14,568		10,599		3,969	73
Royalties											
Transportation, bonds, etc.	1,716		2,449		143	6,864		9,934		(3,070)	145
	9,000	1.9	13,479	2.6	150	36,000	1.9	37,271	2.0	(1,271)	103
Net shipments—Manufactured products	462,000	100.0	518,766	100.0	112	1,848,000	100.0	1,845,337	100.0	(2,663)	100
Factory cost—Manufactured products:											
Material	102,830	22.2	115,167	22.2	xxx	411,320	22.2	397,597	21.6	xxx	xxx
Direct labor	52,114	11.3	54,806	10.5	xxx	208,456	11.3	210,365	11.4	xxx	xxx
Factory expense (standard)	78,417	17.0	82,962	16.0	xxx	313,668	17.0	315,901	17.1	xxx	xxx
Receiving and stores expense (standard)	4,661	1.0	5,064	1.0	xxx	18,644	1.0	18,481	1.0	xxx	xxx
Shipping expense (standard)	2,208	0.5	1,954	0.4	xxx	8,832	0.5	7,269	0.4	xxx	xxx
Subcontract costs					xxx					xxx	xxx
	240,230	52.0	259,953	50.1	108	960,920	52.0	949,613	51.5	11,307	98
Inventory shortage provision	6,324	1.4	7,339	1.4	xxx	25,296	1.4	28,826	1.5	xxx	xxx
Factory burden variance	3,860	0.8	2,896	0.6	xxx	15,440	0.8	6,690	0.4	xxx	xxx
Foundry cost variance			5,555	1.1	xxx			14,536	0.8	xxx	xxx
	250,914	54.2	275,743	53.2	110	1,001,656	54.2	999,665	54.2	1,991	100
Development	39,630	8.6	25,145	4.8	xxx	158,520	8.6	104,538	5.6	xxx	xxx
	290,044	62.8	300,888	58.0	104	1,160,176	62.8	1,104,203	59.8	55,973	95
Gross profit	171,956	37.2	217,878	42.0	127	687,824	37.2	741,134	40.2	53,310	108

Commercial expenses:

Field engineering	11,844		13,418		113	47,376		49,350		(2,154)	105
Commissions	1,815		3,568		197	7,260		4,558		2,702	63
Field correction	6,160		9,656		157	24,640		27,294		(2,654)	111
Application engineering	8,585		12,840		150	34,340		31,127		3,213	91
Advertising	2,563		2,563		100	10,252		10,252			100
Executive sales office	1,423		1,555		109	5,692		6,097		(405)	107
Product improvement	9,702		9,702		100	38,808		38,808			100
Administrative	14,207		14,030		99	56,828		53,979		2,849	95
Executive office	5,716		7,456		130	22,864		22,576		288	99
Miscellaneous over/under-absorbed			(294)					6,970		(6,970)	
	62,015	13.4	74,494	14.4	120	248,060	13.4	251,191	13.6	(3,131)	101
Departmental net profit	109,941	23.8	143,384	27.6	130	439,764	23.8	489,943	26.6	50,179	111
Research	9,240		13,096		142	36,960		67,266		(30,306)	182
Obsolete inventory	2,055					8,220		3,397		4,823	41
Interest on bank loan	10,010		10,828		108	40,040		43,217		(3,277)	108
Miscellaneous other charges	(13,963)		6		85	(55,852)		22		(2,570)	95
Miscellaneous other income	(5,134)		(11,808) (3,478)		68	(20,536)		(53,304) (17,759)		(2,777)	88
Service department	2,208	0.5	8,644	1.7	392	8,832	0.5	42,939	2.3	(34,107)	486
Net income before taxes	107,733	23.3	134,740	25.9	125	430,932	23.3	447,004	24.3	16,072	104
Provision for income taxes	59,000	12.8	74,000	14.3	125	236,000	12.8	246,000	13.3	(10,000)	104
Net income	$ 48,733	10.5	$ 60,740	11.6	125	$ 194,932	10.5	$ 201,004	11.0	$ 6,072	103

TABLE B–5

Otterbein Corporation

Illustrative Form of

Sales Budget and Summarized Report on Orders Booked

Sales Dept.	Products	Total	Atlanta	Boston	Chicago	Detroit
ACCESSORIES	Strainers Other Apparatus Repairs Total					
TURBINE	Mechanical Drive Mechanical Drive Repairs Total Large Turbines Large Turbine Repairs Total					
CONDENSER	Power Condensers Power Ejectors Other Apparatus Repairs Total					
SUPERCHARGER	Apparatus Repairs Total					
BLOWERS	Blowers Other Apparatus Repairs Total					
	GRAND TOTAL					

TABLE B–6

Otterbein Corporation

Comparison of Actual Orders Booked and Sales Budget

District Office _____   For Period _____ to _____ 19 ___

Sales Dept.	Products	Sales Quota	Orders Booked		% Sales Quota	Earned Credit Year-to-Date
			Current Month	Year-to-Date		
ACCESSORIES	Strainers					
	Other Apparatus Repairs					
	Total					
TURBINE	Mechanical Drive					
	Mechanical Drive Repairs					
	Total					
	Large Turbines					
	Large Turbine Repairs					
	Total					
CONDENSER	Power Condensers					
	Power Ejectors					
	Other Apparatus Repairs					
	Total					
SUPERCHARGER	Apparatus Repairs					
	Total					
BLOWERS	Blowers					
	Other Apparatus Repairs					
	Total					
	TOTAL					

Actual District Office Expense to Date

Variance to Date

Ratio—Expense to Orders Booked

Appendix C

MENLO CHEMICAL COMPANY

The following remark on variable budgeting was made by the new Budget Director of Menlo Chemical Company in the summer of 1953.

"Flexible budget is the most dangerous trap in accounting if you do not know its limitations. We started to use flexible budgeting in 1946. But our experience with flexible budget procedure, as customarily used by industry, has not proved satisfactory in that our attempts to base flexible budgets upon percentages of operating capacity did not secure the degree of accuracy for which the system had been designed. Although we are still 'flexing' our budgets, our method used at present differs completely from the one we used seven years ago."

Menlo Chemical Company is a manufacturer of industrial and agricultural chemicals, with a number of plants located along the Atlantic Coast and in the Middle West. In 1953, the company employed over 2,500 people of whom about 1,200 were employed at plants near the headquarters of the company. The following discussion on budgetary control is confined to the company's experience at its main division plants.

Prior to 1946 the company had used an "actual product cost system." Under this system all costs or expenses incurred in any plant were charged to the cost of manufacturing for the products turned out by that plant. Until then, no attempt had been made further to break down cost by department within the plant.

In 1946 the management of the company felt that their cost system did not provide adequate means for cost control and for product costing. Hence, the company employed the services of one of the well-known management consulting firms to study the company's problems. Nine months later a new cost system which was comprised in part of standard cost and in part of flexible budget was introduced throughout the company's main division plants.

Under the new system, responsibilities for cost control were established at points of expenditure. Each plant was divided into several cost centers according to the nature of its operation, and the foreman of each center was made responsible for the performance of his department. For example, the agricultural chemicals plant was divided into nine cost centers as follows: (1) rock grinding; (2) acidulating; (3) pelletizing; (4) material unloading and storage; (5) shipping and related operations; (6) bridge cranes, gantry crane, and electric locomotives; (7) plant building and trucks; (8) pier facilities; and (9) plant management. Shipping and related operations were further divided into five subcost centers: (*a*) rasping, milling, screening, and cleansing; (*b*) bagging; (*c*) bagged shipments; (*d*) bulk shipments; and (*e*) bag-house operation.

The foreman of each department was held responsible for all expenses over which he could exercise control. Included in this category were material, labor, supplies, and the like. Control of depreciation expense was not considered within the foreman's responsibility as it was largely the result of decisions made at higher management level.

Material cost was controlled through the use of standard cost. Standard usage for every product was established by the process department according to the production formula. Standard material price was established by the purchasing department. Purchase price variance was separated when material was issued. Material usage variance was separated when production was completed. Both variances would later be closed to the cost of sales account through a production cost variances account.

Because of frequent changes in the company's volume of business, a flexible budget system was installed to control the company's processing cost which included both labor and overhead. It was expected that, through the use of flexible budget, the company would be able to keep its cost under control as its volume of business fluctuated from one level to another.

At each cost center, budget standards for every item of labor and overhead expenses under the foreman's control were established for different levels of operation. The level of activity was measured by the plant's output in tonnage and was expressed in terms of per cent of normal capacity. At 100 per cent capacity, the plant's production would reach its engineering capacity.

All budget allowances were expressed in terms of dollars to give a common denominator for all types of items. The comparison of actual performance against budget standard was thus facilitated, as all accounting entries were also expressed in terms of dollars.

The establishment of the budget allowance for each cost center was made on the basis of discussions with the foreman of that department. Each foreman would give his estimate of what the cost should be at different levels of operation on the basis of his own experience and judgment. The company had not in the past accumulated cost figures at departmental levels. Therefore, no previous cost record was available to help establish the budget standard.

Budget figures for different levels of operation were tabulated in columnar form at intervals of 5 per cent from the normal plant capacity. The tabulation was done to ease the comparison of actual performance against budget standard.

All budgets were prepared on a weekly basis. Each week a report would be prepared by the plant budget department and issued to the foreman to show his actual performance of the previous week as well as his budget standard. Comparison was also made on a monthly and yearly basis.

The system was put into use for a year. At the end of the period, budget variance amounted to approximately $800,000. Upon investigation, the company discovered that its labor expenses in many producing centers were more or less fixed. Within certain limits, the company could not decrease or increase the number of persons in a crew even if the volume of production changed. Only when the plant's production was changed from a one-shift operation to a two- or three-shift operation, or vice versa, did the labor expense undergo significant change. At such time, an entire crew had to be added or dropped from operation.

The company also found that its highest maintenance expenditure occurred during the period when its plant was at the lowest level of activity. Conversely, the higher the plant's level of operation, the lower would be its maintenance cost. This was due to the fact that, because of the nature of the manufacturing operation, much maintenance work could be done only when the plant was shut down. At such time, there would, of course, be no production in the plant.

In addition, the company noted that the situation had been further complicated by the presence of product mix. In certain cost centers, such as shipping, a great many different products were handled. Under the flexible budget, costs of handling an equal tonnage of two different products would be the same, whereas the actual cost might be entirely different because of variation in packing, volume of units handled, and the like.

Because of the unsatisfactory experience with the system, the company decided that its flexible budget, as then used, was not adequate for management's needs. The system was therefore revised and the old method of "flexing" abandoned. The company's new budgetary system, as now used, comprises a system of fixed budget combined with standard cost and a special feature of "flexing" for items such as labor, labor increment, and utilities.

Under the new fixed budget system, the sales forecast became the backbone of all budgets. Three months before the beginning of the new business year, the sales department of the company would prepare a sales forecast for the coming year by products and by months. The sales forecast was made on the basis of the company's past sales experience, general business conditions, position in the business cycle, degree of competition, and the company's pricing policies and production costs. Maximum use of the market research department was made by the sales manager in setting up sales programs. After the sales forecast was approved by top management, it was transmitted to the budget department and the production department.

Upon receipt of the sales forecast by the production department, each plant manager, in conjunction with the manufacturing vice-president, would establish the level of production for the budget period. The production planning department of each plant then prepared a production forecast of the plant by products and by weeks. The production forecast was established on the basis of shipping requirements, inventory requirements, length of production cycle, time necessary to procure materials, level of production desired, and stability of general business conditions.

The production forecast, when it was approved by top management, became the basis in developing budgets for material, labor, and manufacturing expense. Material budgets by weeks were prepared for the forecasted production level by applying a material usage standard established by the process department and a standard price established by the purchasing department.

Weekly budgets of labor and manufacturing expenses were established for each cost center on the basis of the production forecast. All items of process cost under the foreman's control were budgeted in terms of dollars. The establishment of a budget standard was done through the joint efforts of the plant budget supervisor and the foreman of each cost center. All budget allowances had to be approved by the plant manager.

Budget allowances for labor expenses were calculated on the basis of the number of people needed to carry out the planned production, which in turn would be transformed into dollar figures. A portion of this expenditure was allocated to the direct labor expense and the other portion to indirect labor expense. The amount charged to direct labor expense was based on the time spent by workers on direct productive work. Whenever possible, standard labor allowances would be established.

In comparing the actual performance against the budget standard, budget allowances for labor, labor increment, and utilities would be adjusted or "flexed" to the actual level of production if it varied from the anticipated level of production. No adjustment in the budget allowance was made for other items of manufacturing expense.

Maintenance expenditure was also controlled through a fixed budget. The budget department would study, item by item, the maintenance cost of each of the producing departments in the past year. It would then establish the normal maintenance cost of these departments by subtracting from their total maintenance cost in the previous year all maintenance jobs costing $1,000 or more. The foreman or superintendent of each department would then list all maintenance jobs costing $1,000 or more which he expected to be done in the coming year. This list was submitted to top management for approval. When it was approved, the sum of the listed maintenance expenditure and normal maintenance expenditure would then become the budget allowance for the coming year. By this method, top management was able to control the company's total maintenance expenditure and keep it from becoming excessive.

The selling expense budget and the advertising budget were prepared by the sales department and the advertising department, respectively. Selling expenses which included salaries, traveling expenses, and the like were controlled through a fixed budget, the total amount of which was determined by top management.

The general expense budget included all items of expense which were not included in the cost of production and marketing, except extraneous income and expense. It covered the general management department, treasurer's department, controller's department, central traffic department, central industrial relations department, and research and patent department. The expenditure of each department was controlled through a fixed budget which was prepared by the budget department in conjunction with the respective department head.

The financial income and expense budget included those items of income and expense (or loss and gain) which were of a nonoperating nature, such as income from investments, income from license agreements, net gain or loss from the sale of capital assets, nonproduct service income and expense, and other miscellaneous income and expense. The budget was prepared by the budget department in conjunction with interested department heads and was approved by the controller.

Upon completion, the individual budgets were summarized by the budget department into a profit and loss budget by months and by divisions. The divisional budgets were summarized into a consolidated profit and loss budget for the company. Each profit and loss budget took the same general form as that used for the actual profit and loss statement.

In 1948 the company made a modification in its fixed budget system. Weekly budgets were found to be not very useful for management purposes and their preparation was cumbersome. The practice of preparing weekly budgets was, therefore, discontinued. Henceforth, only monthly and yearly budgets were prepared.

In 1953 the officials of the company were satisfied with their present budgetary system. With this system the company had the means to plan operations more effectively and to institute sounder management. By taking prompt corrective action when the actual operation varied from budgeted standard, the company was able to keep its cost under control through this fixed budget system. They felt that the company now had a system particularly suited to the nature of its operation and its management needs.